African Spirits Speak

African Spirits Speak

A White Woman's Journey into the Healing Tradition of the Sangoma

NICKY ARDEN

Destiny Books
Rochester, Vermont

Destiny Books
One Park Street
Rochester, Vermont 05767
www.InnerTraditions.com

Destiny Books is a division of Inner Traditions International

Originally published by Henry Holt and Company as *The Spirits Speak: One Woman's Mystical Journey into the African Spirit World*

Library of Congress Cataloging-in-Publication Data

Arden, Nicky.
    [Spirits speak]
    African spirits speak : a white woman's journey into the healing tradition of the sangoma / Nicky Arden.
    p.   cm.
    Originally published: The spirits speak. New York : H. Holt, c1996.
    ISBN 0-89281-752-6 (alk. paper)
    1. Spiritual biography.   2. Women shamans—South Africa—Biography.
3. Shamanism—South Africa.   4. Healing—Religious aspects.   5. Women—South Africa—Social conditions.   I. Title.
[BL73.A73A3   1999]   98-52092
299'.698'092—dc21   CIP
[b]

Printed and bound in the United States

10 9 8 7 6 5 4 3 2 1

For my mother
from whom the gift came

Contents

Acknowledgments

There are many people who, like actors in the play that is my life, had an impact on this journey. So, my thanks go first to Margaret and Mario Scheiss, without whom I may never have spent time in the bush and met my seer. Anne Dosher, the Elder, who helped me locate the beginning. Joan Tootle, who always gave me someone to write to. Alina Serote who took my hand. Dennis Arden, through whom I met my teacher and who became our photographer. Doreen Nofal, who first gave us a home on our return to South Africa. My thanks also to my agent Rick Balkin, who believed, and Jo Ann Haun for her sensitive editing. Finally my two families: Joyce Dlangalala and the circle of *sangomas*; my husband Ron, who not only put up with all the trappings of the journey but also paid the bills, and my son Russell, whose droll humor throughout was, and always is, a joy.

Prologue

The old woman with folded brown skin and one eye milky in blindness moves as silently in the bush as an eland. She unrolls the reed mat and sits at its head. Beads hang from her hair, circle her neck, cross her chest. At her side sits the translator.

She empties the contents of a small, dark pouch onto the mat. White, round bones, maybe ten, twelve, some shells, a domino piece. She asks me my name. Her hands, gnarled as old bark, cup the bones and shells, gathering, gathering. She bends low over them, talking in her gently clicking language. Then she throws.

A large shell, conch-curled, tortoise-shell colored, rolls away from the circle of bones, over and over along the reed mat and comes to rest in front of my crossed legs. She laughs, and without raising her head, quickly says something. The translator looks up at me and takes his time before he speaks. "This means you're a *sangoma*,"* he says. I don't know what to think. I pick up the shell and hold it for a moment, its surface cool, smooth. Then I hand it back to her and she throws again. There is stillness as our eyes follow the same shell as it again rolls across the reed mat. I hear my

*An African medicine woman; diviner, diagnostician, herbalist

own blood beat; I feel it in my chest, in my temples. The shell has again rolled three feet from the circle of bones and come to a stop directly in front of me. She pauses for a moment before she speaks, and the translator repeats, "This means you're a *sangoma*."

When for a third time the shell begins its slow roll toward me, I feel a lightness, as though my bones or my blood have become ash. And when it stops in front of me as it did before, she lifts her head and for the first time looks at me as she speaks: *"U xingomantanda; u fanela ku ya dyondza."* You are *sangoma*; you must go and study. And she laughs, but I do not ask her why, I do not ask anything. In my lightness I don't know what to ask.

African Spirits Speak

1

In the Beginning

❡

I was born in South Africa, in Durban, of German-Jewish parents. On weekends I hunched on my haunches under the old avocado tree in the back garden and watched as our "girl," Irene, and Sam, our "boy," washed themselves. They washed in dappled sunlight from large metal bowls placed just outside the *khaya*, the servants' rooms, Sam, stripped to his shorts, as white as blindness against his dark skin. They washed, dipping the cloth in the bowl, then soaping it and starting with face, ears, neck, moving down the body, leaving tracks of wetness glossy as melted chocolate. Each time I watched, it was as though a feast was placed before me.

It was the war years. At night we heard the dull booming of artillery practice coming from the race track below us. "Don't worry," said Sam to my mother. "If the war comes to Durban, I will take her high on my shoulders and run to Zululand." I longed for the war to come to Durban. I pictured Sam's long, strong, shining brown legs, his calves veined as coir, bounding up green hills and across green valleys, pounding the verdant miles away, and I, atop his shoulders, laughing with delight. But the war never did come to Durban or any other place in South Africa. At least not that war.

The other war came later. At first I knew little of it, saw little of it; but one couldn't stop up one's eyes forever. Blacks being harassed, hauled away, beaten into submission. How can one live surrounded by such monstrosity and still look at oneself in the mirror? We couldn't. And so, in 1966, just before my son's second birthday, my husband, Ron, and I left for the United States. We settled in California, became American citizens, forgot cricket and learned the rules of baseball.

Through the years, we read about and watched the horrifying images of human abuse in my native land, my austere, unrelenting fatherland; and I wrapped layer upon layer around my African soul.

We grew to love football, not baseball, and Bill Moyers; I began to explore Native American mythologies. America nurtured me, and I fit easily into its introspective style. Ron talked often about going back, not to stay, although that would have been his preference, but to visit. I couldn't do it. It would be twenty-two years before I returned.

2

The Time of Tears

ᘒ

From the cushion of age I have come to learn that those spirits who guard and guide us often make sport in the ways they communicate, not only in sending the strangest emissaries, but also in the whimsical context in which these emissaries are placed.

As an administrator for a large social service agency, I had gone to New York, to a conference on alternative dispute resolution. During the opening remarks in the elegant, chandeliered dining room, the speaker noted that participants had come from far and wide—one even from as far as South Africa. And he, the one from South Africa, stood so that the audience could see this square, squat Afrikaner who had come all the way to New York.

An Afrikaner! The oppressor race. But I walked over to where he stood and introduced myself, saying that I, too, was from South Africa. We talked briefly. The hated accent grated on my ears and opened an ache in my heart. He said he would look out for me at the dinner that evening. I went late, walking alone through the dark New York streets.

He came over when he saw me, his round *predikant*, or preacher, face breaking into a smile. We talked, first small talk about this and that, and then, as the discussion intensified, I about being an expatriate, he about being a pariah.

We left the dinner and walked the cold city streets, heads down, arms wrapped into our jackets. On and on we talked: I blamed, he absorbed; I made assumptions, he proved them wrong; I grew angry, suddenly ranting, railing against loss. And with each block covered, as each hour passed, the layers around my soul peeled back, until at last we came to that place where our roots twined together in the African earth, and we stood and wept for our lost fatherland.

Perhaps I should have realized that anything under the title of "alternative dispute resolution" might provide a background for change, but that is Monday morning hindsight. What I knew then was that some deep passion had been aroused, a passion to forgive and be forgiven, as well as a willingness to look again at that country of my birth. And so, a few months later we returned to South Africa, Ron and I.

We flew first to London, and then at night with a low, full moon, arced the length of the African continent. We landed at Jan Smuts airport early in the morning, when the sun's light is still pale. From the long, wet grasses along the runway, a black long-tailed widow bird rose clumsily, winging arduously, and I wondered if it was an omen.

We walked across the tarmac to the buses that carried us, load by load, to the terminal. My heart beat wildly; my eyes were greedy, absorbing images in quick frames. In the terminal armed, uniformed white young men stood by each doorway, and I, eager to forgive, greeted them as though they had been as long lost as I.

How strange it was driving the route from the airport. How red the earth; how bright the light. How much space there was. My cells seemed to be turning this way and that, confused, not finding a shape to settle into. We stayed with a friend along the Jukskei River, where the willows curled; and as they purpled that evening into dusk, my bones settled with a sigh, like an old dog into its basket, and I was home. Oh, but I hadn't reckoned with my unpeeled soul.

In the mornings, for exercise, we walk. Up Wordsworth, to Victoria Street. We turn left on Victoria, toward the Jukskei River, and they come toward us, the black ones, in ones and twos. They walk with an easy gait, a swinging gait, even the older ones. I look into their eyes and feel the old pain, the old guilt.

"Good morning."

"*Sa' bona.*" They smile, and I search, in their smiles, for absolution.

Along Shakespeare, then Chaucer and Milton, each fence is flanked with tall graceful gates against which two, three, or four dogs fling themselves, baying "intruder." And I wonder how they feel, the black ones, knowing it's for them.

In the evenings, behind the high fences and locked gate, we have drinks on the patio. Orange-bellied thrushes sway in the berried branches of the Mexican cherry tree. The old mulberry is ripe with dark, fat fruit hanging like replete caterpillars. Weavers, swift silhouettes, flit back and forth from tamarisk to mulberry, streaming supple strands for nest building. The land haunts with its beauty.

On the third morning we leave suburban tranquility for downtown Johannesburg. Along Louis Botha Avenue jockeying buses careen; "green mambas" they used to be called. Casually dressed black men sit on storefront steps; nannies in light blue with matching *doeks*, or headscarves; little boys wearing yarmulkes; gray-haired ladies in beige sweaters walking dogs.

Through Hillbrow—the Haight-Ashbury of Johannesburg—gay, multiethnic, quick-violent like the summer storms. Blond women with brown babies; slim, young, black-slippered men with drug-shot eyes. Down Claim Street now, past the area where we were young. There's Minto Court, where I lay at night watching the old neon sign across the empty lot flash red and green through tired, tearing eyes. GLOSSOP HOTEL! LION BEER! GLOSSOP HOTEL! LION BEER! The empty lot is filled now, but the Glossop Hotel still stands.

Downtown Johannesburg is new glass and steel structures soaring side by side with KwaZulu Muti medicine shops and their shelves of musty herbs and hanging clusters of dried animals. Downtown Johannesburg is the darkening of the land. We park the car and walk. Here the black ones don't come in ones and twos as in the suburbs. Here they horde, in tailored suits, toward me. There is something about it that terrifies me. Too many eyes to look into. Too many to ask forgiveness of. I flee back to the suburbs.

Back on the patio, sipping a soda. A cinnamon dove picks at the spaces in the brickwork around the pool. In the mulberry, brown-bellied bulbuls patter their three-tone chatter. Beneath the yellow privet, a hoopoe waddle-dips, beak disappearing, appearing. The air, soft, strokes all in gentleness. My body cleaves to the land.

For days the sky hangs potbellied gray. Finally it rains. The yellow weavers shriek in the apricot tree and fluff and flutter outstretched wings like children in the first rain of summer.

Driving to Bramley in the rain we stop for two old ones trudging heavy-wet uphill. They have come from the doctor and are returning to Alexandra Township. He, in aged brown suit and wear-cracked shoes, works no more. Divestiture's divestiture. "Who will hire me now?" he asks. "I am an old man." We are quiet save the *swish swish swish* of the wipers. We drop them off on the outskirts

of Alexandra. He takes my hand between his in gentle farewell. My
eyes skitter with shame.

I sit for a week, cocooned in emptiness, soaked in sadness. Swallows hunch in the rain, apostrophes on telephone-wires. From the
willows, hadedas, those black-visaged ibis, draw out their mournful
haw, haw, haw. Rendering judgment? Finally the sun shines, burn-
ing with such intensity as to rob the flesh of its whiteness. I dream
of making love and walking away. And tall black-granite monoliths,
crag-etched with faces, crowding me till fear wrestles me awake
with the pictures still clinging to my retina.

•

It was when the Indian mynahs had picked clean the green berries
from the Mexican cherry tree that we bought a home. A small,
sunny condo that looks into the spreading, lilac-tipped branches of
an old jacaranda and to which we vow to return every year. Why?
Because while the rest of the world shunned, we loved and longed
to show it? Because while my heart broke, my bones had come
home? Because unbeknownst to me, the drum had sounded and
called the dance to life.

3

Where the Only Sound
Is Silence

❧

I don't know when the long slide toward depression began. Whether it was during that visit, or after. Certainly, there I had been sad, but now I was immobilized, depressed beyond caring. It would only be much later that the role this time played would become clear: that here, from this place of emptiness and stillness, a great spiritual journey was beginning. There, in a dark confluence, days become weeks that become months.

We had agreed to return to South Africa at the year's end and I, with neither the energy nor the will to reason differently, allowed Ron to make all the arrangements. By now I barely moved; walking was like wading through molasses. I barely spoke; my brain was empty.

In the little flat in Johannesburg, our sunny condo, I spent hour upon hour sitting on the pink sofa, my back to the northern winter

sun, looking out at the old jacaranda tree. No thoughts, just looking; no feelings other than that of the heat of the sun on my back.
Just before we returned to the States, friends invited us up to their
farm in the northeastern Transvaal and we accepted their offer.

Mario Scheiss, a white-halo-haired Swiss playwright, inherited
the land from his uncle. Margaret, his blond, bubbly and middle-
age-girthed wife is part flower child, part earth mother. She
thought it would help me. We expected cows and chickens, but it
was the bush.

We leave from Pretoria in the Scheiss's well-worn Volkswagen
station wagon, loaded down with food. We are going to the
Timbavati, an area adjacent to Kruger National Park, owned by
about thirty "farmers" in lots that average 2,000 acres. The areas
are unfenced and game migrates freely from north to south
through the Timbavati, and from east to west between Kruger
National Park and the Timbavati.

We head north, driving through winter-yellowed countryside,
fields of maize nubs, gold winter grassland. In Witbank we stop
early to refuel, with toasted sandwiches. *"Padkos,"* say the Afrikaners. Road food. We drive through black tribal land in calm cacti-
studded valleys, past coal mines and land left angrily strip-mined.
Curving into the foothills of the far end of the Drakensberg, we
pass tobacco fields with their drought-empty drying barns.

We climb through craggy, creviced mountain, the rock face
streaked copper red, yellow-lichened, to the Strydom tunnel. On
the hillside, brightly *doeked* black women have set up stalls and are
selling fruit and vegetables: wild bananas tasting of orange juice,
papayas, avocados, marula nuts. Baboons roam freely, waiting for
pickings. We stop to buy, and the bill is tallied in fingered singsong.

"Five rand* for papaya, five rand for avocado, four rand for
tomatoes, and three rand for nuts makes nineteen rand." "Wait a

*One rand is approximately $.29.

minute," Margaret and Mario chorus, "that's seventeen rand." The brightly be*doeked* one sings the numbers to her fingers once again and comes to the same conclusion. "Nineteen rand," she sings out. Charmed by her cheekiness, Margaret gives her twenty rand. She tucks the money away and waves both hands in the air. "No change, no change," she sings.

We are through the tunnel and dropping now into the low veldt; the scrub and shrub is green, the Olifants River, in slow curls, swirls past thick-trunked baobab trees; to Hoedspruit: one-horse hotbed of Afrikaner conservatism. The land levels and winter-silver *doringboom*, or thorn bushes, appear. Onto the dirt road now, each side dull winter-green bush. A giraffe head here, an ostrich there. And finally we make the right turn into Umlani—"Place of Rest." In the days that follow, my stillness will matter little. For here, in this terrain that is not ours, we will all be bonded in stillness.

Ron and I are in a small rondavel a short distance from the main house; thatch roof, reed mats, no electricity. The orange-walled main house, also thatched and reed-matted, with radio phone and no electricity, sits in a clearing in the bush.

Margaret empties the food into the pantry. "Sit, sit" she waves at me as I start to get up to help. I'm grateful and haul my molasses-mired limbs outside.

Stretching away from the clearing, flattening into the distance, scrub, shrub, and tree blend into cumulus contours, broken only by a gap of dry riverbed. Occasionally the head and neck of giraffes are visible as they cross. The air has a soft woman smell, musky and sweet.

In the late afternoon Margaret packs gin, tonic, chips, and ice into an open Land Rover; we jacket up and head out into the bush. Marco, Mario and Margaret's son, who lives here in the bush, is driving, leaning out, watching for spoor. Soon we round a bend and there, ten feet ahead of us, is a herd of fifteen, maybe twenty, elephants. We stop. Marco puts up his hand to make sure we are silent.

The big male standing in front, with ears flapping, looks at us levelly. Ron, in his excitement, snaps picture after picture with a camera that has no film in it. "They're on their way to the water hole," breathes Marco. "We'll back up and meet them there."

We drive over grass-flattened pathways to the water hole, beside which is a tall, broad, heavy-limbed tree with a two-level tree house. Quickly and quietly we climb up the backward-leaning ladder to the second level, with the gin, tonic, ice, and chips, and settle in to the silence at sundown, waiting for elephants under a salmon sky in Africa.

Suddenly they are there. They have come, quiet as shadows, and line up at the water's edge, trunks dipping and lifting the water to their mouths, and when they are done, darkness has folded around them.

Back at base, in a *boma*, or circle of reeds, a large fire has been built. Here we sit after dinner, feet stretched to the warmth, listening to stories of the bush, and now and then in the silences the soft coughs of lion, till it is time to take a candle and go to bed.

In the morning, well before sunrise, we drive out again in the Land Rover, in the direction of last night's lion sound. The earth smells of ripeness. The cold air bites into our cheeks, our eyes tear, and we roll high our collars. The sun rises orange-balled. Thorn bushes scrape by. A herd of impala leap crazily ahead of us and then off into the scrub. A giraffe slowly chews at a few winter leaves and watches us from soft, long-lashed eyes.

The Land Rover edges down steep gullies, pitching us forward, and across dry riverbeds. Every now and then a mature tree is down on its side, roots exposed. "Elephant," says Marco. "In winter when there aren't many leaves on the trees, they will uproot a tree to eat from the roots. They don't eat much, they usually just nibble at the roots." The tree lies dying.

杰

Each night we sit around the fire, our feet stretched out before us, our heads sometimes cupped back in our hands, watching the sparks whirl away into blackness. Marco tells bush stories of attacks and escapes, while we listen to the lion cough, the shrill pitch of the hyena, the night sound of sudden killings. Now and then we shine the flashlight out into the surrounding night and catch a sudden orange glint of eyes.

On one such night, after we had gone to bed in our candled rondavel and fallen asleep, I dreamed of a lion at the foot of the bed, launching himself at me. I screamed a long, curdling no-o-o-o-o-o, and Ron threw himself across the room onto my bed to hold me, to reassure me, skinning his knees on the reed mat.

It was the day before we were to go back to Johannesburg that Margaret asked if I'd like to meet with a *sangoma*. Perhaps she thought I might gain some insight into the gripping morass of my depression. My answer came without thought. I said yes.

She is wrapped in a red skirt. Her feet are bare and cracked. She unrolls the reed mat and empties the bones from their pouch. They are small, as the knuckle bones of a monkey would be small. Then she gathers the bones, asks me my name, and throws. She speaks, low-voiced, in her language, the translator bending toward her. "You are suffering from a sickness of the spirit," he says, "a sickness of the heart."

I nod, and she speaks again in her language.

Again the translator turns to me. "You are feeling a great emptiness in here," he says, pointing to his chest. "And here," he says as he holds his head.

Again I nod. "Ask her," I say to the translator, "what I must do about this sickness."

He turns to her and speaks, and she answers. "She says you must keep taking the white doctor's medicine."

As we rise, she gathers her bones back into their pouch, rolls up the reed mat and turns back to me and speaks. "You must not be afraid to sleep in the bush, the lion will not get you." And, while I stare after her, she is gone.

4

Morongo Valley, Meditation, and Mother Earth

ᠬᢣᠥ

If you take Route 62 northeast from Interstate 10, the road climbs into the San Bernardino Mountains. And as you crest the pass you may see a sign: MORONGO VALLEY, POPULATION 1300.

If you happen to notice the sign, you might be surprised at how few residences you see as you drive on, through to Twenty-nine Palms or beyond. Not many people stop at this dusty "middle of nowhere" other than to get gas. The desert dwellers don't hang out the welcome sign in Morongo Valley. This is Southern California, high desert. Dirt roads wind off Route 62, back into the scrub, where the creosote and cholla close around the desert homes. In the foothills, catsclaw and desert apricot hide most of the signs of human habitation.

Jenice had moved here after her husband died, to heal. This is where I came to visit her. She lived on Elm Street, a rutted, rock-strewn dirt road, in a small, creosote-embraced house.

It was summer, and it was hot. On the broad, east-facing veranda we sat in two rocking chairs, listening to the hum of the heat. In the late afternoon we spread out scratch, and doe-eyed rabbits came gently out of the scrub, and tail-thumping desert squirrel, and quail, like little old plume-clothed ladies looking for something they'd lost.

Around us fold the hills, dun-colored during the day, purpling into evening. In the southwest, Mount San Jacinto, like a great bird with wings outstretched, hovers over the valley. I'd come for one night and stayed three; I could have stayed forever.

I visited often. In the late summer, tropical storms en route to Mexico swept across the valley, and from the ground rose such a sweet, sensual fragrance that my heart ached.

In the winter, great candelabras of rivered snow etched the great wings of San Jacinto, and now and then the valley itself was white-cloaked, the creosotes' long limbs lowered, like offerings, to the ground. And always at night, the great whorl of the Milky Way, diaphanous clouds of stars, thick enough to fall into.

I could die here I thought.

And so when we sold a piece of property and talked about what we should do with the money, I told Ron I'd like to buy a home in Morongo Valley, and he, with love, suggested we do it.

It was the second house we looked at. It sits high on a hill on the western rim of the valley. Inside is a cocoon of raspberry carpeting. Outside, to the north and south, the curving arms, the layered hill-tops of the San Bernadinos surround it. Across the valley, five or six miles away, the undulating tiers of the Little Bernadinos complete the circle.

It was only later, after I began to do the medicine wheel and found myself always returning to sit in the west, that I realized the little house, too, sits in the west of the wheel that is Morongo Valley. West, the place of nurturing, of Mother Earth, the woman's place. The place of darkness and introspection. The place where we enter the silence, ready to listen and receive.

Here I began meditating, yoga style, on my breath. And here, where the dark-skinned ones of the Americas had once made their wheels, drummed their drums, chanted their prayers, I found places in the hillsides, small circles of clearing, that drew me into their midst.

I stood for long hours chanting the song of the east, greeting the sun as its tongue first flicked across the valley floor even before its golden eye crested the eastern hills. Or I turned into the face of the wind as it swept hard from the south, its force rocking me, its sound streaming around me.

Ron's work was taking him out of town more and more, and so I came out often to the little house on the hilltop, spending first one night, then two and three.

Each day of each visit brings gifts. The thin, blood-red line of dawn upon the hills. And I give thanks. The two early-morning-soft jackrabbits playing such a gentle game of tag, stopping now to touch noses, now to leap straight up into the air, nuzzling, with closed eyes, one into the chest of the other. And I give thanks. The slow, fat drops of morning rain releasing from the earth a smell so erotically womanish, so evocative, that some archaic part of the brain celebrates the recollection of it. The old manzanita tree grows so strong out of the rock face, and once a year, snakelike, sheds her red skin. Each time I pass her, I stop in greeting and leave an offering. The curling surround of hills and mountains burnishing apricot in the setting sun; the big mountain, San Jacinto, and two airy escort clouds shimmering a deep salmon.

There is no language for this. I lay my body on the earth, stretching out my arms. I put my face into the earth. Then I stand and turn to each of the four directions, giving thanks, giving thanks.

∾

A spring passes, painting the hillsides with great swathes of yellow and blue, bringing passages of new birds in their migrations: western bluebirds and yellow orioles. I stick orange halves onto the yucca tips for the orioles, and the finches discover the new delight and bicker in flurries over the fruit.

And with the passage of the spring, a change has taken place; the time of depression has passed. As silently and as inexplicably as it had settled, so has it now withdrawn. In reflecting then on the two years of its dark possession, it seems to have had a reason, although as yet its meaning is not clear.

One day, after meditating, and bending to touch the earth as I do often, I find I have drawn three shapes with my finger: S shapes in the ground. I look at them and wonder what the shapes represent. There is only one connection I make: S, I think, looks like a snake.

The first one appears the next morning; she is lying in the small circle where I meditate. She isn't large, maybe two and a half, three feet long and has a pink sheen. I stop; for a while she doesn't move, then slowly she slithers out of the circle and away. I feel elated; it is the first time that I have seen a snake in the desert.

It is a summer of lingering sunsets, and the next evening I climb up into the hills to watch the sun settle behind San Jacinto, the sky turn from apricot into dusk. I sit on a large boulder amid the cactus and the sage. The wind is still. My eye catches movement, and there she is, the second snake. She crosses slowly, almost languidly, in front of me, and disappears into the scrub. The third snake came the next morning as I stood with my arms around the trunk of the umbrella tree, my nose in a branch crook, smelling the sap. She moves across the small stretch of flat earth in front of me, for a moment raises her head, and then dips down the hill and disappears.

I knew then, as I had always known in some unknown part of me, that I do not dance this dance alone. I called this other, the silent partner. And as I felt the earth take me deep into her care, as the woman shape in the northern hills resonated in dialogue with me, I gave the dance over to the silent partner, the one who leads.

"I have given up directing my own evolution," I say to my friends who are all busy goal-directing theirs. "I am conducting an experiment with my life. I'm leaving life decisions to the universe; I want to see what shape that unfolding will take."

"Thy will be done," I breathe now, facing the east, place of illumination. "Thy will be done," I breathe into the wind from the south, place of beginnings. "Thy will be done," I breathe to the woman shape in the north, where the four winds meet. When I walk now in the mornings, I chant to myself, "Trust." And, "Trust," I say as I lie in bed at night.

5

The Weaving Thread

❡

In August, when the sun sits high in the sky and bleaches all shadows from the desert hills, we leave again for Africa. The night before flying out of San Diego, while walking after dark, a meteor as large as a tennis ball trailing a fiery lightning tail streaks across my span of vision. I am sure it is an omen.

The little flat welcomes us, shining with sunniness. Outside, the spreading old jacaranda is still winter bare, but Jean, the archaeologist just moved back to South Africa from Madagascar, puts out seed and fruit so that it is always filled with birds.

I decide to learn Zulu, and twice a week go back to Wits University, where we had been teargassed so many years ago. Now it overflows with all races.

Mehlo, quiet, elegant in her long African dashiki, starts me with the traditional greeting:

"*Sawubona.*" (Hello.)

"*Yebo.*" (Yes.)

"*Unjani?*" (How are you?)

"*Ngikhona, wena unjani?*" (I am well, how are you?)

"*Cha, nami ngikhona.*" (No, I am well.)

She is "*utisha,*" (teacher) I am "*isitshudeni.*" (student).

Time seemed to fly. When Margaret called to invite us once again to the bush, three weeks had already gone by.

The veldt is again winter yellow, occasional willow trees making elegant silhouettes. The drought has not yet broken, and in the country, miles of maize fields lie, sunburnt brown. The thorn-treed bush is silver bare, and for the first time I realize how it and the high desert are similar: They are both sufficient unto themselves and they are both unforgiving. The earth shall abide, they affirm, which gives reason for hope.

Once again Margaret asked if I would like to have the bones thrown. Again I answered yes.

The *sangoma* comes the day before we go back to Johannesburg. She wears a red and black wrap and her beading. And it is now, now that the long sickness of the spirit has passed, that the large and conch-curled shell rolls three times to come to rest in front of me. It is now that she says, "You are a *sangoma*, you must go and study."

Later, in the blackness of the bush at night, Ron and I talked about the strangeness of it. "Will you do as she said?" asked Ron.

I answered slowly. "I must." I knew then that the meteor that had flown across the San Diego sky had indeed been an omen, that the universe had spoken. And the next day when we arrive back in our flat, as if in confirmation, on the balcony lies an eagle feather a foot long.

Like most white people in South Africa, I knew nothing about *sangomas*, least of all how one would train to become one. So I call Wits University and receive a telephone number for the Traditional

Healers Council. A man by the name of Pip Erasmus answers the phone. I tell him the story about the bones, that I know nothing about *sangomas*, and that I am looking for a teacher. He suggests that I meet with him.

The home is large and rambling, Pip is short, upright, and mustached. He is in the midst of writing a book on traditional healers and hopes to help make them participants in the changing South African political process.

Traditional healers, he explains, play the role of diviner, doctor, priest, herbalist, and psychologist. "There are different levels of traditional healers; there are those who cure by the use of herbs, and those who use divination as well as herbs. The *inyanga*, who is usually male, does not divine, but prescribes herbs much as doctors will prescribe drugs for different ailments. The *sangoma*, who is usually female, uses divination to diagnose the problems of the patient, which may be physical or emotional, and then will also use herbs, along with other ingredients, to cure."

I ask about the percentage of blacks he believes are influenced in one way or another by traditional healing. "In the rural areas about one hundred percent," he answers. "In the cities, eighty percent." It seems that traditional healing is a layer of black culture, alive, well, and influential.

He gives me the name of a male *sangoma* from Zimbabwe who has an office in town.

The building is Third-World seedy, the elevators out of order. Every landing reeks of hair-perming solution and, indeed, when I reach his floor the first two or three offices are beauty salons.

His office is impressive. From the walls hang dried animal skins. Sheets of newspaper line the floor, mounded with dried roots, bits of bark, powders. Under the windows, a large zebra skin on which he sits wearing a suit, a tie, and a leopard-skin cap; in his hand, a buffalo-tail whisk. Other than the fact that he wears socks but no shoes, he looks, for all the world, like an African potentate.

There is a small wooden chair in the middle of the room and on this he tells me to sit. I feel as though I'm being given an audience.

He leans his head, listening as I tell him about the *sangoma* Maria, and the bones. He says nothing. When I finish there is silence. Then he gathers up a pile of small white bones that have been lying beside him on the zebra skin, and throws. For a while he looks at the lie, then speaks. "Yes," he says, "you do have the spirit and I will train you, but we need to come to an agreement on the price."

"How much," I ask, "would it cost?" But this is clearly not the way fees are negotiated.

"You must go away," he answers, "and think about how much you want to pay." As I wonder how to create a framework for thinking of an amount, he provides it, adding, "And remember, if we were in the village, you would come on your knees and bow down in front of me and offer me many head of cattle." My head swims. Many head of cattle! I go away and make several calls, trying to find out just how much a head of cattle would cost. "Between a thousand and fifteen hundred rand," I'm told, and I shudder at the cost of several head of cattle.

I call Pip, who suggests that I make him an offer, but when I return with my proposal he laughs, tilting back his leopard-skin cap. Yet he clearly doesn't want to lose a potential customer and begins haggling, as though bargaining at market over a fish. I find myself wondering whether his interest is not purely pecuniary and slowly take my leave.

Next I am told of someone whose maid is training to be a *sangoma*. "Would you like to meet her teacher?" I'm asked.

"Of course," I say, "of course."

We drive to Bellevue, an older, single-family-home suburb. We are led through the side garden gate, around the house, past rose-bushes in a green lawn to the *khaya*, the little building in the back where the maid sleeps. The room is small and light, the bed high off the floor and covered with crisply ironed white cotton, intricately embroidered in red. On a hot plate, a large pot with herbs simmers; the contents fill the room with a wet sweetness.

A woman comes in and sits on a small stool beside the bed. Her face is milk-chocolate brown, her smile warm and welcoming. I tell her the story of the throwing of the bones, how the shell rolled three times to land in front of me. I tell her about the instruction to go and study and that, while I would like to study, I do not want to be seen as a crazy white woman doing this as some kind of lark. I also say that I don't want to offend her or the ancestors, for I had learned from Pip the importance of the ancestors.

At this time a man comes to the door. He is black, tall, dreadlocked, and wrapped in beading, and as he walks in he trails a strong smell of *dagga*, marijuana, which fills the room. He sits down on his haunches next to the *sangoma* and for a while they talk together in their language. It is clear in the exchange that he is the one in charge. Eventually she turns back to me. Yes, she says, she will train me. But there is something about the marijuana smell, something about his dominance that I find disturbing; I tell her I need to think about it, and leave.

"You know," says Ron's brother, Dennis, that evening over dinner, "I think Mercia's maid is a *sangoma*." Mercia is his current lady friend.

And so there was Joyce.

Tub-round body in a tidy pink maid's uniform, her pug face dour under a matching pink cap, she, too, agreed to test me to see if I had the spirit, for if not, she said firmly, she would not train me.

We set a date, and on the given afternoon I knock on the door to her room. Joyce the *sangoma* opens; Joyce the maid is gone. Circling her roundness is a red skirt fringed with beads. Beads cross her chest, ring her neck and her head; her hair, freed from her cap, drops in a hundred woolly rolls to her shoulders.

With her is another woman, also red-skirt wrapped, bead bedecked. This is Miriam, toothless, bespectacled Miriam, who, Joyce informed me, would be doing the testing. Joyce brings out a short, white candle in a blue tin holder, unrolls a reed mat, and tells me to take off my shoes and sit at its head. Miriam sits across from me, Joyce next to her. Joyce tells me to light the candle.

For a few moments we are all quiet. Then suddenly, startlingly, loud, high-pitched wails burst from Miriam, her toothless mouth wide. Flailing her whisk, whirling it about her shoulders and beating her shoulders, she reaches back, back to the ancestors. Now her voice drops low, now rises high again, she is writhing, bending, beating the air with the whisk. It is a dazzling performance and I catch myself wondering how much is show and how much possession.

After several alternations of high and low wailing, she seems to be talking to me rather than the spirits. Joyce translates: She says you are having headaches. Yes, I reply. And she says that your eyes get sore. Yes, I reply. And your tummy gets upset easily. Yes, I reply. She says that you have the spirit. And I am quiet. I look at Joyce, at her round face, her pursed mouth, her almost angry chin thrust forward. It seemed I had a teacher.

We agree on a fee (not nearly the cost of several head of cattle) and that I will start at the next visit. Joyce wants me to have several months clear with which to begin, so I will come ahead of Ron.

"You will buy a mattress," Joyce says, "and bring it here. You will come here at six o'clock in the evening and sleep here with me at night so we can do our work and you can tell me your dreams."

"And during the day?" I ask.

"During the day you can do whatever you want," she answers.

6

The Emerging Pattern

ॐ

Well," said Anne, elder of the Fireweed Eagle Clan, "there is certainly great elegance in this unfolding. Now you not only have a reason for going to South Africa, which will keep Ron happy, but you have your direction for the next several years."

Indeed there is such elegance to this emerging pattern that I wonder if experiencing these patterns could be the experience of a greater truth. I had always believed that there are many truths, like relativity, each to her own truth. Yet, as I've grown older I have come to believe that there are overarching patterns, which, if we could only step back far enough, we could see.

Is the dance with the silent partner the dance of a greater truth? Reflections of a larger pattern? A larger memory?

And in these musings I remember a man I had met, a year or so ago, not a young man but with a child's face in a cloud of red hair. He seemed enchanted, both serene and radiant. And I was enchanted, watching him, enchanted and envious. I wanted to hear his story but he was reluctant to talk, his story clearly not for the telling.

When I persisted, he thought for a while before replying. "There is a lesson," he said, "that I learned several years ago. I had wanted to make a change, I needed a renaissance in my life." He looked up at me, "A renaissance of the spirit, you understand?" I nodded. "I went to Venice, city of renaissance, where I stayed for two years. But nothing changed. Before I came back here, to America, I went to London. There I met the man who would become my teacher. And the first lesson I learned was that before there can be a renaissance, there must be stillness."

And now, recalling that encounter, I see the role the depression played, its place in the pattern; it brought me to my stillness. And out of the stillness came the unfolding dance.

And then each piece, each gossamer thread becomes clear: The chance meeting in New York that stripped the layers from my soul; my beautiful, bleeding fatherland that reclaimed my heart; the beloved desert where the spirits first answered. And finally, like a seer coming out of the bush, the old woman with folded brown skin and one eye milky in blindness, pointing the way.

7

The Work Begins

ॐ

So in March I fly back, back to Africa, back to follow the words of the old *sangoma*.

As always, we cover the length of the African continent at night, and, as always, I look down into the vast darkness that seems always more compelling than any other. Because it is Africa; because I am, after all, an African.

Harry, a brother-in-law, meets me with gun on hip at the airport. To him I am a pinko, commie liberal; to me he is one of the achingly unmoving—unable to flow with impending change, dammed in anger, cemented in fear. He drives me to the flat, talking all the while of the ANC, the African National Congress. His lips curl in loathing. He believes them to be totally inept, these people who will shortly govern. There is not a word they utter, not a move they make that he does not seize upon and lift to the light of his own terror.

In front of the apartment building the rose trees are blooming great white-tissue whorls, and along the brick wall the bignonia vine trumpets red.

Gentle Elias, in his blue coveralls, is polishing the front doors. "You are back!" he says, his weatherbeaten black face creasing wide with a smile.

"Yes," I answer, "I am back." But it is not until Harry has left and I have pulled open the drapes, not until the African sun stretches its morning arms around the salmon walls and I greet the spreading, old jacaranda and the flitting yellow weavers that I am truly back.

It has been a good summer in drought-ridden southern Africa, a rain-filled summer; the gardens are green and lush. The early air is satin soft and only a slight breeze stirs the feathered jacaranda fronds. My bones resettle with a sigh.

Then I call Joyce. She is already working, and I wait while she is called to the phone.

"Hello, Joyce." I'm almost singing with anticipation. "I'm here."

"Hello," she answers, her voice downward with reserve. For a moment I worry, then realize that she is on her "madam's" phone and often those white madams don't like it when the maids use the phone. The conversation is short.

"I will start on Monday," I say.

"You remember how to get here?" she asks.

"Yes," I answer. "I will see you at six o'clock."

"O.K. I will see you Monday," she says and hangs up.

For the rest of the weekend I restock the little kitchen with food that grows increasingly expensive, reconnect with friends, and sit quietly on the balcony, feeling the air, listening to the bulbul's sweet three-note call, the alarm clocklike *trrrrr* of the orange-costumed barbet.

ⓖ⤚ⓐ

It is Monday, a quarter to six, almost time.

Yesterday I bought the mattress, three-inch-deep foam, wrapped in a sunny blue and yellow cotton. The African who carried it out of the store asked if I was going to sleep in the car. No, I answered, I'm going to study with a *sangoma*. His response was unexpected. "Hau," he said in the traditionally African expression of surprise, "you will make a lot of money."

My red sheet and green blanket wait by the door; the mattress is rolled up in the car. Just before I leave, the heavens drum the earth with a flash flooding of fat drops, almost too white to be rain, too soft to be hail.

Last night I dreamt that a small dark figure stood as though hunched on the right side of the bed. As it receded and grew, receded and grew, did I wake? Later a bright light shone onto my lids, but when I opened my eyes I saw only the dim hallway lights through the bathroom window.

The streets steam from the sudden storm as I drive the short distance to Bordeaux, where Joyce works. I drive slowly, aware that my life will not be the same again, tasting the warm, sweet, tarry aroma of the wet street, my eyes lingering on the clouds still looming in great gray billows.

Joyce is waiting, her stocky roundness in baby-blue maid's wear framed in the doorway, her face still bulldog dour. I climb out of the car feeling awkward, but she takes my hand gently in hers. Behind Joyce stands another woman whom she introduces as Sylvia and who also wears the wrist, neck, and ankle beads of a *sangoma*. She is broad-faced and broad-beamed, and smiles white-toothed wide, a black fedora perched merrily on the back of her head.

"Hello," she says, her voice singsonging, "nice to see you," and she also takes my hand. The soft warmth of their hands holding mine relaxes me.

I will later learn that Sylvia was trained by Joyce, as were most of the women who will become the circle of *sangomas* of which I will be a part, including toothless Miriam. Sylvia helps me take the things from the car, and we go inside.

There is first an entryway that also doubles as a kitchen. On one side is a gray Formica counter and, above and below, off-white kitchen cupboard doors, a couple of which dangle at crazy angles. Against the opposite wall, a small white-painted wooden table with magazines is flanked by two wooden chairs. To the right, just beyond the wooden table and chairs is the door to the bedroom. Before we go in, they tell me to take off my shoes and they take off theirs.

Beneath two high, barred windows sits a single bed covered with a pink candlewick spread and raised high on bricks. Many Africans have their beds raised high, either on blocks or on bricks. I had been told that it is so that the *tokoloshe*, a small, mythical, wicked being, cannot get to them during the night.

A large black-and-white television set is switched on and a black presenter is giving the news in Zulu; on the adjacent wall is a towering two-door wooden wardrobe topped with a pink laundry basket and several rolls of blankets. Between the two, from string stretched wall to wall, hang several of the black, red, and white wraps that are part of the *sangoma's* trademark wear. And on the floor, under the wraps, filling the corner is an assortment of forty, fifty, sixty small bottles and jars, candles, matches, holders. There is a soft musky odor in the room.

The room is small, and as I look around, I wonder how we'll manage, and where I'll sleep since there doesn't seem to be enough room to unroll the mattress. For now we lay it and the pillows on the bed, and my bag containing cleansing cream, night cream, makeup, pajamas, book, glasses, slippers (did I think I was going to camp?) under the bed.

Joyce points to my stomach: "Your tummy here, is making pitta, pitta, pitta, pitta," she says.

"Yes," I answer, "that's because I'm nervous." And I am. She laughs and takes my hand. I tell her that I don't know what to expect.

I had decided, before starting this training, to go with an open mind and to allow myself to stay subjective. And so I avoided what little literature there was on traditional healers and their practices. I wanted whatever happened to be a fresh experience, free of other people's descriptions and interpretations. "You will learn, little by little," she says now, "slowly, slowly."

Joyce and Sylvia settle down on the floor in front of the television set; Joyce points to a stool and I sit, expecting them to begin something—an introduction to what I'll be learning, an explanation of the process. Instead we watch television, and it is strange after all the waiting, the anticipation, to be doing something so mundane, so everyday.

Sylvia, I will quickly learn, is a television buff, and on the days she is with us the television is never switched off. The programs we watch are usually in Zulu: in the early evening, when I arrive, the news; later on, sitcoms and soap operas that they sometimes translate. During one of the commercials, Joyce reaches under the bed and brings out a large tin container. From it she takes a handful of rust-colored filaments and goes out into the little entryway-kitchen. I am curious, but since I'm not sure yet whether it's rude to question, and she doesn't say anything, I don't ask. She comes back in and we return to watching the news.

When the news is over, Joyce reaches under the bed again, brings out a hot plate, and puts it on the floor in the shower stall just beyond the bedroom door. The black cord runs across the bedroom to the plug under the nightstand. All the while the two *sangomas* chatter to one another in Zulu, ignoring me. I watch, wondering what is being prepared, sensing that it's for me. "Patience," I say to myself, "you will find out."

Again Joyce leaves the room and then reappears with a large pot that she puts carefully onto the hot plate. Now Sylvia stands, stretches, and with Joyce begins to lay newspaper on the floor around the hot plate. Next, on the newspaper they put a stool that they also cover with paper. I breathe deeply to stay calm.

They tell me to undress and sit on the stool.

"Even my bra and pants?" I ask.

"Everything," says Joyce, and I strip and fold my clothes on the bed, feeling awkward in my tall whiteness.

When I sit on the newspaper-covered stool, it is close enough that my feet are on either side of the hot plate and my knees on either side of the pot. The pot is filled with a red simmering liquid in which filaments float. Joyce and Sylvia arrange a blanket over me, making sure that I am covered to the ground, tucking it under so that no light enters the tent I now make. I am told to keep my eyes closed.

Beneath me the pot bubbles and steams; the smell is sweet and yeasty, the heat feels hard on my face. I hold my arms in a circle away from my body, elbows on my knees so that the steam will reach as much of my body as possible.

Almost immediately sweat begins to drop onto the newspaper, beginning with the sound of the first fat plops of rain, then gaining in speed. I feel another blanket thrown over me and then another. The weight pushes down on my neck, and for a moment I panic as I struggle to raise my head.

I don't know how long I sit, enclosed in the warm, wet, dough scent, my eyes closed, listening to the steady fat drops of sweat into the pot, onto the newspaper, the two women and the television chattering in the other room. Maybe twenty minutes, maybe more, maybe less.

When the underparts of my arms begin to burn, and my neck aches with the weight of the blankets, I am told to open my eyes.

In the beginning there is only blackness, then slowly, as a winding tornado dances over plains, ghosts of golden smoke wisp in a circling scrim. My eyes delve into the unending pitch. Yellow orbs like leopard irises float up from the unseen.

"What do you see?" Sylvia asks. Her voice has joined another world. The darkness pulses in waves. Incandescent streaks flare, make shapes, contract to ultraviolet pinpoints and dip like dying fireworks into the dark.

"Do you see anything?" Joyce asks, and my ears hear her voice and my eyes recede from a great depth. With effort I move my mouth to speak.

"First I saw smoke and then lights that looked like the eyes of a leopard and then streaks and flares . . ."

"Good, that is very good," they say after each description.

When they remove the blankets they are excited, Sylvia all smiles. I sit wetly pink, feeling light after the weight of the blankets, like a stranger back in this setting. "This is very good, this is very good," they say, "because this means you have the spirit." And Sylvia tells me of the day she knew she had the spirit, when she was spun around by some unseen force and dropped to her knees. And while she speaks my self seems to gather together again, to return from the experience of the steaming, and settles back into the room.

In the past, and still today in rural villages, the *sangoma* tradition is hereditary and runs in families. From an early age a child will become apprenticed to a parent or grandparent from whom he or she will learn the craft of traditional healing. But the ancestral spirits are whimsical and many choose to inhabit anyone, either appearing in a dream, telling the sleeper that he or she must go and become a *sangoma*, or someone might become possessed, exhibiting the symptoms of having the spirit, or *ukuthwasa*.

The symptoms take various forms but share certain commonalities: There is sadness or depression, a heaviness around the back of the neck and the shoulders; there are headaches that can't be treated, pains throughout the body for which western medicine can find neither cause nor cure. Once thus inhabited, those possessed must "take the spirit" if they are to be free of the symptoms; in other words, say yes to the condition and begin the training that takes them on the road to becoming a *sangoma*.

We go into the bedroom, where the television is still on and where I stand dripping while they exclaim their delight over and over. There is no move to offer me a towel, so I tell them that I have one in my bag but they say, no, I'm not to dry myself.

Joyce opens the big cupboard door and takes out a red wrap that she ties around my waist and a red, white, and black-patterned wrap that is tied around my shoulders, covering my back but leaving my breasts bare.

"You can sit down," says Joyce, and she pulls out the small stool. We sit, Joyce and Sylvia on the floor. I tell them about the American Indian sweat lodge and ask whether this is a similar thing.

"Yes," they say, "this is to open you up and to clean you, but it is also to make sure that you have the spirit." And again their faces light up and they reach out to each other and talk quickly in Zulu. They are clearly still delighted at what I had seen.

On the television, the program in Zulu has given way to David Frost interviewing President De Klerk, and I delight in this strange juxtapositioning of cultures as I sit wrapped in shawls with my still-pink breasts bare.

After watching Frost for a while, Sylvia stands and removes her blouse. "We must show you how to dance now," she says. The two women begin singing softly together and clap their hands, finding the rhythm. Then Sylvia moves, swinging in place slowly from one foot to the other, her body relaxed, her arms flowing with the movement. Gradually the rhythm increases and she double-times her movements and eventually comes to an end with a low, fast gallop.

I watch her feet, allowing mine to feel for the movements as one more time she demonstrates. There will be an occasion, not too long hence, when I will be most grateful for these first few lessons in dancing the diviner's dance.

"Now you do it with me," Sylvia says, and I stand next to her and let my feet follow hers. We go through the movements together, first the slow side stepping, then gathering speed and finishing off with the low, quick gallop. As we stop, panting lightly, she swings her arms around me in a great hug, my wet pink breasts against her brown ones. "My darling," she says, "that was so wonderful, so wonderful. It took me so long to learn this that I would cry, and you are so quick." And Joyce reaches out and hugs me and then Sylvia again.

Once again they are ecstatic. "That was so good, so good," they say over and over and I feel as delighted as a schoolchild getting a gold star. Then slowly we settle back down, Sylvia reaching out every now and then to touch my hand. On the television, the interview is coming to an end.

He is doing the right thing," says Sylvia.

"Who is?" I ask.

"De Klerk is right," she answers, "we must do this slowly, slowly. We cannot go fast because these white people are too afraid. But you see it is not them, it is not their fault, it is their grandparents and their great-grandparents who have done these terrible things to our people. They are afraid now that we will come back and want our vengeance. But things are different now for us," she says. I am surprised.

"In what way?" I ask.

"Well, before," she says, "I couldn't use the same cups and saucers as the people for whom I was working. I just had to have my tin cup and my tin plate. Now I can use the same cups and plates."

More gently now, David Frost has begun interviewing Nelson Mandela and again we sit quietly and watch.

Joyce takes out a candle from a blue packet, puts it in a blue metal holder, and lights it. "It's time for you to do your herbs," she says, and a small gust of fluttering breath passes through me.

In the corner of the red, white, and black shawls, among the small bottles and pots, stands a round, ocher clay bowl filled with water. Bits of woody chips float on the surface. Across the top of the bowl lies a twig, about a foot long, with one forked end. Sylvia demonstrates how I am to go down on my knees in front of the pot, clap my hands three times with cupped palms, then carry the pot while still on my knees to the doorway where a piece of news-paper has been laid out.

I kneel down and, following her directions, clap three times, carry the pot to the doorway, and put it down on the newspaper. Now I'm to clap three more times, pick up the twig and, putting the forked end in the pot, begin to twirl it between my palms so that it acts as a beater till a foam rises.

I lean over the pot, twirling and twirling, raising nothing more than a few bubbles in the pot and beads of sweat on my forehead.

"Here," says Joyce, and she takes the fork from me and with swift, well-practiced movements raises a quick froth worthy of six egg whites. She hands the twig back to me.

"Now," she says, "put your hands behind your back and take a mouthful of the foam and spit it out onto the four corners of the newspaper." This, explains Joyce, brings the four corners of the earth in around me.

Next I am to take mouthfuls of the foam and swallow them while thinking of all my ancestors. I must start with my male ancestors, my father, my grandfathers, my great-grandfathers, and then move on to my female ancestors. I must do this until my stomach is full.

I lean forward, my breasts swinging free, and take a mouthful of foam and swallow. It has a somewhat woodsy taste, not unpleasant. I scoop up mouthful after mouthful, spitting out bits of wood.

I think about my German-Jewish father and grandfather, my German mother, my German grandmother, but that feels so incongruous in this little room, so of another dimension, that I switch to thinking about the black ancestors, not mine but of this continent, of Africa and so also mine. After a dozen mouthfuls my stomach is full and I stop.

Next, Joyce tells me to scoop up a mound of foam and rub it onto the top of my head. This is to help "open" my head to receive the spirits. Then another scoop is rubbed onto the back of my head. Again I dip my hand into the foam, gently spread the foam between both hands and cover my face with it. I feel bits of wood clinging to my face, my eyelids, my lips. Then another scoop that I spread on both arms, then once more for each leg and foot. Then I carry the bowl, on my knees, back to the corner containing the jars. I put it down and repeat the series of three claps.

When we have settled back onto the floor, I ask why we eat the foam. "It is for opening you," says Joyce, "to help you 'see,' so that when people come to you, you will know what is wrong with them and you can help them."

"We must know," Sylvia says, "what is wrong with someone when they come to see us. Sometimes I will know even long before they come."

"How do you mean?" I ask.

"Well, I will be perfectly fine during the day and then suddenly like this," and she clicks her fingers together, "I will get a headache, or a sore neck or something, and then I know that it is the sickness of the person who is coming to see me."

"How do you know that it's not just you getting a headache?" I ask.

"No," she answers, "you see, if I wake up with a headache, then I know it is me, but if it comes suddenly, during the day, for no reason, then I know it belongs to somebody else."

It is ten-thirty when Joyce asks me at what time I normally go to sleep. "Round about now," I say. She nods and goes over to the corner with the wraps and takes one of the little bottles out of the collection. She empties a small amount of a fine brown powder onto my palm and tells me to inhale, half into each nostril. Like the foam, this is a *muti*, a medicine, that will open up the top of my head so I will be able to divine. As I inhale, it burns pinpricks in my nostrils and my eyes tear; I wonder briefly what it is I'm inhaling.

We pull the mattress down onto the floor, and by pushing the foot end under Joyce's bed, it just fits along the length of the room. I brush my teeth over the little sink in the kitchen and climb into bed. Joyce puts a roll of toilet paper beside me that I will use through the night as my nose runs and runs. Sylvia takes a load of blankets into the little hallway where she will sleep.

Joyce climbs into her tall bed wearing a red, black, and white wrap knotted in the middle just above her breasts, which are full and pendulous. Her dreadlocked hair stays wrapped away under a nylon stocking.

My nose burns, and each time I move my head the back of it sticks to the little cupboard behind me. For I while I can't make out why, then realize that it's the foam I rubbed in earlier and that has grown sticky. My eyes get heavy and finally Joyce blows out the candle.

I listen to the rustlings on the tin roof, leaves dropping, cats scurrying; strange night sounds, different night sounds. But they lull me in some way remotely reminiscent, and my body, still warm from the steaming and the dancing, lies relaxed on the mattress.

The membranes in my nose swell until I have to breathe through my mouth and I wonder briefly whether doing this constantly will damage my nasal membranes.

After a while Joyce gets up to go to the toilet. She has to walk on the mattress to reach the door. I roll away with my face to the corner, toward the collection of *muti* bottles, which give off a thick, musty odor. I'm not aware of falling asleep.

•

I am awake almost as she reaches to wake me. It is five forty-five and time to do the herbs again.

Once again it is hard for me to raise a foam and Joyce kneels beside me and helps. Again, as I swallow mouthful after mouthful, it is difficult to picture those German ancestors and easier to think up African ancestors, but when I tell Joyce later, she says no, I must not think of any other than my own.

After I have returned the pot to its corner, Joyce says that I can go home now. I drive back to the flat. It is six-thirty.

I am ravenous and feel hung over. I eat three pieces of toast, take a cup of tea into the bathroom, and steep, deep in warm water in the long tub. But when I get out I am not refreshed and for the rest of the day feel depleted. Two of my fingers are blistered from the friction of the twig.

8

The Second Night

ᵔᵥ

At six P.M. I am back in the little room. Once again the television set is on although Sylvia is not yet there. Joyce is busy working at the Formica-topped counter. There are two buckets standing on the floor, one blue and one orange. I watch as Joyce mixes fronds of reddish-brown herbs, boiling water, and tap water until she fills one bucket completely and one bucket to just over halfway.

"Tomorrow morning," she says, "you *phalaza*."

"What is that?" I ask.

"You will vomit," she says.

A sense of foreboding seeps in.

Sylvia arrives and we sit in the warm little room, toes touching, until Joyce tells me that it is time for the foam.

Afterward we watch television: a black soap opera in Zulu, which Sylvia explains as we go along, then a game show—the money or the box. Joyce and Sylvia play along, avidly calling out along with the audience. When the second contestant wins the car, Sylvia is totally carried away with delight. She jumps up, ululating, and we do high fives and clasp hands in every possible way to celebrate. And I am amazed at how easily they delight, how close to the surface lies their joy, for they have been so harshly ruled for so long.

After dinner, Joyce opens the doors of the little white cabinet against which my hair had stuck the night before. As the door opens, roots, branches, corms, baby-blue tin cans, and bundles wrapped in plastic tumble out.

Joyce and Sylvia are on their knees in front of the cabinet. I sit on the stool and watch. As they pull bark, roots, leaves, and fronds out of their wrappings and containers, they begin to explain what they are, and after a while it is clear that this is to be my first lesson in herbs, so I settle down on the floor beside them.

"This is *insulansula*," they begin, and they push a brown rootlike piece toward me. "It is for *phalaza*, to vomit, and also to cleanse. You can mix the herbs in a bucket with water and spray outside at night to chase away animals like monkeys and horrible things."

"What kind of horrible things?" I ask.

"Things like horrible spirits," they respond. "And if you *phalaza* with this, then the two of us can't see you, it's as if you were just gone."

"Gone?" I ask.

"Yes, we would just talk about you as though you were not here, as though you were out, and if you talk back to us, we would be surprised that you are here."

"Why would I want to be gone?" I ask as my western mind wraps around the unexpected thought of becoming invisible after vomiting.

"Because it's to find out your bad people—the ones who don't like you. Because then you can hear the bad things they say about you. And then when you want, you can just say 'I'm here,' and they will be so embarrassed."

I nod blankly, feeling somewhat incredulous, and catch myself thinking that this is not quite what I had expected. But there is no time to ponder as they press on.

"This is *imphepho*," they continue, showing me the strands of lightly colored dried stems and small flowers. "You burn it before you fortune people to clear out any other thoughts." I bury my nose in the thick bundle of slim, tightly massed stalks; it has a soft, sweet, tobacco smell. They push the *imphepho* to one side.

"And this," they say, unwrapping a plastic bag, "is *isimpinda*. You use it if someone is doing something bad to you, like funny tricks," Joyce says.

"What kind of funny tricks?" I ask.

"Like when someone is making you sick, for example, then you must use this and it will make all the sickness go away. You can drink it or mix it with other herbs, or you can spray it around outside to keep your house safe. And sometimes you can cut yourself here and here," she indicates her joints, "and rub it in and then the bad stuff goes back to the person who sent it."

"How does it go back?" I ask.

They laugh. "No, it just goes back."

And thus begins a phenomenon that will happen time and again: When I ask a question, a question such as how does this work, or why do we do such and such, their response will be to laugh, to say, "No, we just do it," or, "No, it just happens," as though the hows and whys have not been recorded, are not important; this is the way the old ones did it, this is the way it has always been.

Later I will understand that there is as much faith in this system of belief as there is in any other. In fact, on one occasion when Joyce gives a young man some herbs to take, she says after he leaves, "This will not work."

"Why?" I ask.

"Because he doesn't believe," she answers.

"This is *impila*," they now continue without pause, moving the herbs around on the floor like chess pieces. "You can spray it outside to make your home safe, put it in things that you drink, and it's good when someone is dead."

"When someone is dead?" I ask.

"Yes," they reply, "you can just make the ground where they are buried nice and smooth, and then sprinkle it there and then nobody can do anything bad there."

"Nobody living or a spirit nobody?" I ask.

"No, nobody who is living. Also," they go on, "you can cook it in water and keep a bottle of it to drink to clean your blood. See, it looks like the skin on an elephant's leg." It is indeed gray and wrinkled like elephant skin. My head begins to swim with information, not only of the different herbs, but in response to this new way of looking at things, a way of conjury and superstition. But they have more.

"The elephant is a very good animal. It is bigger than all animals so it is a strong potion. We also make up a herb with elephant poop to keep a home safe."

"Elephant poop!" I exclaim, and they look at me and laugh.

"And we use the fat from many animals also, like the elephant and the lion. We often call on the animals. We mix many animal skins: snakes, monkeys; you can get it from the chemist already mixed, it's called *inyamazan*. You can also burn it before you sleep to keep the bad things away."

I look at all the pieces on the floor around us; I had been so careful, before I began, not to build expectations, not to design what I thought would happen, and yet, and yet, I must have. I knew there would be roots, bark, herbs; but the world of evil intentions meant to harm, spraying around a house to keep it safe from evil designs or rubbing *muti* into cuts in joints to send those evil designs back to the sender—that was a world that did not settle easily into mine.

My enchantment slips a little, my quest for the spiritual soul of Africa somehow subverted by witchcraft.

I ask if they use herbs to do bad to someone else. "No," they say, "we don't use the herbs to do bad things, only to defend. There are some people who will do it, for the money. But we are not allowed to. If we do bad things our spirit will run away from us and all the herbs in the world won't work."

It is after ten when Joyce puts the roots, bulbs, and bundles in the cabinet and we unroll the mattress. Again, I sniff the reddish-brown powder and go to bed. For a long while I hear Joyce and Sylvia talking in the hallway, and even though they are quiet, I lie awake. Under my eyes, my sinus cavities ache, and I unroll sheet after sheet of toilet paper as my nose runs and runs.

●

It seems no time has passed when Joyce is shaking my shoulder. "It is time to *phalaza*," she says. I sit for a while on the mattress, my knees bent, my hands holding my ankles as though to detain myself. I do not want to do this. Eventually I realize I cannot keep sitting, and slowly get up and roll up the mattress.

The two buckets stand on the floor, one in the shower stall where I had steamed, and one on the floor in the little doorless toilet. Each contains a pink liquid, the orange bucket in the hallway perhaps a gallon and a half, the blue bucket in the toilet about two and a half gallons. Beside each bucket stands a cup and a large round plastic basin.

"You will *phalaza* here," says Joyce, pointing to the bucket in the hallway, "and Sylvia will *phalaza* in there," pointing to the toilet. "You will take the bucket and pour the liquid into the cup and then you drink, and when you feel your vomit coming, you put your fingers down your throat and you let the vomit come."

I kneel on the newspaper in front of the bucket. My throat feels so firmly closed against the pink liquid that I don't know if I can drink it, let alone puke it up again. In the meantime Sylvia had begun dipping her cup into the bucket and I know I cannot just kneel here wishing this away; I have to start.

I dip the cup into the liquid, take a breath, and drink. Surprisingly, it does not taste bad and I drink as quickly as I can, emptying the cup.

"Now drink again," says Joyce, who is standing watch over me. I scoop out another cupful and drink. When I am halfway through I begin to gag, but only spittle comes out of my mouth. Sylvia, meanwhile, is gushing vomit.

"Drink again," says Joyce, and I drink another cupful. Again I gag. "Now pour it and drink again," says Joyce. I pour out and drink another cupful, this time quickly. I gag again.

"Put your fingers in your throat," says Joyce, and as I insert three fingers deep in my throat, about a cupful of the pink liquid comes up and out. "Now drink," says Joyce. I pour another cupful.

In the meantime, to a steady sound of retching and gushing, Sylvia has emptied half the contents of her bucket into her tub. Again I drink and again put my fingers in my throat. About a cupful of the pink liquid comes up. I am sweating now. I pour another cupful and drink.

Sylvia is down to the last fourth of her bucket, methodically, almost cheerfully, pouring, drinking, and puking, pouring, drinking, and puking. Again I throw up my cupful. The contents of my bucket creep below the halfway mark. Once more I drink, gag, and puke, but, as I next raise the cup to my lips, my throat closes. No more, it says with inarguable finality.

"I can't do any more," I say weakly to Joyce.

"Don't worry," she answers, "slowly, slowly it will come and you'll be drinking just like Sylvia."

I sincerely doubt her words as I get up on shaking legs and sit on the stool in the little bedroom. I feel exhausted.

"Now you eat the foam," says Joyce. At this, every fiber of my brain, throat, and stomach contract into tight refusal; but I wrap the red, white, and black shawl around my shoulders, kneel in the corner in front of the clay bowl, clap three times, and carry it to the doorway. There I twirl the forked stick in the mixture until it foams, take a mouthful, spit in the four directions and then, hands behind my back, begin to eat. But after three or four swallows my digestive tract firmly shuts down.

"You must eat some more," says Joyce.

"I can't," I answer. "My stomach is full." And I finish spreading the foam on my head, hands, and feet and return the bowl to its corner spot.

"Come here," says Sylvia, and she leads me out into the yard where she breaks a twig from a bush. Back inside we go over to her tub, filled with the pink liquid she has thrown up. She swirls the stick through the contents and pulls from it sheets of clear mucus. "This," she says, "is what you must vomit out. This is the bad stuff inside you. We *sangomas* like to *phalaza* to keep our insides clean."

I look at the clear, clean mucus and my western mind snaps. No, no, no, it says, this stuff is meant to be inside me. This is the mucus that lines my digestive system. But I nod and sit on the stool, leaning my head against the wall wondering whether this training could be dangerous to my health.

I suddenly remember with some relief that Joyce had said that her mother had died recently at ninety-eight, and I ask her if her mother had been a *sangoma*.

"No," she answers, "but my grandmother was a *sangoma*."

"Oh," I ask hopefully, "was she also very old when she died?"

"No," she answers, "she died before I was born."

I drive home in an early morning drizzle. I feel lousy. At home I pull out an old blanket and collapse on the sofa. I am bone-shivering cold but don't have the energy to get into bed. And so I doze and sleep till one o'clock, when I wake with a foul taste in my mouth.

I stagger to the bathroom to brush my teeth. In the mirror my face is yellow, with dark rings under my eyes. I feel drained and close to tears, and when I blow my nose, blood runs out.

On this third day I come close to calling the whole thing off. When during the day I visit Harry, he takes one look at me.

"Girl, you look like shit."

"I feel like shit," I reply.

"Do you really want to be doing this?" he asks.

"Yes," I answer, "but not if it's going to kill me."

I call a friend, a physician. I tell her what I've been doing and how I feel. "Do you know if anyone has died from this?" I ask.

She laughs. "No, but I know of people who have died because they have continued to see a *sangoma* when they should have been getting medical treatment. By the time they get to a hospital they are so sick there is little we can do for them."

I tell her about the vomiting and the mucus Sylvia fished up. "Do you see many people with stomach problems?" I ask.

"Not really," she says, "and if we do it's usually because they've gone onto a western diet rather than for any other reason."

But when I tell her about the snuff I inhale at night, she urges caution. "That stuff can really do damage to your nasal and sinus membranes," she says, and from then on I use only the smallest amount possible as infrequently as I can.

9

Herbs and Politics

❧

At six o'clock I am back in the small hallway sitting on the wooden stool. When Joyce finishes her chores in the white madam's kitchen, she comes in, takes off her shoes, and plunks herself down on the other wooden chair.

"Unjani?" she asks. How are you?

"N'kona," I reply, *"wena unjani?"* I am well, how are you?

"Ngisaphila," she answers. I am well.

But although I had said that I was well, I tell her how I felt during the day and how I still feel. "If I were twenty, or thirty," I say, "I wouldn't be worried, but I'm an old woman." She laughs and shakes her head. "Well on fifty. I also have a lot of problems with my stomach, and sometimes when I've been sick and *phalaza*'d I can't stop and I'm worried about that."

She takes my hand. "I was thinking," she says, "that we will leave the *phalaza* for now and we will just go slowly until you are ready to try again." And, feeling salvaged, I give her a hug.

Again the metal cabinet with its botanical and animal magic is opened and again the lessons in herbs continue. There is the pink cream you rub on yourself so that you glow in the dark. And the piece of brown root that you put in your pocket during a storm so the lightning won't strike you.

Sylvia arrives late. She takes off her shoes in the hallway and comes into the bedroom. Joyce puts away the bottles and jars, and for a while they chatter in Zulu. The television set goes on and we sit on the floor eating. The staple food for most Africans is mealie pap, or cornmeal porridge, and stewed meat. We eat with our right hands, holding the plates in our laps. As we eat we watch two Zulu sitcoms and the news. Sylvia translates.

Even before ten-thirty I am tired, but neither Joyce nor Sylvia shows any signs of fatigue. At eleven, boxing comes on and they plunge into it, fisting the air and shouting their encouragement. Joyce, I discover, is a great boxing fan. I pull out the mattress and lie down, but it is close to midnight before Joyce empties the brown powder into my hand and I inhale just a little, carefully, into each nostril.

And so the routine that will follow for the next several months is established. Some evenings Sylvia is present, more often now she is not.

Sometimes Joyce and I walk around the suburb's streets with plastic bags, collecting herbs that grow as decorative foliage around houses and gardens. I ask her if the people living in the houses know that these are herbs for healing. No, she answers, they think that they're just plants.

Bordeaux is an affluent suburb with tree-lined streets and well-kept lawns that stretch beyond the walled enclosures down to the road's edge. At lunchtime the maids in their pastel uniforms lounge on the grassy inclines, their legs stretched out in front of them, and share gossip. Every now and then one will call down the length of the block to another, as people out in the country, separated by distance, might.

Sometimes we walk out into the veldt just beyond Bordeaux, and Joyce points out wild geranium and wild spinach; she will fill her bags with the wild spinach and, that evening, will cook it to have with her meat and pap.

There are certain things that I cannot eat or drink now. No eggs or milk, no ice cream; I can have the white people's spinach, but not the wild spinach that the blacks pick and eat; no pork or fish. I miss my cup of tea in the morning; it is not the same without milk, and I miss bacon and eggs, particularly as the bacon here is so meaty and the eggs so rich.

When we get back to the house after walking, we empty the bags on the floor while Joyce explains what this one or that one is used for. Eucalyptus for steaming when you have a cold; an iceplant leaf for a sore throat; amaranthus root for nausea, the leaves mixed with bacon fat for crab lice.

When I have difficulty sleeping she drops little red, green, and yellow incense pebbles on to hot charcoal so that they sizzle and melt, releasing plumes of scented fumes into the little room. And the smoky sweetness lulls me to rest.

One night, when my back aches, she pulls out an Estée Lauder mascara box filled with porcupine quills and runs their points up and down my back with quick light pricks, chanting softly in Zulu, and I doze off before knowing whether it has worked or not.

My sinuses still ache and my nose bleeds from inhaling the brown powder, and I try, surreptitiously to inhale less.

For the last ten days or so, the neighborhoods have been plastered with notices of a meeting called by the Democratic Party to explain the proposed new conditions of the employment act for domestic workers. I ask Joyce if she is going. Yes, she says, she wants to go, as does Sylvia, and toothless Miriam, who had first tested me to see if I had the spirit. Madota, who is Miriam's *thwasa*, or student, also joins us.

The five of us climb into my little car and set off on a sunny weekend afternoon for the school grounds where the meeting will be held. It is the first time I have seen Miriam since the day she tested me, and she throws her arms around me and smiles wide her toothless smile.

I meet Madota, a quiet initiate in her red skirt and black and red wrap, who will later invite me to her graduation party, the party where she will kill a cow and a goat.

Crowds are already streaming onto the grounds when we arrive. Black women in their dressy weekend wear, some men. White women of the Democratic Party hand out literature: pamphlets telling about the party, a pamphlet describing the proposed new law, a pamphlet on voting.

It is hot in the sun, and we make for one of the big trees on the school grounds and settle on the grass. In front, there is a table around which cluster several party members, mostly white. When we are all eventually seated, I count three whites in the audience of nearly five hundred people.

The meeting is opened by the Democratic Party's representative for the area, one of the white men. He welcomes the audience in English and invites the presiding bishop to say the opening prayer.

Then the representative takes over the microphone once more. "Apartheid is gone," he intones seriously, and there is a dissenting growl from the crowd. "Well," he says, "it is gone in the laws." There is another dissenting rumble. "But maybe not in some hearts," he says. The crowd is quieter. "The group areas act is gone." There is a scattering of applause. "Pass laws are gone." More scattered applause. He goes on to describe other changes that seem clearer to him than to the black audience.

"Can you agree with me," he says finally, his voice rising, "that the police have changed?" To which he receives a resounding, collective, "NO!" "No?" he responds quizzically; he seems honestly surprised. "Well, if you are being harassed by the police, you must report it at the police station." At this a low buzzing is set afloat from the audience while the speaker seems oblivious to the incongruity of his statement.

Now comes the party pitch. "The Democratic Party has always been working on your behalf. And because of our hard work many things were changed." The audience remains quiet. "Parties like the ANC and the PAC (Pan African Congress) were unbanned. Mandela was released from prison. Don't you agree that these are good things?" At this there is a resounding "Yes!," but whether this indicates Democratic Party approval is suspect.

Then comes an explanation of democracy. "Democracy is listening to everyone with respect." And an explanation of the running process. "Many parties will come and speak to you, and we hope you will listen to them with respect. But only the Democratic Party can make your dream of a home of your own, a secure job, better schools, a crime-free neighborhood, health care for all, and a growing economy come true." How this is to be attained in a country with high illiteracy, 50 percent unemployment, a diminishing tax base, and illegal immigration that makes the influx into the States look like a children's tea party is not made clear.

Next comes an explanation of the voting process. "It is very important for you to know that nobody will know who you voted for. Some people will try to intimidate you but no one will know how you voted." At this there is a silence that reeks of suspicion from these people only too terrifyingly familiar with the tactics of intimidation as the ANC and IFP (Inkhata Freedom Party) engage in their deadly brokerage of power.

Then on to the interest of the day for the audience, the proposed changes to the employment act. "All of you domestic workers have to work long hours." Much vocal acquiescing. "Well, under the new law you cannot work more than forty-six hours a week." Sustained applause. "You will have to be paid annual leave." Sustained applause. "Sick leave and meal breaks." Sustained applause. Later when I talk to white employers, all claim to be already paying for three to four weeks of vacation a year, sick leave, and meal breaks.

On the drive back home I ask the women what they thought of the meeting. "Mandela did a lot for us," Miriam says, and they all agree. And they go on to talk about the changes wrought by Mandela, those same changes that were just claimed by the Democratic Party.

When we part, Madota goes down on one knee, claps her hands twice, and says the word that I will also soon be using as a greeting and a leave-taking: *Thokoza*.

10

Spirit Riffles and Porcupine Quills

❧

This evening when I leave the flat, the sun is wrapping the western sky in great swathes of fiery orange. The heat of the last few days is finally breaking, and there is a gayness, a lightness in the air that comes with change.

For a few days now, the newspapers have been free of reports of violence, and it is as if the land, too, is breathing its relief, this land of weeping willows and silken birdsong that is still so heavy with the anguish of its people.

Joyce is just finishing in the kitchen, and I sit at the little wooden table until she comes in and toes off the heel of each shoe. We sit for a while, talking about the day, about the breaking heat, about the violence that is quiet now but is never far off.

"It's no good," she says, shaking her head, "it's no good."

I ask her why she thinks there is so much killing, black killing black, brother killing brother.

"I don't know," she says, shaking her head, "they are mad."

We sit for a while in silence, then I take off my shoes and we go into the bedroom.

Joyce reaches under her bed, pulls out a foot-long, newspaper-wrapped bundle, and opens it. The dry, dull, gray-brown twigs and small yellow flowers of *imphepho*, a herb I will use every day from now on, emerge.

From the corner she pulls a metal saucer toward her, then twists a three-inch-long section from the bundle. She puts it in the saucer and lights it with a match. It takes a while for the twigs to catch, and when they do, they smolder rather than flame. The smell is sweet and tobacco yeasty. The smoke and aroma play in the space around me, and some ancient vestige of memory is roused; some field around me riffles. Around my face, my head, my hair I feel the movement. It sighs in ancient whisperings. Like steel shavings to a magnet, cells long dormant are drawn. The earth stills on its axis; my eyes close, my breathing slows.

When I open my eyes Joyce is watching me. "Do you feel it?" she asks.

"Yes, I feel it," I answer. I don't ask what it is, I don't want to disturb or rationalize the feeling.

That night I sleep deeply, heavily, and wake sensing that I have been some time far away.

All through the morning the gossamer thread to that far something stirs. My cells remember, still aroused. Yet surrounding me is calm, warmth. I sit for a long while out on my balcony, feeling both within and without the same soft stirrings of the air that feather the jacaranda fronds; hearing, both within and without, the sweet, liquid call of the bulbul.

Later in the day, when I go to my Zulu lesson, I tell Mehlo about how let down I felt when Joyce talked about sending bad things backward and forward, and then the experience with the *imphepho*.

"Well," she says, "it is clearly not all hocus-pocus," picking a term I had used. "There are some things that one cannot explain, and this can be very powerful."

This evening I know that there will be clients waiting to see Joyce, and when I arrive there are two women, like patients in a doctor's office, one sitting on either side of the wooden table and paging through the magazines. The older woman, maybe thirty, in a pink maid's outfit, has swollen wrists and ankles. The younger woman, about eighteen, is slim and withdrawn.

I greet them with *"Sawubona,"* and join them in the little hallway. I ask the woman in pink how long she has been coming to see Joyce. "Since October," she answers.

"Is it helping you?" I ask.

"Very much, yes," she says. "When I first came here I could not open my hands or move my fingers, I could hardly walk, and now," she flexes her fingers, "I can move my fingers well and I am walking well."

Joyce comes in from the main kitchen, where she has been clearing up. She talks in Zulu with the woman in pink, who pulls an empty Pepsi bottle out of a plastic shopping bag. Joyce fills it with a light-brown liquid. Then they take off their shoes and go into the bedroom. Joyce calls to me to follow.

Joyce takes the Estée Lauder mascara box with the porcupine quills from her white *muti* cabinet. She takes out one quill and, with quick rhythmic pricks that just touch the skin, starts tapping, with the pointed end, from the top of the woman's head down her face. Then she hands the quill to me. "You do her arms and her legs," she says. "I must go and get the pot ready to steam." She gets up, saying, "Always move the quill downward, not back up."

I take the woman's hand in mine; I am shaking with excitement. I begin to prick, prick, prick from the top of her arm to her fingers, the quill tottering a little as I shake. As I do this, in my mind I talk away the sickness as Joyce had taught me earlier. "Please leave this woman," I intone in my mind, "leave this woman so that she may be whole."

When I am through with both arms, I ask her to sit on the stool and I take each foot in my hand. I feel a warm gentleness toward her as I turn and prick her legs from her thighs down, and then down each toe. After about ten minutes I am through and we rejoin the young girl in the hallway.

When the woman leaves I ask Joyce about her condition, what it is. "I don't know," she says, "she just came with pains and swollen legs and arms."

I ask her about the treatment she used. "First," Joyce says, "she had to steam and *phalaza* and then start with the pricking and the *muti*."

"What is the *muti*?" I ask. But the herbs she mentions are unfamiliar. There are so many of them to learn.

I ask the young girl what she is here for. She is here, she says, because she is looking for a job. She smiles at me shyly while she speaks. She is from Newcastle, she says, in Natal, where there is no work. But she hasn't been able to find work here, either. It is for her that Joyce has put the big pot on the hot plate, and when it simmers Joyce moves it to the smaller hot plate in the shower stall. She will steam.

"You cover her with blankets," Joyce tells me while the young woman strips. Carefully I drape three old blankets one at a time over her, tucking in the sides and corners until she is completely covered. The blankets give her a slim, ghostly appearance. After ten minutes she has had enough, and one by one I remove the blankets. Her brown skin shines with sweat, and with her forefinger she pushes rivulets down her legs.

When she is dressed I ask her if she feels this will help her. "Oh, yes," she replies, smiling. After she last steamed she got a job right away, but it is only for one day a week; so now she is doing this again so that she will get another job.

11

Alina

ॐ

Today I meet with Alina, gray-haired Alina whom I first met in South Africa four years ago when she was the director of Women for Peace. Then she had taken my white hand in her warm brown one and said, "Come home, we need you." She is in her seventies now, no longer director of Women for Peace but one of the most respected women in Alexandra, someone whose presence is always requested, whose input is always sought. She is greeted as "Mama," a term of respect.

"You are not to drive into Alexandra," she says, and because she is Mama, and because it is truly dangerous, I listen. I wait for her outside the Tecknikon that sits on the border between Alexandra and its neighboring white suburb, Kew.

I am watchful as I wait here on the outskirts; there have been so many incidents of murderous car jackings, not only around the townships but all over Johannesburg, that Harry has given me a can of mace that I keep in the car-door pocket. Now I keep my hand on the can and my eyes on the alert.

They pull up in a small truck; her husband has brought her. She gets out, and I cross to hug her. A few more gray hairs crisscross her head, a few more lines deeply score her face.

I had told her on the phone that I was doing "the *sangoma* thing." "Oh, Nicky," she had said then, "you are playing with the devil." Now, sitting next to me in the car, she looks at me sideways. "I'd like to take you to my church," she says. "To save my soul?" I ask. She laughs.

Here in my comfortable white suburb we sit on the balcony looking out on the green that is Africa in this season of rain. She sits quietly for a while as she always does, her age-etched face lifted to the color, the quiet, the peace. Finally she looks at me and asks, "Why are you doing this?" I know she means the *sangoma* training.

I wonder momentarily if I feel defensive, but it is caution that I feel. "For several reasons," I answer. "Because I felt the bones called me to this journey. Because it takes me to a level of African consciousness I would otherwise not experience. Because this belief is so prevalent among black people and so ignored by whites. And," and here I feel the caution, "because my soul might catch the echo of some ancient African spirit."

She sits quietly, looking out at the jacaranda trees. "My father would tell me," she finally begins, "that we are here for three reasons. The first reason is to interact with others, to share with them the experience of life. The second reason is to experience and appreciate life fully—"

"To see the beauty," I interrupt.

"Yes," she says, "but this happens through our minds. It happens here," she says and puts her hand to her head. "The third reason is to awaken our spirit and to join it with that greater Spirit that is God. And this happens here," she says and places her hands between her breasts.

I had told her of the moment the spirit took hold of Sylvia, how it had spun her around and dropped her to her knees. This was not the spirit her father had spoken of. "Yet Sylvia believes in God," I say; "this other is separate, apart from that belief."

"But what is it that you are trying to find?" she presses.

"Well, I'm not sure I'm trying to find anything," I answer. "I am doing this because it seems to be a life pattern that unfolded before me, and I chose to trust its unfolding as being part of a larger truth."

"Yet," she says, "you talked about catching an echo of an ancient African spirit."

For some reason I cannot tell her that I stand on a hilltop on Indian land in California and feel the resonance of the Indian spirit. I cannot tell her of my dialogues with the woman shapes that lie in those same hills. I cannot tell her that it is this same resonance I want to experience here, that it is the experience of black ancestral resonance I seek.

While we eat lunch she talks about her father. "He was the first black teacher in the Orange Free State," she says, "and when I was going to school all the young girls were having things done to them by their *sangomas* so that they would be the best students. They would scarify their arms here," she says and indicates above the wrist, "and they would wear *muti* around their necks. But my father was an educated man and he believed that all this stuff was nonsense. 'You watch,' he said to me, 'if you study and apply yourself to your work, you will do well.' And so I studied and did my work, and it just so happened that I was always the best in the class." She looks at me sideways to make sure I heard the message.

Later she tells me that she has been invited to a planning meeting for a prayer rally for the mothers of Alexandra later that afternoon. "I really don't want to go," she says. "I'm so tired of these things. All the talk, talk, talk that never goes anywhere. Nothing changes, the violence never ends. But," she says and sighs, "several people asked me and I guess we have to keep trying, so I should go." I tell her I would like to go with her.

The meeting is in an industrial building just north of Alexandra.

When we arrive, on time, there are only two or three women there. But this is Africa, where time's uncoiling flow is less hampered by the constraints of minutes, seconds, hours. We go into the meeting room where twenty, thirty chairs have been set out, and take an agenda.

Slowly women drift in—working women, some in work overalls, some in dresses. One young woman in tight jeans. An elegantly dressed woman arrives and we introduce ourselves. She says she is from Lesotho, she is with the United Nations and is here as an observer. Alina raises her eyebrow at me and later wonders why someone from the United Nations would be at this sort of meeting.

Two whites arrive: a white-haired, ruddy-faced bishop from England and a neatly coiffed woman in a flowery dress, and then another, a tall, balding man who seems to know several of the women. We four are the only whites.

By now thirty women have arrived. There is much conviviality and shaking of hands. Little Martha of the children's crèche, whom I also met four years ago at Women for Peace, gives me a giant hug although she only comes to my waist. I am introduced around: to the mayor of Alexandra, to Patience, the new director of Women for Peace.

Patience calls the meeting to order, and asks Alina to lead the group in prayer. After the prayer, while Patience is going through the agenda, four young men stride in, their feet punching out sound, one shouldering a traditional weapon, a spear. This defines them as Zulu.

They are grim-jawed and tensed, ready to do battle. They stride to the front and fill the remaining empty seats in the front row. They are followed by ten unsmiling women who settle themselves behind them. Patience finishes her preamble and then asks each person in the audience to introduce themselves and say where they are from.

The front row begins with the four young men. Each one leaps up and loudly and proudly says his name, followed by IFP. Behind them the women, less boldly, give their names and add IFP. As we move through the audience people give their names, but other than the IFP followers, none give their affiliation. Many women in the audience add that they are displaced. This happens as an area becomes a stronghold of either the ANC or the IFP. The people with a different political affiliation who live in those areas often move out because they are afraid of intimidation, or they are forced out through intimidation.

Once the introductions are over, Patience, who is angelic-faced and is shortly to become the very model of her name, moves on to the next item on the agenda, an explanation of how the idea for a prayer rally came about. She introduces the tall, bald, white man who begins to tell a story of women from different sides of Alexandra coming to him seeking a way to create peace in the area.

"I then had a vision," he intones, his voice rising in a passion and cadence not unlike that of Martin Luther King, Jr.'s, "a vision of hundreds, no, not hundreds, thousands of women, mothers, coming together." He raises his arms and swings his body in a rhythm of vision. "Coming together and joining their voices in prayer."

As he orates, I am very aware of his whiteness, his maleness in this his call to the black women of Alexandra. For all the cadence and rhythm of his call, he himself is a jarring note. When he finishes, Patience asks for responses, for a vote of approval, from the audience.

First one, then two and three women stand and with deep passion embrace the concept. "We are the wailing women," says one, and the others murmur their agreement. "We weep as a nation that is rising against Jeremiah."

Suddenly the traditionally weaponed one, the young man with the spear, leaps up. "I am not satisfied," he shouts, and we all sit up in surprise. "I am not satisfied. We have come here and openly said that we are IFP. Nobody else has said which party they belong to. I am not satisfied." And he abruptly signals to his followers and leads their exit from the room.

Patience sends an emissary to recall them, and when they return several of the women in the audience stand to say that they had believed this meeting was to plan a prayer rally and that it had nothing to do with political affiliation. One woman questions why, at a planning meeting for a women's rally, men are present at all since the fathers clearly, she adds pointedly, do not want peace.

The leader of the IFP makes as though to walk out again, then the tall white man stands to explain. "The men," he says, "are from the Interim Crisis Committee for Alexandra, the local peace committee. They were invited here, as were their ANC counterparts, to be observers," he says pointedly, "not participants." At this the young leader turns his back on the head table and for the rest of the meeting faces the rear.

Again women stand to support the need for a time of common prayer, a moment of healing. Again the IFP supporters angrily demand affiliation. Again they walk out and are patiently recalled.

Finally it is abundantly clear that a consensus to move forward will not emerge, that people are not ready to plan, let alone pray. In a brave saving of face, one of the IFP supporters, a woman, stands and suggests that maybe not everyone here has come with a clear knowledge of the purpose of this meeting. And with that as an agreement, we all file out.

As Alina and I are about to drive off, the young man of the traditional weapon knocks on the car window. When I roll it down he takes my hand firmly in the African triple clasp and says, "I want you to know that I, too, am for peace." In my surprise, I can't think of anything to say.

A month later, in an ambush on his home, his wife and baby son will be murdered and he will be paralyzed by a bullet in the spine. "Oh no," I lament, remembering his fiery youth, "who would do that?" "His people," was the reply. "They probably didn't like what he was doing anymore." And the old, familiar ache, so long dormant, returns to my heart.

Alina is weary as we go for coffee afterward. She has been working at peacemaking for over twenty years. All we do is talk, she says, and nothing changes.

12

Herbs to Cure, Herbs to Hide, and Spirit Names

ოჯი

Joyce and I walk through the streets of Bordeaux with our plastic shopping bags, collecting herbs, she with her rolling gait. "This," she says, "is *imbozisa*." It is fennel. "We take a handful of leaves and just hit them a little bit to crush them, and then we boil them for five minutes in a cup of water, and then you drink a little bit every day for when your tummy feels as though it has something hard here," she says and points to her diaphragm area. I ask whether it is when you feel as though your tummy is puffed out, like with gas. "Yes," she says.

We walk on. "This is *isidletshene*." We stop in front of a mound of kalanchoe and pick a few leaves. "You use it for sore ears. You first make it warm, and then you squeeze a little of the water in your ear. Or if you have a bruise, you make it warm and put it on like this," and she demonstrates, touching it to her calf again and again. "Or if you have a sore that is beginning to heal, you touch, touch, just around the sore and then it will heal fast."

We walk on, crossing from one side of the street to the other as she points out different plants. "This is *isikhothokhotho*." It is the tall, thickly patterned leaves of sansevieria, mother-in-law's tongue. "You can also use it for your ears when they are sore."

Sometimes the plant she shows me sits just within the gate of a home, and I sneak in and quickly remove a leaf or a twig and feel like a child again.

When we are back in her room with our shoes off, she opens her white *muti* cabinet and takes out a small, light-brown piece of root with long, thin, spreading tendrils. It looks alive, like a grasshopper about to leap from her fingers. "This is *phayi bashimane*. We use this when someone does not want the police to catch them. Like sometimes when the people come from Zimbabwe and they are not supposed to be here [by this she means that they are illegal immigrants], then they take a little piece of this," she indicates perhaps a quarter of an inch, "and they put it in their pocket and just keep it there, and they can just go around and the police won't catch them."

"Has anyone come back to you later and said that it didn't work," I ask, "that they were caught and they want their money back?"

"No," she answers, "nobody." I wondered quietly to myself if perhaps it was because they were in jail.

"And this," she says and pulls out a large dry clumping of small bulbous roots, "this is *inyathelo*, we use it when somebody wants to drive and they don't have a license. Then we break a small piece," she indicates about a half inch, "and we put it together with a piece from a Zulu broom" —the small, straw whisk broom— "and we put the two together and then we blow on them," and she makes a soft, explosive blow, "and then we put it in their hair, here in the front, and then the police won't catch them."

I'm aghast. "Isn't it dangerous? What if the people you give this to can't drive; they may kill somebody."

"No," she says seriously, "if they can't drive they won't come to me for this." And once again I am amazed by the naiveté of her response.

When I lie on the mattress that night, I wonder at the simplicity of the teachings. Not the simplicity of what is taught, but rather the simplicity of the belief. And yet, I reason, is it any more simple than any other pattern of belief? The secret lies in the agreement.

If, together, we all believe that this will work, or that something has power, then indeed it has power and it will work. Is this no less true when, for example, we celebrate the Eucharist? There, too, we have an agreement. We have agreed that the wine and the wafer represent the body and blood of Christ and are an expression of His continuing presence. It is a communion, a possession in common of a deep understanding. And their understanding, although different, is no less common and no less deep.

There has been violence again in the city, but this time it is different. This time the victims are members of a white family, killed as they were driving their children to school. The story reverberates in the press.

It was all less horrifying while they were only killing each other—this thought is palpable in the white community, but no one says it. Only the ANC points out that the police reaction far outstrips any that would have been taken, that indeed has been taken, when the victims are black.

Three times a day I light the *imphepho* and breathe in its haunting aroma, and eat the foam atop the woodsy *isitundu*. When I light the *imphepho* at home, I sit in front of it with my legs crossed and my index finger and thumb making a loop, yoga style, in the way that I often sit in front of a half shell of smoking sage in California, emptying my mind. And now, in Africa I sit again, in a strange bringing together of East, West, and Africa.

And one day, when I am seated so, from the base of my spine, from a place deep where I sit, the snake uncoils. She rises through me, through my spine, through my diaphragm. Deep between my shoulder blades, behind my breastbone, rising through my neck, my head, smoothly sinuous, until my arms echo her passage and I become her. She sways through me, arcing to the left, to the right, weaving high, bending low. Hands stretched high, I am engulfed, possessed in a movement that is not mine but hers. Consciousness becomes no more than the flow of motion, sure and strong; all else falls away. In timeless space we weave.

Slowly, slowly, a soft, three-tone call drifts through space toward me.

I reassemble, coming together. Around my closed eyes the room reassembles, the carpet underneath, the sun warm on my shoulders. Breath moves down, in and out, lifting my diaphragm, filling my chest, warming my nostrils. It is a long time before I open my eyes. The jacaranda fronds show green through splashes of sun and shade; somewhere a bulbul sings.

I sit for several minutes, unmoving, unthinking, then wonder at her wanderings, like Kundalini, through me. The snake: She had come three times once before, and now is here again, in Africa. I reach back through memories. What did I know about snake beliefs? Only that in some societies they are seen as an embodiment of spirit, acting as intermediaries between God and Her people. Other beliefs were easier—the immortality of shedding skin; the infinite wisdom of Kundalini; the totemic form of the Great Mother. I am loathe to probe too deeply—the magic is in the experience; in examination it is lost.

Tomorrow," Joyce says, "a man is coming who has a difficult court case. He was caught with a gun and doesn't have a license for it. His court date is set for Thursday." I ask her what she will do for him. "When he comes," she says, "I will make a small cut here," and she indicates a spot high on her forehead just at the hairline. "I will rub *muti* into the cut. Then he must *phalaza* for the three mornings before the trial. But on Thursday morning, when he is finished with *phalaza*, he must take the vomit out into the street in a tub or a bucket, and throw it away hard," and she makes a forceful throwing motion, "and he must say: 'This is nothing, this case is nothing,' and then he must walk away and not look back.

"Then," she continues, "when he goes into the courthouse he will put under his tongue a small piece of this root," and she hands me the small brown stick piece. "It is called *icalakalithethwa. Icale* means case, and the rest of the word means 'it is nothing.' It will stay under his tongue the whole time in court, even when he is talking." And again I wonder at the simplicity of the belief. Yet perhaps the ritual and the symbols add a resolve that strengthens.

Later that evening as we sit on the floor in the bedroom, a soft warmth fills the room. Not a temperature warmth, it is not the air and yet it is in the air. A feeling of great good surrounds me, settling in soft waves. I feel cushioned in a great contentment. The skin around my lower cheeks and chin begins to glow, then the skin on the backs of my hands and my arms. I sit quite still, afraid of interrupting the experience.

"There are good spirits in the room tonight," I say softly to Joyce. She looks at me, surprised.

Suddenly I wonder if it has something to do with the way I'm sitting and I change position. But the sensations continue. "Joyce," I say quietly, not wanting to stir, "my chin and my arms feel as though they are glowing." She reaches out and touches me. "No," I say, "you can't feel it, but I can feel it."

Joyce smiles. "You are getting the spirit," she says quietly. And I remember the snake moving through my being and tell her about it. She looks at me intently. "The snake is your spirit, it is a very powerful spirit."

Then, as though this has allowed me entry to another level, for the rest of the evening she increases the pace at which she pulls herbs and shells and roots out of her magic *muti* cabinet while I scurry to keep track of all she is saying.

Later, when I'm lying on my mattress, I tell Joyce that I never remember my dreams, and ask her for some of the powder *muti* I have seen her give to help people remember. And before I go to sleep, she puts a little on my forehead and sprinkles some on my pillow.

I wake in the morning coming fresh from two dreams. In the first I am dressed as a bride, in a long dress, all in white. I am at a large gathering with men, women, and children in which there are other women also dressed as brides. The air is joyful and clearly festive; there is much swirling movement, and music and singing and dancing.

In the second dream, the one I have just prior to waking, Ralph Laubscher, a long-deceased friend, appears standing next to the mattress where I sleep. He speaks to me. "Your name is Melisande," he says. And then I wake.

When I am through doing the foam, I tell Joyce the dreams. She doesn't respond to the first, but when I tell her of the second she takes my hand. "You have your spirit name now," she says gently.

"My spirit name?" I ask.

"Yes. It is our ancestors who bring our spirit name to us in our dreams. We must get our spirit name before we can become *sangoma*. Your ancestors sent your friend to bring you your spirit name." And she strokes my cheek as she murmurs, "Melisande."

13

The Initiation

᳅

I drive home with the name like a butterfly in my head—
Melisande. It alights with soft wings first here, then there. Melisande. It goes back almost thirty years.

In the flat I soak in a bath and wash my hair. I feel as though I'm
going to a party, and for the last week it has increasingly seemed as
if we are. The *sangomas* are going to Lenz, the village where Miriam has her house, for the weekend, to drum, sing, and dance.

I know Joyce has been excited. All week she has been asking me,
"Are you going to be all right?"

"Why?" I ask.

"Because we are going to be dancing all night," she answers.

"The whole night!" I exclaim in mock alarm.

"The whole night," she answers solemnly, forewarning.

There will be four *sangomas* going, and it hasn't been easy for them to get this time together. They all work as maids and don't have every weekend off. So to negotiate a weekend when all four are off together takes some doing, and for several weeks the conversation has centered around which weekend we will be doing this. Even so, Sylvia will be late.

Joyce arrives in full *sangoma* regalia like a steamship all beflagged. Her hair, normally wrapped away in a stocking and tucked under her maid's cap, is released in glorious dreadlocks. She is twice wrapped, around waist and shoulders, with shawls emblazoned with red lions' heads. Around her head is a band of white beads. Across her chest from each shoulder to her waist, there are three, four strands of large red, green, black, and white beads; around her neck, blue and white beads, and, of course, about her ankles, wrists, and neck the red and white beads that she always wears.

We will be taking one of the minibus taxis to downtown Johannesburg, those same minibus taxis that careen at breakneck speed up and down the city's main roads, stopping and starting sans signals with seemingly chaotic randomness. The vehicles are crammed with more bodies than the automakers imagined in their wildest dreams, the drivers' goal to get as many people to and from their destinations in as short a time as possible.

It is rumored that the often fatal attacks on passengers who travel by train occur at the instigation of the taxi owners, who would rather see the profits of travel in their own pockets.

Whites rarely use these minibus taxis; most would not know how to flag one down. There is a complex array of finger signs to indicate destination; and they are, of course, quite horrified at the prospect of my taking one.

Joyce tells me what to pack: my clay pot, my stick, a white T-shirt, the tape recorder, a camera, something to sleep in. From the beginning I've kept a tape recorder at Joyce's place to record what I'm learning, and often she asks me to play back an evening's work while she listens, nodding occasionally.

We walk up the hill to the taxi stop on Jan Smuts Avenue and wait. Every now and then a black man or woman passing by bows his or her head in acknowledgment to Joyce in her *sangoma* wear, and claps hands twice, saying, *"Thokoza,"* and Joyce claps back and says, *"Thokoza."* Occasionally someone walking or driving past gives me a long look as I stand with the other blacks at the stop; I gaze back levelly.

We wait for almost an hour, then Joyce begins to worry about the time and I suggest that we take my car. So we go back to the flat and load our bags into the trunk.

We curve down Jan Smuts toward Rosebank. The avenue narrows; tree-lined with old oaks and gracious old homes, it was built before there were any thoughts of snarled traffic and rush hours.

On the left now, the zoo, on the right, Zoo Lake; then farther down Jan Smuts, approaching Wits University, the curving wall reserved for graffiti, every two weeks or so repainted white for new messages; this week the usual political excoriations and personal heartache. Then past the university and across the Queen Elizabeth bridge and into town.

On the way downtown, Joyce tells me that I must buy a wrap for each of the four *sangomas* who will be there, so we drive first to Diagonal Street, which is where many of the *muti* shops and the shops that sell *sangoma* beads and wraps are located.

The gods are with us and we find parking almost immediately. We walk down Diagonal, narrow, crowded with cars, past deep shops with dark interiors: fabric stores, hardware stores, incense stores, a *muti* shop with clusters of dead monkeys hanging, like bananas, from a pole, all run by Indians. Vendors line the sidewalks, hawking fruit, tape recorders, dried herbs spread on newspaper.

Old, balconied buildings, some still with ancient, scrolled porticoes, tightly crowd the street, trapping sound and fumes. From shop doorways bored voices call to passersby, urging them to buy this or that item. Crowds push and jostle, black, Indian, almost no whites; every now and then we are stared at—Joyce sailing ahead like a queen in her *sangoma* trappings with me in my whiteness trailing.

We round the corner onto Pritchard Street. On the corner a small crowd has gathered and we hear the word "body." "Don't look," says Joyce, and she takes my arm and steers a wide swath around the crowd. I keep my eyes straight ahead, but fibrillate with the heady allure of danger.

We pass one fabric store still too close to the crowd, and go into another three down. Racks line the walls from floor to ceiling, disappearing into dimness. Each rack is striped with colored squares of folded cloth. The store smells of long-folded fabric.

The squares of cloth are precut into just the right size for the wraps the *sangomas* wear, although these colors and patterns are different from the red, white, and black worn when the *sangomas* practice their craft.

Joyce knows what she wants and gestures to a section from which different patterns emerge. The Indian saleslady offhandedly tosses them onto the counter. "What do you think?" asks Joyce as she fingers the fabric, holds the colors to the light, deliberating about pattern. And I am aware of the instant change in the saleslady when she realizes that I am with Joyce, her brusque style becoming more accommodating because I am white.

We choose two peacock patterns, one in blue and one in gold for Miriam and Melita, brown with red umbrellas for Sylvia, and the same pattern with green umbrellas for Joyce. I pay the now more sweetly dispositioned saleslady.

We pop into the incense store next door, another dimly lit, narrow store, a tall, long-faced Indian at the till who holds his nose high, as though besieged by a bad smell. Rows of bottles holding powders of pinks, blues, yellows, mauves, and greens, so vibrant they assault the eye, and customers, mostly black women, stand three deep against the glass counter.

Joyce makes her selections, and we head back to the car. The body on the corner has gone, the crowd has dispersed. We drive through the frenzy of Johannesburg traffic, all gunning action, toward the center of town where we will pick up Melita and Miriam. I have not yet met Melita, but she will be the fourth member of the small circle of *sangomas* who take me into their care.

We meet them at the terminal where the minibus taxis gather, load up their gear, overnight bags and drums, and then head south on the M1.

The area is first industrial, then opens on to veldt. The three women chatter a while in Zulu, then, switching to English, Joyce complains about her madam who wants her back early the next morning to bring her scones in bed at eight o'clock. "You know what I will do with those scones," she say threateningly. "I will throw them at her!"

"Why didn't you just tell her that you couldn't be back to make her scones at that time?" I ask.

"No," she says, "I just say nothing, but she won't get scones at eight o'clock. She'll get them when I'm ready."

Miriam joins in. "When the new domestic law comes in Parliament, then I will tell my madam to pay me one hundred rand overtime for bringing her tea in bed."

I contemplate explaining that the new law for domestic workers won't allow them to reap those kinds of benefits but decide against it, and they fall back into Zulu.

We loop around the far outskirts of Soweto, and then again we're into open country, still green from the summer rains. It is hot out now, and we roll up the windows and I turn on the air. After another fifteen, twenty minutes of travel Miriam says, "We turn off here," and I take the fork to Lenasia and Lenz.

Lenasia is an all-Indian community of neat brick houses, some grander, almost mansions, set in cleanly cultivated gardens. As we drive through, I remember a conversation we had some years ago with an Indian store owner about conditions then in South Africa.

"I don't want to be like them," he said of white South Africans. "I just want to live where I choose. But," he added after a moment's reflection, "I would probably stay where I am, because that is where my family is, where my friends are, where my children play."

And now that the group areas act, the law that regulated where people could and could not live, has been gone for some time, there has been little noticeable shift. What movement there was came ahead of the changing laws as middle-income blacks moved into high-density suburbs in what became described as the graying of Johannesburg, and a few wealthy Africans began to move into the high-priced areas.

We drive only a few blocks through Lenasia, then leave its trim orderliness and turn left onto a red-dirt road. The recent rains have left the road terraced with ridges and water-filled potholes, and we travel slowly, weaving this way and that, bouncing up and down while the old car groans.

First on our right, then on both sides, the red-earthed land is separated into lots by tall, rough-cut upright branches, some leaning at crazy angles, some strung with wire to make fences; each square of earth meaning ownership, each with its center, its home of corrugated tin.

The road dips, lifts, plummets, straightens, I worry about the shock absorbers, then, "Turn in here," says Miriam, and I pull into the gap in the branched fencing. "This is my home," says Miriam, smiling proudly.

It is a corrugated house, as are the others, its silvered tin walls shining in the bright sun. Alongside the door, a bright blue painted stripe from ground to roof, brighter even than the sky. Two small windows with white drapes, and a red, shining *stoep*, or veranda. Morning glories spread random, green and deep lilac along the wire fence.

I park alongside the house, and we get out into the baking heat. Miriam's daughter comes out of the house to greet us, followed by Madota, in red skirt and white bra, who arrived earlier.

Walking into the house is like entering a sauna, the wet heat a solid wall. But the moment we've taken off our shoes and stepped inside, the *sangomas* throw reed mats onto the floor, pull the drums between their legs, and begin to drum, the metal barrels making each beat sharp and urgent.

I am startled by the suddenness of it, and then startled again when Madota begins wailing much as Miriam did when she tested me to see if I had the spirit. But Madota is singing the first high notes of the call to the spirits and Joyce gestures for me to come and sit beside her on the mat as the *sangomas*, their voices high, join in.

Madota dances, holding the stick that all *thwasas* carry out in front of her, her feet first in a stepping movement and then increasing to a gallop.

The drums and the singing stop. Madota kneels in front of Miriam, and in a hoarse growl-speak welcomes her. Then she rises, and once again, in a high pitch, sings down the spirits, and dances again, first stepping, then increasing to a fast gallop. Once again the drums join her, and then the *sangomas*, voices rising and ululating.

Three times in the dulling wet heat of the tin room the cycle of drums, dance, and growl-speak repeats, until finally, with sweat running down her face, Madota collapses on her knees in the corner where *sangoma* shawls and clay bowls make an altar to the spirits.

The *sangomas* put aside the drums and begin to chatter in Zulu. I look around the little house. It is one room, maybe ten by twenty feet. Close to the door there is an aluminum-legged rectangular kitchen table covered in a flowered oilcloth, three or four kitchen chairs, a tall white metal kitchen cabinet, and two paraffin cookers that release a steady smell of gasoline. On the cookers sit two large pots, emitting steam in steady puffs from under their lids.

Here, in the area of the kitchen, the floor is covered with linoleum. Farther into the room, felt carpeting lines the floor under the queen-size bed with the bright pink, blue, and yellow floral comforter. Next to the bed, a bathtub is filled with blankets and suitcases.

Miriam's daughter, slim in yellow denim jeans and black blouse, the tips of her hair dyed blond, sits and fans herself at the table and picks idly at grapes. She seems an anomaly among these women in their bold wraps, with their bones and beads at wrist, throat, and ankle.

I wonder fleetingly about toilets, and less fleetingly about water, but then notice, in the kitchen area, two large barrels sitting in the corner, and gratefully discover that they hold water.

After a while, Madota comes around to each of us with a basin of water and a towel. One by one we dip our hands in the water and dry them on the cloth. Then she comes around again, this time with mealie pap and chicken on tin plates. We sit on the reed mats and eat with our right hands, the left holding the plates. At one point I put the plate down on the mat and I am quickly reprimanded; the plates may not be put on the mats. The women continue their Zulu talk. I sink into the food and the heat and the chatter.

When we are through eating, Madota collects the tin plates, fills a small tub with water from one of the drums, and washes the dishes. The midday heat bakes into the corrugated room. One of the paraffin stoves has remained lit, a large simmering pot of water adding thin billows of steam to the hot wetness.

Miriam's daughter takes off her blouse, crosses to the bed, and throws herself on her back spreading her arms wide. Almost stupefied by the heat, I lean back against the bed and stretch out my legs. I am thirsty, but no one has asked for something to drink, and since there doesn't seem to be a toilet, I assume drinking is kept to a minimum.

My mind slides back again to the dream I had after Joyce sprinkled the dream powder on my pillow. First the wedding dream, where I was dressed as a bride and moved in a throng of similarly clad people, and then the second dream: Ralph Laubscher standing by the mattress, saying, "Your name is Melisande."

How strangely life cycles and spirals. Many, many years ago, Ralph had introduced me to my first husband, and later, when that short marriage came apart, he unknowingly led me to my second husband. And then one day Ralph blew his brains out in the Glossop Hotel. That same Glossop Hotel across from which I had lain at night, decades ago when I was young, watching its neon sign blink red and green.

At two o'clock Miriam stands, stretches, and says, "It's time to go and buy the chickens." I had known we would be buying the chickens because Joyce had told me so earlier; but when I asked her what for, she'd said, "No, you will see."

We put on our shoes and wander up the red-earth road bordered with crook-branched fences. On each side, clean-swept red-earth yards, a patch of grass, a tree, sudden gusts of flowers in neat, tended beds. An elderly couple under an umbrella, a young woman playing with a puppy, a young boy pushing a hoop on a wire.

We walk slowly, it is too hot for anything else; the *thwasas*, Madota and I, slightly behind the *sangomas*—Miriam, back erect, her head held high, round Joyce with her rolling gait, and Melita with arched back, full behind. As we walk, easy country greetings go back and forth.

The small market crammed with goods is run by Indians. Outside a three-layered coop holds twenty or so white-feathered chickens. Joyce and Miriam look through the wire, talking, prodding, assessing. We ask the prices. The top layer, says the black man in coveralls, is twenty-four rand, the next twenty, and the lowest eighteen. As they choose two from the top layer, I feel a slow build of feeling, a sense of ill-boding.

The man opens the coop latch and with a curved wire reaches in.

The chickens clamor and flap. He loops the first and pulls it out by the wing, and then the second. Small white feathers fly. Quickly the chickens' legs are bound together and I pay. We start back, Miriam and Madota each carrying one of the chickens upside down by its bound legs.

And as we walk on the baking road, I talk about how far we whites in our western ways have come from the act of killing as part of the act of sustenance, how difficult I find it to buy something that lives, knowing that we will kill it to eat. They don't seem to understand. Perhaps they haven't come as "far."

Once back in the house, the chickens are thrown onto the linoleum floor where they squawk and flap until they find a position in which their bound legs allow them to settle. The women settle back on the floor, fan themselves, and begin their chatter. The daughter is still lying on the floral bed covering, arms outstretched, small breasts pointing skyward. Madota busies herself with cleaning.

She had been very quiet the day we first met, en route to the Democratic Party rally, and I thought her shy. Later I will find out that the *thwasas* all keep to themselves and are quiet around their teachers and that Madota will turn out not to be shy at all.

Every now and then one of the chickens tries to change position and flaps and squawks as it topples this way and that on its tied legs. First one, then the other empties its bowels with a sudden squirt, and my eyes open wide. The *sangomas* pay no attention, not even Miriam, in whose house the chickens are shitting. It is clearly not important, and Madota wipes it up.

Since we came back with the chickens, and they joined us so casually on the floor, I drift back and forth between looking at this afternoon scene from afar, mentally shaking my head at the oddness of it, sitting in this baking corrugated tin room with the *sangomas* and the evacuating chickens, and then being in it, listening to the *sangomas*, now and then picking up a word I understand and joining in the conversation.

Melita comes and sits next to me. She has large, expressive eyes and is missing her two top front teeth. "You're living at Gatwick?" she asks. Gatwick is the name of the apartment building in Johannesburg.

"Yes," I answer.

"Me, I'm working at Gatwick in number five."

"One day you must come and visit me." And I wonder how Ron would react to a visit by a Gatwick maid.

At four o'clock, Miriam stands. "It is time," she says. I have no idea what it is time for and watch, curious, as she takes off her dress and petticoat and puts on her traditional clothing: the pleated, beaded skirt and short overskirt, the beads, the wraps. Joyce and Melita already wear their *sangoma* wear, and just retie their skirts.

They carry the three reed mats out to the front yard and lay two of them out at one end. The third is placed in front of the first two, a couple of yards away from them. Alongside the single mat two sticks are pushed into the ground and one of the traditional red, white, and black shawls is stretched between them, making a small screen. The three drums are carried out and put on the two adjacent mats and a couple of chairs are brought out.

In the meantime Melita and Joyce tell me to undress. A red, black, and white sun-centered shawl is wrapped around my waist and pinned at the back. Another is pulled tight under my armpits and pinned. I don't ask what is happening, I know they will only tell me that I will find out.

When I am wrapped, Madota picks up the two chickens and goes out with one under each arm and crouches in the road just outside the gateway. Melita tells me to go and crouch next to her.

When I go out, I notice that while I was being prepared inside, six or seven of the village folk had arrived and are now sitting on the *stoep*; an elderly couple, he white-haired and wearing a suit, she with silver-streaked hair, are on the chairs, a couple of younger men in slacks and sports shirts are beside the drums.

Crouching in the gateway I begin to feel apprehensive; this is clearly not just the *sangomas* dancing, there is something else going to happen. Melita joins me in the gateway and explains what I'm to do: that Miriam will call me; that I am to run into the yard and sit on the single reed mat facing away from the drums. I must sit with my legs straight out in front of me and with my hands in my lap, palms turned upward. I nod, although I am now so jittery that her words seem to float by me. My bare feet hug the earth, muscles tensed.

The first plaintive call to the spirits rises and the drums start. The signal is given but I don't hear it and Melita yells, "Run." Madota and I bound forward. I sit on the mat, legs stretched out straight, hands turned up. The women's song joins the drums.

For an instant I notice a few people gathered in the gateway, then I feel something hard pressed against the top of my head and hear Joyce's voice, above me, intoning in Zulu.

Suddenly, water, in cascades matching the cadences of Joyce's intonations, is poured over my head. My eyes close and I gasp at the sudden coolness. The drums pound, overwhelming the voices. Cascade after cascade runs down my face, my chest, into my lap. As it runs down my face, I smell and taste the familiar woodsiness of *isitundu*.

Water runs into my mouth and I quickly swallow, then open my mouth again and breathe and swallow. Small pieces of *isitundu* run into my mouth; the liquid pools in my lap.

"You must shake your hands," shouts Miriam, and I shake my two upturned palms.

Suddenly it stops and Miriam stands before me. She takes both my hands and pulls and I start to rise, but she barks, "Sit," and I stay seated. She pulls at each arm, stretching, and then my feet.

My attention leaps around in fragments. Like pieces of a puzzle I notice the growing crowd in the gateway; I catch sight of Miriam's cracked brown heels, my thin white calves, my feet sticking up, my long white toes, the red earth under my legs; I long for another pair of white eyes to be seeing this.

Suddenly Miriam shouts, "Run, run into the house," and I run wet, confused. A tub filled with pink-colored water now sits on the floor. Melita quickly strips off the wet wraps and tells me to wash first my hair, then my face, arms and legs and feet in the tub. "Quickly, quickly," she says, and I kneel over the tub, rinsing first my hair, then my face, my arms, my legs.

"Get in," she says, "get in with your feet," and I stand in the tub. "Now get out," and as I step out she begins to dry me and then helps me pull on a T-shirt and a fresh wrap. This is too strange and happening too fast for me to register, and I just dumbly do what I'm told.

Melita hands me one of the squares of colored fabric that Joyce and I bought earlier, and tells me to run out with it and tie it around Joyce's neck. I run out to Joyce, but my fingers are shaking so much that I have a hard time tying the knot. When I am finally done, Madota and Miriam run with me back into the house. There they each tie around their calves the broad leather bands stitched with soda-can tops. When they move their legs, the can tops rattle together and make a clattering sound.

These rattles were originally made of seed pods attached to leather strips, and probably out in the country they still are. But here, tradition incorporates modernity, and besides, the *sangomas* prefer the louder rattle made by the soda-can tops.

The three of us run out again, following closely behind one another. Miriam, her voice rising high, introduces the rhythm, *"Kwasa, kwasa ngihleli ebaleni,"* and the answering voice of the women join in, *"Kwasa, kwasa ngihleli ebaleni."* Then the drums begin, pounding into the voices, carrying the beat deep into the earth, high into the air.

Miriam and Madota begin the dance, moving their feet in unison, first the slow easy step from foot to foot. I watch their feet, my eyes riveted, and follow their steps, giving thanks for the lesson with Sylvia. The pace increases and their feet move faster and faster, to a gallop, and the women clap and break their singing to cheer us on. Then we slow again.

By now the crowd has swelled, spilling into the small yard, men, women, and children watching and clapping. As we stop between dances, I am suddenly aware of my whiteness and I am strangely embarrassed, but then Miriam leads the chanting into the next round of singing and dancing and again we move from the slow pace to the fast gallop while I concentrate on moving my feet with theirs.

Women ululate, their voices rising above the rattling of the ankle wraps. My thighs are tiring, but a third song is introduced, and again the pace increases, the insistent drums pushing it along. Finally we slow and stop.

I sit on the mat, my chest thumping. Miriam begins a round of spirit-speak, moving back and forth in front of the seated *sangomas*, whirling her whisk, telling each one of them what she sees, drawing on her powers of divination. She concludes each sentence with *"Kanvume,"* Is it true? and the crowd echoes *"Siyavuma,"* Yes, it is true.

Then Madota takes over, repeating the ritual of spirit-speak, the same thrusting sentences ending with *"Kanvume"* and the crowds reply *"Siyavuma."* Then she leads the drums into the next song. With each song, one, two, or three of the *sangomas* dance, the women ululate. At the conclusion of each dance there is laughter and hugs and chants of *"Thokoza, thokoza."*

Sylvia arrives and immediately joins in. Each of the *sangomas* takes her turn speaking the growling spirit-talk, moving back and forth in front of the seated others, whisks drawing stories in space, then leading solo-voiced into the song, the other voices joining, followed by the hard beat of the drums. Then the feet move in the prescribed steps of the dance.

It is all in Zulu and I don't understand anything, but the driving energy and the hoarse spirit-speak, the swirling red skirts and pounding feet sweep me along like a magnet. Every now and then I hear my new name, my spirit name, Melisande, and I know they are saying something about me.

While we have been dancing, the chickens, their legs still tied, have been lying on the red earth close to the wrap that had earlier been stretched between the two sticks.

Now Madota picks them up, again tucks one under each arm, and goes out to the gateway where she crouches; again I am told to crouch alongside her. At the signal, once again we run into the yard. This time we stop and kneel before the upright shawl. In front of it, on the reed mat, are three small, tin dishes: in one a mound of cornmeal, in another a mound of tea, and in the third a small amount of snuff. It is as though an altar has been made with offerings.

I hear Miriam chanting behind us, and Madota transfers the chickens from her arms to mine. I put them on the ground carefully, so that their tied legs will keep them upright. Kneeling between them, holding their necks with each hand, I stroke their feathers, knowing it is their time to die. I speak to them quietly, apologizing, asking forgiveness.

The *sangomas* chant in Zulu, stopping now to take a pinch of cornmeal and sprinkle it on the ground, now a pinch of snuff and sprinkling that. Small stones dig into my knees. Then I am told to leave the chickens and sit on the mat where the drumming *sangomas* sit.

The sun is at its most liquid now, spilling its golden redness onto the earth. Around me the women's voices rise, and on each side the drums start up their beat, swelling, the sound hammering into my head, into my chest. In front of me the dancers' feet pound, lifting small clouds of dust; as my mouth fills with the dry, red earth, between their flashing legs I see the knife and the bowl into which the blood from the chickens will run.

And I remember their feet, as they sat with their bound legs beside me, like little old ladies' hands, with long, tapered nails, women's nails. I see wings beat once, twice. As the drum sound fills and spills in and around, tears run down my cheeks, into my mouth. Madota carries the basin into the house, the quiet white wings spread over the rim.

Once more the act is repeated, once more the blood drains slowly into the bowl, the bird is held down until the wings slowly stop beating, and then is carried into the house. Outside the dancing continues. Inside Madota quickly plucks out the white feathers. And when I come in they are clean.

By now the crowd has grown even larger. Men and women, even some of the children, join in the dancing. Six, seven, eight, nine, ten dances. I sit on the reed mat and watch. A couple of the children sidle around and stand near me. I smile at them and they run back and hide behind their mothers. Joyce comes and sits next to me. She puts down a fifty-cent piece. Someone has asked me to dance.

"No, give the money back," I say, "I'll dance, but not for money."

"No, you must take it," says Joyce. "It's for luck." I ask Miriam to dance with me; I'm not yet confident enough to dance on my own. In her full voice she introduces the music, the singers and drums take up the tune, and we dance. I watch her feet and follow, the crowd claps and ululates, and finally, as my body relaxes into the rhythm, I am thankful not only for the lessons with Sylvia, but also the obligatory, but hated, ballet training of my youth.

The sky is darkening now, and Miriam calls me into the house. She seems to be hoping that with me out of sight the crowd will begin to go. We watch out the window, but the singing, drumming, and dancing continue in endless rounds, the people show no sign of leaving.

"Do you always have a crowd like this when you dance?" I ask.

"No," says Miriam, "this is because of you; this is your wedding dream." I look at her nonplussed. "Your wedding dream," she repeats. And suddenly I see it: the women, the children, the activity, the several of us dressed alike in wedding dresses—*sangoma* dresses. I look at her and she laughs, her scalloped gums wide.

Finally some of the crowd begins to break up, but a large number follow the drums into the house. Beer, home-brewed and store-bought, appears from nowhere and the partying continues. People standing, sitting, cramming into corners; only a small center of the room is left unbodied and here the dancing continues.

I sit on the bed wedged between Melita and Miriam's daughter. Inside the tin hut the drum sound is shattering, the ululating spirals and bounces off the walls, sound fills even the smallest crevice. The paraffin burners hiss and heat, and add their gasoline smell to the thick, sweet closeness of the crowded bodies. In front of the altared corner the uncooked half of one of the chickens lies on a plate, next to it the bowl of blood.

Much later when we eat, I notice that half of a cooked chicken has also been added to the corner. I am given a leg and mealie pap; I eat some of the pap but I cannot eat the leg—I had too recently held the bird—and give it to Madota.

There are fresh faces in the house now. Again someone asks me to dance. Joyce, being watchful, says that it is late now and I am tired, but I want to dance. I am beginning to find a liberation in this dancing; liberation from the rigid constraints of that dancing of my youth with its judgments and requirements of talent; and more important, liberation from the inhibiting shame at my awful lack of talent. Now I begin to dance freely, allowing only the sound and the rhythm to move my body. And as the beat quickens, my feet fly in sweet deliverance and my soul soars. Afterward, as I stagger back to the bed, my legs shaking, people hug me, touch me, hold me.

Two men, young men, sit across the room; one of them speaks to me but the singing and the drums drown out his words. I move across the room and kneel by his side. He seems stern.

"This is not a game," he says slowly, "this is not play. This is serious." I am startled. He repeats it again, and since I don't know what else to say, I repeat back what I heard from him. "Yes," he says, "you understand."

Then the other man speaks. He is taller and bearded. "This is not something for you to play at," he says, reiterating what the other man had said. And then he adds his own thought, one that will stay like a mantra in my head. "You hold our people like leaves in your hands," he says, cupping his hands. "You must treat them gently."

I am suddenly moved, and feel my throat tighten and tears prick at my lids. There are no words, so I put my hands in his.

•

It is well past midnight when people begin to leave, but the *sangomas* still have work to do with Madota. She has not yet been given her spirit name and, since she is soon coming to the end of her training, it now needs to be called forth.

Earlier, while we were sitting on the bed, Melita had leaned close to me. "You are so lucky," she had said.

"Why?" I asked.

"Because you have got your spirit name."

And at different times during the afternoon and evening one or another of the *sangomas* had come and asked me the name I had been given in my dream. "Melisande," I'd said, "Melisande." And they had repeated it to themselves, almost dreamily: "Melisande."

"But why am I lucky?" I asked.

"Because you can go quickly now."

"Quicker than if I hadn't gotten my spirit name?"

"Yes," Melita answered.

Madota now sits cross-legged on the floor and is covered with two sheets. The *imphepho* is lit and held in front of her. The *sangomas* form a tight circle around her, holding tight the sheets. Miriam begins the singing, her daughter shakes the rattle, Joyce blows a whistle, and the drums begin. The sound builds until it crashes about the room like a storm.

Madota's hoarse spirit voice begins from under the sheets. The women answer her, *"Yezwake, yezwake."* On and on goes the singing, whistling, drumming, and rattling. Again and again Madota spirit-speaks and the *sangomas* answer.

Under the sheets Madota begins to shake. The sound increases, her shaking increases for five minutes, ten, fifteen, I think my eardrums will explode, then the *sangomas* give a loud final shout, *"Yezwake!"* and she has her spirit name and the sheets are lifted.

Later, when I watched yet another *thwasa* be blanketed under sheets and held tight with the steaming herb and the stupefying sound, I wondered if her spirit name had come to her just so that she could get out from under; perhaps it doesn't matter.

Finally we go to bed. Miriam's daughter and I share the bed. Several blankets and an eiderdown are pulled out of the bathtub. These are laid out in a row across the room at the foot of the bed. Eight women share this. Madota lies on a reed mat in front of the altar. The *sangomas* take off their shawls and beads and settle down on the eiderdown and blankets. The two candles are blown out and I settle on my side.

But sleep doesn't come easily. At the bottom of the bed, in the darkness, the *sangomas* chatter quietly.

I think about Miriam, standing in the doorway, looking out at the crowd, saying, "This is your wedding dream." I think about Ralph Laubscher, standing beside my bed saying, "Your name is Melisande."

Melisande, the name Starbuck gives Lizzie in the play *The Rainmaker*, the play in which Ralph played Starbuck, the rainmaker. And here, on this dark continent, where rain is regarded as the mystical link between past, present, and future, where it is regarded as the eternal made manifest, rainmakers are revered, for they are the means whereby this link with the eternal is created; the rainmakers, the people say, "know the words of God."

How the patterns swirl through time and space; how our lives twine and circle, now braided garlands, now separate strands, now reaching back to braid once again.

And how I love growing older, this gift of age, which allows us to see the garlands of our dance through time. How can we doubt that there is design to this dance when there is such grace, such elegance to the patterns, as beautiful as the swirls and butterfly wings that trace the pattern of chaos into order.

The women chatter on and on and finally I doze.

We leave early the next morning after a cup of tea and the use of a neighbor's outdoor toilet.

All around, in the slanting sunlight, women with straw whisks are sweeping their red-earth yards. Across the road a little girl of five or six is helping her father kill a chicken. Perhaps they, too, will leave half for the spirits.

We head back, north on the M-1 through the clear blue morning air. Joyce's madam will not have her scones at eight o'clock, but she may have them by nine.

14

Learning to Divine

After dropping Joyce off in Bordeaux, I race back to Hyde Park to call Ron. My excitement spills out and tumbles across the continents. "Oh, I really wanted another pair of white eyes to be seeing this," I say; and then, "No, no, it would have changed it." Then, "It was Ernest Hemingway in Africa . . ." On and on, and Ron, dear Ron, knowing just how to listen, just how to answer, until I have talked myself out.

Then I blissfully sink my body in the old bathtub that is, unlike the ones back home, long enough so that I can stretch out my legs, and I let the water run until it laps just under my chin.

I think back to the water, poured over my head like an ancient baptism rite. Water, the first element, the feminine element. And water gave birth to spirit. But that was an old pagan belief that the

Christians borrowed. How odd to find it here in Africa, and yet here it is. It is in the water that the spirits reside and it is water that gives rise to spirit. How wonderful to have been a part of so ancient a ritual.

*O*riving back from Lenz in the silver morning light, Joyce had said that now she would begin testing me to see whether I could "see," and at the dreaded word "testing," my stomach clenched.

Learning to see is the most important part of the *sangoma* training. When a client comes to a *sangoma* for help, the *sangoma* must be able to see, or feel, what is happening with that person. A client does not tell a *sangoma* where she has pain; the *sangoma* must know and tell the client.

As with their bodies, so the *sangoma* must know what is happening with their lives: whether their wives or husbands are cheating on them, whether someone has put a spell on their house, whether they are pregnant, or whether they will find a job soon.

So when I go over to Bordeaux that evening I am nervous. So nervous that I forget to take off my shoes when I into Joyce's room. "Take off your shoes," she says patiently, "and eat the foam."

I kneel in front of the little ocher and black clay pot. "Should I do it here?" I ask, the ritual suddenly totally forgotten.

"No," she says, rolling her eyes, "bring it to the doorway."

When I am finished Joyce brings out several loops of small beads, some red and white, some white. These are the beads I'll be wearing while I am a *thwasa*, and some, like the red and white beads that wrap around my ankles and neck, I will always wear.

"I'm going to hide these," she says, "and you will tell me where they are. Now go and wait outside."

I wait in the little hallway, pacing. Soon her voice rings out. "Come in," she sings, "sit here." She unrolls a reed mat on the floor and I sit on it.

"Where are the beads?" she asks.

For a few moments I sit with my eyes closed, then sense that the answer lies to my left. I slowly move my left arm up and out, hand turned down. "It is on this side," I say.

"You are correct. Where on this side?"

I slowly move my hand forward a little and then back a little. "It is somewhere around here," I say after a while, the sensing seeming to occur in the downturned palm of my hand.

"You are correct. Are they on the floor or in something?"

I try to sense this but get little from my hand. "On the floor," I say eventually.

"No, you are wrong," she answers.

But I know they are on the floor, but maybe not directly. "They are in something on the floor," I say.

"You are correct. What are they in?"

I know that my hand is hovering somewhere near her corner filled with scores of little bottles, and for a moment I panic. Then I breathe deeply and empty my head. My palm feels a presence. I move it just slightly back and forth, and as though there is a magnet, it responds to the position. "They are here," I say.

"What are they in?" she asks again.

I see a picture of her clay pot with the water and *isitundu*. My mind quarrels: She would never drop them into the pot with the water and herbs.

"What are they in?" she asks again. My hand hovers over the spot, feeling the attraction. "Are they in the pot?" I ask.

"No, don't ask," she says, "tell me what they're in."

My hand is sure, but my mind quavers in inner dialogue.

I will learn later that inner dialogue absolutely cuts off any intuitive response and that I must clear it out of my head as quickly as possible.

"They're in the pot," I finally say.

"Open your eyes."

My palm has been over the pot.

"Now bring the pot here."

I pick up the pot with both hands.

"Now take the stick and lift the beads out," she says. I pull out the red and white beads: the set of ankle beads and the necklace, and the two strings of white beads that will cross my chest. I have left one item behind, and she fishes out the white beaded double loop that will go in my hair.

"Come here," she says, and I kneel in front of her. She feels around the crown of my head, moving hairs this way and that. Then she seems to find a suitable strand and begins to fasten the loop to it.

Warmth laps my crown, oozing out from her working fingers like heated honey. When she is done she asks if I felt anything. I tell her of the lapping warmth and she claps her hand to her mouth.

"What?" I ask, almost alarmed.

"It means your head is opening," she says.

It is important that my head "opens," because this means that the spirits will be able to enter and tell me what I need to know.

She ties the two shorter red-and-white beaded strands around each ankle, measuring carefully so that they rest just above the bone. Then the longer red-and-white strand goes around my neck. Wherever she touches me, works the beads around me, the seeping warmth infuses. Cells come deliciously alive, delighting in this process. Then I slip the white strands over my head and across my chest and I am complete. There are no more beads to be received until the final test when I graduate.

Next, she opens the wooden cupboard and takes out a red skirt. It is simply made, with a cord running through one length.

"From now on you will wear this," she says, and I take off my slacks and she ties the cord around my waist.

"Now wait outside," she says again.

In the hallway I look at my ankles, the red skirt, feel the beads in my hair. Do I feel different, I wonder, now that I am dressed as a *thwasa*? Not yet, not yet.

"Now what else did I hide?" she asks when she calls me back in. I sit with my eyes closed. The picture of something round appears.

"It's something round," I say, "no bigger than this." I make a small circle with finger and thumb.

"You are right," she says. "What is it?"

"It shines," I say.

"You are right. What is it?"

The picture of a coin enters my head, but again there's the inner quarreling. I plough on. "It is round and it is small and it is shiny."

"You are right," she says. "What is it?"

I want to say money, but the inner dialogue gets in the way. "Is it a key?" I ask.

"No, it is not a key," she answers.

Eventually, I stutter it out. "It's money, it's a coin."

"You are right," she says. "Where is it?"

"Under the carpet," I say. I lean forward and play my palms over the carpet edge nearest her bed, feeling for a response. I don't feel anything. I come back closer to where I sit.

"No, it's not there," she says. I go back to the edge close to her bed and again play my palms over the carpet edge. A slight pull. I lift the corner, and there it is.

"You are learning to see," she says softly.

That night, as I listen to the rustling of leaves on the corrugated tin roof, my cells come so joyfully awake that I laugh out loud.

"What is it?" asks Joyce.

"My spirits are happy," I answer. And indeed they are.

My sister-in-law laughs her smoky, sultry laugh when she sees me in the *thwasa* regalia. "You're not really going to run around like that?" she says. "Yup," I answer, "I am."

Now when I walk in the shopping center across the road, or go into the supermarket, I am greeted with stares. Hyde Park tends to the elegant and, unlike Southern California, most Johannesburg women still dress up to go shopping, all high heels, red lips, and earrings. The sight of me in my red skirt, white T-shirt, and red, white, and black wrap emblazoned with a bold sun raises some eyebrows. Among blacks, the stares have a different quality; they know what the emblems mean.

"*Hau*, are you *sangoma*?" I'm asked again and again.

"No, I'm *thwasa*," I reply, and I feel their eyes following me.

A woman coming up the stairs while I'm going down sees my ankle bands first and has clapped her hands and said, "*Thokoza*," before it sinks in that I'm white, and she looks as though she's seen a ghost.

In the supermarket the African staff call to each other to come and see, and they gather around and take my hand and ask who my teacher is. And through all the attention I try to stay serene, battling a little with both aspects of the divide: my ego with the black population, and a slight embarrassment with the whites.

I have my own clay bowl that I take home, and three times a day I whip up and eat the foam of *isitundu* and light the *imphepho* and inhale its sweet lift smell. Sometimes I am aware of the region of my third eye humming with activity. Sometimes, in the quiet of my inner ear, I hear a command to face the sun, and I go outside and turn to the east. And then my American meditation rises: It is my father the sun, it is the place of enlightenment; and in the enchantment of the blend of African and Native American I stand for a long while drinking in the light, then begin the completion, facing next the south, the place of new growth, the west, place of my mother the earth, and then north, where the four winds meet.

Sometimes my third eye vibrates even as I move through the day, and then I return to the pot and scoop up a small bit of the remaining foam and place it between my eyes and ask that this third eye close.

The routine of seeing or divining will occupy every evening from now on, but it becomes contained within the full *thwasa* ritual.

Now, when I arrive at six o'clock, we each go down on one knee and clap twice saying, "*Thokoza, unjani, ngikhona, thokoza.*" Sometimes, before we go into the bedroom and begin working, we sit on either side of the little table while Joyce relaxes for a few minutes.

Or Mercia has not yet finished eating and Joyce still has to clear up and wash the dishes.

It is a long day for them, these maids, and I'm not surprised that they'd like to earn overtime. They usually begin early, at seven in the morning, and sometimes they don't finish till seven at night. And the days seem to be filled with endlessly repetitive chores designed only to keep them busy, sweeping areas that couldn't possibly have gathered dust since the last sweeping.

Joyce is clearly not happy with Mercia; almost every evening when I ask how her day has been, she rolls her eyes heavenward. But, as will be the case with every maid who talks about issues with her "madam," she will not talk to Mercia about whatever is troubling her, and resorts instead to balkings and bickerings.

Eventually Joyce will say, *"Masingene endlini,"* let's go in, and I take off my shoes and we go into Joyce's room. I now cross the threshold to her room on my knees, both when entering and leaving. In the room, I pull off my T-shirt and Joyce wraps the sun-centered shawl around my bust. In the sacred corner with the shawls and little bottles, I light the *imphepho* and lean over it a while inhaling, slowing my breathing, allowing the *imphepho* to clear and open my head.

Joyce has carved a stick for me, about eighteen inches long. All the *thwasas* carry such a stick, and when not in use push it down in the back area between the shoulder blades so that it is held in place by bra and T-shirt.

Now the stick is standing upright in the corner, and when the *imphepho's* smoking spirals thin and I am steeped in its stillness, I pick it up. Then Joyce begins to clap and sing.

Sometimes when I arrive Sylvia is there with Joyce. Then the two *sangomas* sit on the floor and sing.

"Siyabingalela ngonyama ihawu legoso," and I dance, moving one foot in front of the other, first slowly and then faster, from foot to foot and ending with a quick gallop. *Umdawu* dancing, dancing to make magic.

When they stop and Joyce calls, *"Yezwake,"* I go down on one knee and quick-click my fingers: *"Shaya ngikutshele, shaya ngikutshele,* Clap your hands and I will tell you," I say.

"Yezwake," they respond.

"Shaya ngikutshele, shaya ngikutshele," I say again, waiting for a picture, a beginning place.

"Yezwake," they respond; and so we continue until finally I say, "It is big."

"Yezwake," they answer, their voices rising.

"Is this thing outside or inside?" they ask.

"Shaya ngikutshele, shaya ngikutshele, Outside," I answer.

"Yezwake," they say, their voices rising.

"Who made this thing?" Joyce asks.

"Shaya ngikutshele, shaya ngikutshele, God made this thing."

"Yezwake." Their voices rise again.

"Shaya ngikutshele, shaya ngikutshele, It is a tree," I say.

"Yez." Their voices drop; this means no.

"I'm going to dance," I say, and I get up and dance while they sing and clap their hands. Often when I feel stuck while divining, I get up and dance, and the action seems to jog me beyond the sticking point. When Joyce says, *"Yezwake,"* I drop back onto my knee and again begin to click my fingers.

"Shaya ngikutshele, shaya ngikutshele."

"Is this thing on top or on the ground?" Joyce asks.

"On top," I say.

"Yezwake," they shout.

"What color is this thing?"

My fingers click. "It is bright," I say.

"Yezwake." Their voices rise high. "What is it?"

"It is light," I say.

"Yes, yes, yes, it is light." They are falling into one another's arms in anticipation.

"The sun," I shout, and we all collapse into each other in a heap.

"Thank you, God," says Joyce, and Sylvia ululates. "Beautiful, beautiful, my darling," she says.

But I am not yet finished. I still have to put the sun on the ground in front of me. I reach up with both arms and, miming, carry the sun down from the heavens and place it on the ground. Then I run to the corner, take up a pinch of ash, sprinkle it on the sun, put first one foot and then the other on it, and begin to dance again while they sing and clap until, *"Yezwake,"* Joyce says, and the process begins again.

Usually we go through three, sometimes four such rounds of dancing and divining, by which time my thighs are shaking and I am sweating and panting.

Then, between gasps, I give thanks to my parents, to my grand-parents and great-grandparents, then to all my higher spirits, asking that they may keep opening my head so that I may see. Once more I am up and dance, then facing the sacred corner, the one with the bottles and wraps, I sit down quickly and stretch each arm forward, stretch out my legs, and then take my toes with opposite hands and pull out, stretching the joints. This is telling my spirits that they may leave me now.

"Oh, you are so quick," they say, and Joyce leans forward to stroke me.

"Oh," I answer, "I thought I was slow."

"No," they answer, "you are so clever and quick."

And it warms the cockles of my heart to be so praised.

When we have finished dancing and divining, we cook dinner; always mealie pap with a few pieces of chicken, or stew, which we eat sitting on the floor watching television. Then we go through the herbs. Herbs to get pregnant; herbs to take while pregnant; herbs to boil string in to place around the newborn baby's belly to keep him healthy; herbs to draw closed the soft spot on his head.

Joyce takes a thick piece of eggshell out of the cabinet. "Do you know what this is?" she asks. I shake my head. "It is ostrich shell. We use it when a baby is vomiting. We grate it fine, fine, fine, and put it in the baby's food and give it to him until he stops vomiting. And eggshell, when your eye is sore and red, then you take some eggshell and make it just like powder and put it in a little water and drop it in your eyes."

"Eggshell," I say, dubiously.

"Yes, eggshell."

One night we talk about lightning; perhaps it was a stormy night. If you're afraid of lightning, says Joyce, you take water that is running down the street from a rainstorm and mix it with tap water, and drink it until your tummy is full, then *phalaza*. Or there's *ikatazo*, a little piece of brown woodiness. You put it in your pocket and you won't be scared. Then to get rid of the lightning, you bite a little bit of it and spit it out in four directions and say go, go, go, go, and the lightning will go.

I ask Joyce how she learned about all the different herbs.

"Sometimes," she answers, "I just dream that I must go and walk in the veldt and pick this one or that one and use it."

"Don't you worry that it might be poisonous?" I ask.

"No," she says and laughs. "If it was going to be poisonous, then my spirits wouldn't show it to me."

Will my western mind ever think this way? I wonder.

One evening as I sit panting after divining, I ask Sylvia and Joyce about the practice. "Fortuning" is what Joyce calls the process of divining. It differs from the concept of "telling one's fortune" in that it does not necessarily predict future happenings but rather addresses what is currently going on in a client's life. "Why doesn't the client just come in and tell you what's wrong?" I ask.

"No," they answer together, shaking their heads. "When you go to the doctor you don't tell him what is wrong; he must know that you have this wrong with you or that wrong with you."

"No," I say, "when I go to the doctor I will tell her that I have a sore throat or a bad stomach."

They look totally aghast. "And you pay them for that?!"

15

The Work Goes on and Western Worries

༄

A month of nights with Joyce goes by quickly.

"You must try and *phalaza* again," Joyce said a couple of times, and I begin a modified version, working with small amounts of the pink liquid. I also continue to inhale the deadly snuff, though my nose is still constantly blocked or running, and every now and then it suddenly bleeds, no matter how small a pinch I take. Often now the region of my third eye feels aroused, drawn forward, in a sensation that is almost painful, and occasionally the east calls and I face the morning sun and meditate on light, on enlightenment.

And one morning while I meditate, eyes closed over the wisping smoke curls of the *imphepho*, my shoulders curve into a different shape, my nose lifts differently to the air. A rolling motion begins, starting with my shoulders; it is strange, yet familiar. And I am gone.

My front legs tread in sure footfalls, shoulders rolling. I walk on substance, yet in space; untethered, unleashed from belonging. All is consumed in the motion, in the liquidly repetitive padding, in the smooth sweep of the shoulders.

As with the snake, this creature has become me, my body—her host. We travel through an insubstantial surround where no sound penetrates, where there is no sense of time.

The return is slow, reluctant. Sound returns first, then sensation. When I open my eyes, the contours of the furniture seem hard and square.

Joyce looks at me long and hard when I tell her. "What kind of animal?" she asks.

"I'm not sure," I answer, "not a lion, more like a leopard." She nods but doesn't answer.

Ron is due to arrive shortly, and for these last few days alone I'd been worried. All my concentration had been going into working with Joyce; there was no one else to tug at me.

And indeed, once he is here I seem to feel immobilized. During the day I don't eat the foam regularly or inhale the *imphepho*; my attention is split between the *sangoma* work and him. Not that he does anything to distract me, it is just the fact of his being here. From the beginning Joyce had been clear that we were not to have sex while I was in training, and aside from the occasional nudges, he holds to the agreement.

I soon feel mired. The thought of driving to Bordeaux becomes galling and I stall and arrive late. When I dance I am slow to see.

"Your spirits are not coming up today," Sylvia says one night after a laborious session of dancing and divining.

"No, they're not."

"Don't worry, we all go through times like this while we are training. Sometimes it feels like we just want to say, forget this, but you must fight this feeling, just fight it and keep going, and the spirits will come back up." And I feel relieved that it's not just me.

One evening after I have been particularly slow and sit in embarrassed silence, a woman comes to visit Joyce. Her name is Emily. She is plump, dark-skinned and pink-cheeked.

As she and Joyce speak in Zulu, I become increasingly aware that my hands feel hot and prickly, my face sweaty, my mouth dry, and somewhere in my legs an ache begins. After a while I interrupt. "Emily, do your hands sometimes feel hot and prickly?" I ask.

"Yes," the woman answers.

"And your face," I ask, "does your face also sometimes feel hot and your mouth dry?"

"Yes," she says again, and she says something to Joyce in Zulu. Now they are both looking at me.

"And your body also," I say as the heat moves from my face down my chest.

"Yes," she answers.

"Your legs, they also hurt you?"

Her eyes are wide.

Something clicks in my head. "Do you drink a lot of water?" I ask.

"Yes," she says, "even at night."

I am suddenly sure that she is diabetic. But how to say it? How to leap across the cultures? Also, I cannot undermine Joyce, and I feel that by saying something I would be doing just that.

Later, when she is gone, I ask Joyce if she has been prescribing anything for her. Yes, she says, she is giving her herbs to *phalaza* and steam herself, but, she adds, the sickness is because she must take the spirit and become a *sangoma*. Her spirits are calling her.

That night I wrestle with the conundrum of my western worries and traditional practices. What if this woman is diabetic? What if she goes on believing it's the spirits calling her? The next morning when, back at the flat, I see Jean out watering her little garden below, I go down and talk to her about it.

"This is why doctors can't stand *sangomas*," she explodes. "Here this poor woman could well lose her sight or her legs. You've got to say something to Joyce."

For a few days I mull this over, unsure of how to raise the issue. Finally, one night I tell Joyce of someone I knew who had similar symptoms and was diagnosed as diabetic. "Perhaps Emily should go and have a blood test," I suggest, "because it's something that could become dangerous."

But Joyce's eyes close down and I know this will go no further.

My dreams lately have been filled with images of men with no legs or with only stumps for legs. When I tell Joyce about them she says that it is my spirits. "Your spirits want to be picked up again, because when Ron came they went down, down, down."

"What must I do?"

"No, you just keep eating your foam and doing your herbs and you will be all right."

Later on we talk some more about dreams.

"If somebody keeps dreaming she's having a baby or she's sleeping with a man, or a man with a wife, that's not good."

"Why?" I ask.

"That means," Joyce answers, "that there is somebody sending you horrible things. It's when you dream that same thing again and again."

"How," I ask, "do people send these bad things?"

"I don't know," she answers, "because I don't know how to do it."

"Why do people do these things?"

"Because they're jealous," she responds. "Like I'm working, and maybe they think I'm getting lots of money and they want the job. Or they want my house or the things inside. It's only the jealous ones who do those things. They go to people who are willing to do bad things, and they pay the money and they take *muti* and come to your house and put it around there. And that's why I give someone *muti* to spray outside their house; it's to kill those bad things."

"When you spray, will it take care of it forever?" I ask.

"No," Joyce answers, "you see, when you spray, then the bad things will go back to the one who sent it. They'll see those things coming back in a dream, or they will start itching, and they will say, 'Oh, I see these things are coming back to worry me,' and they will try again."

"So it's a case of who can last the longest," I say.

"Yes, who can last the longest. You see, instead of taking the money and buying something nice, like a dress or something for the house, they buy the *muti* to do the bad things."

Later, when I'm lying on the foam mattress, I think about the conversation I had with Pip Erasmus six or seven months ago about *sangomas*. He had said then that so much of their belief is based on superstition. That, for example, if your car drives over a nail and your tire is punctured, it is not a random act of chance, rather it is that the nail was "put" there by somebody because they were jealous of you or had a grudge against you.

And I remember his almost cavalier attitude toward *sangomas*, and then the story he told about being awakened one night with his bed shaking and continuing to shake until he commanded the spirits to leave. And here I am now, wedged between my western being and experiences for which there are no explanations.

The amount of time we spend on the herbs is less now; most of the time is given over to dancing and divining. One night while divining, as soon as I drop onto my knees to say *"shaya ngikutshele,"* a picture of the pug dog that lives across the road pops fully formed into my head. And when I say it, Sylvia throws up her arms and shouts, "Oh, my God," and breaks into a high, loud ululatation, and she and Joyce throw themselves into each other's arms, then into my arms. This is the first time that an image has revealed itself so quickly.

Eventually Joyce regains control and starts to sing again as I reach for the imaginary dog and place it on the floor in front of me. I then take a pinch of ash and sprinkle it on the spot where I put the dog, place each foot on the ash, and begin dancing. And there are other times now when the picture of what Joyce is thinking appears almost immediately, like a photograph, in my mind.

Oh strange, strange process, strange only to me though, swaying in some never-never land, neither an unquestioning African disciple nor Eurognostic.

One evening, while we cook, we talk about customs. Sylvia tells how, in her culture, a girl passes from childhood into womanhood. When a girl has her first period, she is kept at home for ten days, after which she is led to the river where she washes herself and puts on new clothes that are special for the occasion. Young men, from the ages of seventeen to twenty, are taken up to the hilltop where they are circumcised by the medicine man. They stay there, usually in a group of eight to ten, for about three months, until they are healed.

Sylvia says that her son is now nineteen and will soon have to be circumcised. She will probably take him to a hospital to have it done, she says, rather than back in the village.

And I am just amazed at the transition Sylvia represents, that so many of these women represent, one foot planted in the world of old tradition and the other in the white, western ways of being.

And I wonder whether they have given up more than they have gained.

A man comes to see Joyce. He has been feeling as though there are spiders' webs all over his face and he has sore joints and a pain in his side. Joyce prescribes, first, steaming for him, every other night. For the pain in his side she takes a penknife and makes quick prods around his waist with the knife point, not breaking the skin, just a light touch, touch, touch from side to side, and then when she is done, she touches the point of the knife to the floor. As usual I want to ask why, and as usual I know the answer: No, we just do it that way.

I worry about whether there is something severe going on with his liver or gallbladder that should be looked at by a medical person, but I hold my tongue. I cannot question her judgment, and I have to suspend my western thinking. But it's hard.

*N*ewsweek has a long article on AIDS, and I take it to show to Joyce and Sylvia. We had talked about AIDS before, after I met Daniel, Joyce's twenty-year-old son.

"Straight up," my physician friend Viva had said about the rate of AIDS increase in southern Africa, so I urged Joyce to speak to Daniel about using a condom. But she had seemed disinterested.

Now I show them the tables giving the numbers of HIV-infected people on each continent. Sub-Saharan Africa has the highest number by far, with 7.5 million. They are stupefied. They didn't know there were that many people on the face of the earth!

I ask them what black people are saying about AIDS. "They say how is it that only white people are talking about this; that is what black people are saying."

Now I was showing them the figures, and it was clear that they were amazed. But again, once I begin to speak, to suggest that Joyce speak to her son about the dangers, to suggest that both of them, when they cut people, use a fresh blade, they quickly lose interest. It seems that when I move into the role of teaching them about western responses to illness, their eyes glaze over and they pull away.

*M*eanwhile, my other, daytime life continues. Ron and I spend days looking at furniture or pictures for the flat. He has a hard time walking around with me in my *thwasa* wrappings, but he enjoys the attention. "That skirt makes you look like a sack of potatoes," he says. But he is good-humored about it.

Often we drive to Hillbrow, that Haight-Ashbury of Johannesburg, where we have delicately flavored Greek lunches, or toasted cheese sandwiches at sidewalk cafés and watch a world sometimes as strange as *Star Trek* revolve by. Burly Greek men with their shirt sleeves rolled high and their biceps bulging; slim young men of indeterminate color in skintight pants sway by sensuously.

A young man dressed in leather with studs and with bleached hair carries a monkey on his shoulder; two brown prostitutes come to blows over a pale German tourist; every now and then an armored car with men in green carrying rifles. Black men, some boys, some old, hustle to direct cars into parking spaces for small change, and two-storied buses cloud the narrow street with fumes.

While the country gentles into fall, the days have been sunny and warm. Everywhere there is a mix of hope and despair. The radio is filled with optimistic talk of the new South Africa. Cars sprout bumper stickers calling for peace. Meanwhile, in the townships, on the trains, the blacks kill each other.

Among our friends, it is the white men who seem to be having the hardest time with the upcoming transition, moving farther and farther to the right, their speech peppered with epithets such as "kaffir," their jokes diseased with racism.

But not all of them. Dennis, Ron's brother, says, "We are witnessing a most remarkable period in history. Do you know this is the first time a government will be voting itself out of power?"

When I go for my twice-weekly Zulu lessons I watch Mehlo's mouth making sounds that I know mine will never wrap around.

"*Chk,*" she says, "*chk,* like you're calling a horse."

"*Chk,*" I repeat, perfectly able to make the sound unattached to the rest of the word, but once attached, my tongue and lips flail.

And the rules! "If the left-most of any vowel juxtaposed is either *i* or *u* or *ou*, it changes into a semivowel; or, if the left-most of two vowels is *a*, *e*, *o*, and the right-most is *i*, *u*, then *i* becomes *e* and *u* becomes *o*." And I had been told that Zulu was the simplest of the African languages!

One night when I come into Joyce's little kitchen, there are two men waiting to be "fortuned." This evening Joyce tells me that I will start, and I am immediately panic-stricken.

We go into the little bedroom while Sylvia, who is also at Joyce's, waits outside. Joyce wraps the *ibayi*, the traditional white shawl with the red sun in its center, around my shoulders.

The men sit on the floor on the reed mat in front of the pink-bedspreaded bed, their legs stretched out in front of them. Their socks have holes in them. The lighter-skinned one moves with a nervous quickness; he holds a match between his teeth that he rolls with his fingers every now and then.

Joyce lights the *imphepho* and I breathe deeply, hoping that its sweet smoke will bring some illumination into my mind, which at this stage is frighteningly empty. Nothing comes. Dear spirits, I beg, a little illumination, please. Joyce gestures to the candle and I push it into the center of the room.

The one with the lighter skin places a ten-rand note on the floor between us and I tell him to light the candle. I sit looking first at its flame, and then long into his eyes. He looks directly back at me, mockingly. I wait. He rolls the matchstick between his lips. Then I start, and I talk without thinking, allowing the words to come out of my mouth.

"You have a tightness around your head." He shrugs slightly. "You get headaches here," and I gesture to over my eyes. He shrugs again, and I don't know whether he is saying yes or no. "Your neck often feels tight, and your shoulders." Again he shrugs. Joyce says something to him in Zulu, and he responds by answering, "Sometimes."

I feel him thinking, *No white bitch is going to tell me what's going on—least of all a white trainee.* But I continue. "There is a sadness deep in your belly," I say. He takes a while to answer, rolling the matchstick between his teeth, then nods and says, "Yes," almost mockingly.

"This sadness has to do with someone else in your life, someone close to you."

Again he rolls the matchstick around in his mouth. Then, "My life partner," he says.

Joyce tells me that is enough now, and she calls in Sylvia. I move to the stool.

Sylvia comes in and goes to the sacred corner where she takes down the whisk, and two sets of beads that she pulls over her head so that they cross her chest. She wraps an *ibayi* around her chest, and faces the corner where the *imphepho* smokes.

Deep growls rise up, like smoke, from her belly, move cavernously through her chest and out, filling the small room, warm and musky now with its five bodies, with its laboring animal sound. Her eyes are closed, she is on her knees, the candle is before her.

She begins to flail at herself with the switch, hitting from shoulder to shoulder. Then she starts: *"Shaya ngikutshele, shaya ngikutshele."* The words erupt as deeply cavernous as the growls; she crawls this way and that on her knees, hitting her shoulders with the whisk, eyes closed, head moving from side to side like an animal sniffing the air.

The sound crowds out all thought; we are riveted to her, melted down by the depth, the primitive essence. She begins to speak, first to the light-skinned one who has quickly taken the matchstick out of his mouth. She speaks rapidly, in Zulu; he answers, she talks. While she talks to him her voice is normal, then *"Aiyeh, aiyeh,"* she wails, pushing the air out of her body, panting, as though in the throes of labor. Again her eyes close, she moves from knee to knee, sweat pours from her face. She whips the switch. And again she talks.

I am awed by it all, wavering in and out of thoughts of theater.

How lame I must have seemed. This is worth something. For half an hour she continues, then she is done and she sits panting, wiping her face with her fingers. The men put on their shoes and leave.

When they've gone I say to Sylvia, "Wow, that was incredible. What did you see?"

"That man has got a lot of problems. His head here," she motions to her forehead, "is very tight, and down his neck and across his shoulders is very tight."

"You did see this also," Joyce says to me.

"Yes, but he was having no white dame tell him what was wrong with him."

They laugh. "You're right," Joyce says, "and some people don't want to have someone who is in training working with them."

Sylvia continues, "He wants his wife to leave the house they are in, but if he forces her out, the comrades will come after him and kill him. She is a schoolteacher and she can get the comrades to do this."

"Why doesn't he just go see a lawyer and take care of it legally?" I ask.

"Because he is afraid that then the comrades will get him," Sylvia answers. Those "comrades," the ones who would kill for a song, are often no more than children. They are the ones who have seen too much: too much violence, too much hatred. They are easily manipulated toward whatever cause, political or personal.

"What did you tell him?" I ask.

"No, it's very difficult," she says, "he should be putting *muti* down around the house, but if he does, she will find it, so he can't do anything at home."

After we eat and watch television for a while, Joyce helps Sylvia prepare to make a home safe. Sylvia has a client in Bloemfontein who has been experiencing strange things around her house: footsteps on the roof, fleeting figures that she sees out of the corner of her eye, strange sounds and strange illnesses.

Joyce has gathered about sixteen five-inch sticks made from

small branches that she has sharpened at one end, and six smooth river stones. Joyce takes a beaded horn out from among her *muti* bottles, and with her finger reaches in and hooks out lumps of a black, tarry-looking substance. I ask what it is. "It is herbs," she says.

She puts the horn aside and opens a small jar and hands it to me. "This is lion's fat," she says. I smell it. It smells musty. She adds half a teaspoon. Then she opens a second small jar. "This is horse's fat." I smell it also. It smells rancid. She adds a small amount of that as well. Then from a small, slim bottle she pours a half teaspoon of a dark liquid. "It looks like old car oil," I say.

"Yes." She mixes the ingredients and then takes each sharpened stick and smears the mixture around them, leaving the sharpened ends free. Then she takes the river stones and spreads the mix on them.

While she is preparing the sticks and stones, she explains that Sylvia will dig holes around the house and bury them, creating a barrier against anything bad that someone might be sending.

Once those are done and packed away in a plastic bag, she rummages in her *muti* cabinet and pulls out a handful of aloe leaves and snake-lily root. Sylvia begins pounding the leaves on a large flat stone with a smaller round one until what she has is a mushy mess. The bulbous roots are roughly grated. Joyce gives it a final looking over, then scoops it into a plastic bag and ties the ends together tightly.

Now Sylvia needs to be made safe so that she will not absorb any of the bad things, so she will be immune. She takes off her top and her skirt and tucks her petticoat into her panties. Joyce looks among her bottles and pulls out a small packet from which she takes a razor blade. I note that it is not a new one. Joyce stretches out the blade toward me. "Do you want to cut her?" she asks.

"Oh, God," I say, "I shake too much, she'd have zigzags."

Sylvia kneels, and Joyce parts the hair on the top of her head, then quickly makes a tiny cut with the razor. Then at the wrist, elbow, shoulder, throat, between her breasts, on the hips, knees, and instep. She waits a minute to make sure drops of blood have formed. Then she takes a black creamy substance from a small bottle and rubs it into each cut, starting with the head. When she is done Sylvia stands still with her arms out from her sides.

"Does it hurt?" I ask.

"It stings," she says. She stands until the *muti* has dried and then dresses again. She will leave the next morning for Bloemfontein.

The man who has been complaining of the sensation of spiders' webs around his face and a pain around the side of his abdomen has been coming every second day for his regimen of steamings. He strips down to his underpants and sits over the simmering herbs for fifteen minutes.

"*Hai, uh uh,*" he answers, shaking his head, when I ask *Unjani*, "How are you?" "The pains are getting worse," he says. Again I'm wracked by my western worries that something is clinically wrong, and also by guilt, that I'm not doing anything to help him get to qualified help. Then I shake my head. As far as he is concerned he is getting qualified help. *Oh God*, I pray, *let his belief be sufficient.*

While he is steaming, Joyce says that he is very worried because his peepee won't stand up. "Well," I say, "if he is very worried, then it won't stand up for sure."

She laughs and slaps my hand. "No," she says, "I must make him some *muti* to drink to help his peepee, and tomorrow he must *spuyt.*" She scrunches her lips and points to her butt. As hard a time as I have with *phalaza*, Joyce has with enemas.

In the little shower area I'd seen the white metal jug with the pipe coming from it, ending in a small spoon-shaped lip. I wonder whether she uses the same insertion tip for everyone. I'm sure she does, but better not to ask.

When he leaves we both sit scratching at our faces, at the sensations of spiders' webs he has left behind.

Four days later Sylvia is back from Bloemfontein. I see her walking down the street with her overnight bag balanced on her head and rush to meet her, unbalancing her bag, and we both laugh and struggle to catch it. "How did it go?" I ask.

"No, it went fine," she says, "but I am tired."

She comes in and takes off her shoes. We kneel and greet each other formally: *thokoza, unjani, ngiyaphila*, clapping two claps each time. Then Joyce and Sylvia kneel and do the same.

"So, tell us what happened." I am anxious.

"Let me first have a cup of tea," she says.

Finally she finishes her tea and we go into Joyce's room and settle on the floor. There is always a *gemütlichkeit*, a feeling of family, when we do this, sitting so close that parts of us almost overlap, sometimes taking each other's hands. And I notice now how much easier it has become for me to touch, to be touched.

"No, it was all right," she says again. "It took me a long time to get there, so it was already in the evening when I dug the holes and buried the sticks and the stones." She describes how she sprayed with a whisk first inside the house, then around the outside with the grated leaves and roots. After that, with the *muti* in the beaded horn she made crosses above each door and each window. Then, with a blade she cut each member of the family on all their joints, at the neck front, on top of the head, and between the breasts and rubbed in *muti*.

"That night," she continues, "the woman of the house had a dream that there was a large animal pawing at the gate to the yard, but he couldn't get in so she knew that the house had been made safe. And in the morning, when we went to the gate, there were marks there, like something big had been scratching."

My eyes widen. "Are you serious or are you playing?" I ask.

"No, I'm serious," she answers, and my spine tingles.

The *sangomas* had been planning a trip to Miriam's house in Lenz, to drum and dance for the weekend, but there's been trouble again in the townships and attacks on the minibus taxis.

"Why don't you all come over to the flat on Saturday afternoon and drum and dance there?" I say.

"Will it be O.K. with Ron?" Joyce asks.

I know Ron won't mind.

So on the Saturday morning I go around to inform all the neighbors, above, beneath, stretching away on both sides. Most of them know by now what I have been doing since they've seen me around in my strange *thwasa* wear. I tell them that there will be drumming and dancing and invite them to come and watch or join in. Most decline, but Jean from downstairs says wild horses wouldn't keep her away.

At two o'clock they begin to arrive: Joyce with her drum, Sylvia, Miriam with Madota, and Melita, who brings her husband, George. I immediately recognize George with his curly crop of silvering hair. He also works in the apartment building. He is a sweet man somewhat given to overimbibing and becoming downright schmaltzy.

As the *sangomas* arrive, we greet each other first formally, going down on one knee, clapping, *"Thokoza, thokoza,"* and then we stand and hug. And Miriam, as she wraps her arms around me and croons "My *nu-nu*, my ba-ba," waters deeply some long-dry portion of my soul.

They seem a little more reserved here in the flat than at Lenz, and for a while we sit in a circle on the floor while Ron makes a wonderful host, offering wine, tea, cookies. Soon, however, Joyce pulls the drum between her feet and Miriam starts the singing with her high, spiraling note.

Madota begins the dancing; the *sangomas* have hidden things for her to find: the television set, a drum, her purse. When she has found them, we all join in the dancing, jostling each other in the small space.

Melita dances a different style, Zulu style, and as my feet follow hers, they seem to remember this, even my body seems to remember this from some time long, long away. What is this old memory that infuses my bones? Perhaps when I was very young I was taken to watch tribal dancing; but surely the steps would not have lodged with such sweet remembrance within my being?

The *sangomas* say that we dance to awaken the spirits so they rise up within us. Perhaps, I think, it is a collective memory that infuses me. But those thoughts come later; while I dance I am swept by such a rush of joy, such jubilance, that I feel literally to be dancing on air.

When the drumming and singing stop, Melita and Sylvia go out onto the balcony to have a cigarette. I can never get over the anachronistic sight of *sangomas* smoking, and I tease them mercilessly about it. Now, as I follow them outside, we notice a crowd of black women standing under the jacaranda tree, looking up.

They are the women who work in the building, and this must surely be the first time they have ever heard such sounds coming from a white person's apartment. We invite them up and they shyly join us, and for the rest of the afternoon Ron is a gracious host to an ever-increasing audience.

16

Return to the Bush

❦

Margaret has called and invited us back to the bush. I tell her that it is unlikely, since I'm staying and working with Joyce every night. But then, suddenly, Joyce has to go to Newcastle for a funeral, and so the gods open a way.

Again the smell of African bush: earth smell, woman smell, animal smell. The land is lushly green with new growth, and as hot as the fire feathers of the red bishops who nest in the rivers' long reeds. During the day we loll listlessly in hammocks; at night large, black-winged moths hang lazily from the thatching, and we unroll the mosquito netting from its spired beam.

One morning we leave early for a hike through the bush. Marco is back in Pretoria; he has malaria. Dry-humored Leon, Marco's right-hand man, leads us, rifle in hand. He is tall, gangling, darkly tanned in his khakis, as all the men are here.

First come the rules: "If we come across lion, make a tight circle and hold on to one another." His speech is thick with an Afrikaans accent. "Nobody must move." The reason we hold on to one another is to make sure that no one will make a bolt for it, a lone bolter being sure lion fodder.

"If we come across elephant, run behind a tree." We don't ask what to do if there aren't any trees.

We tramp through the high grasses, our socks quickly becoming leached with sharp seed spurs that bite and scratch. For almost an hour we wade, ankles ablaze, until Leon holds up his hand. "Can you hear?" he asks quietly, and we freeze in mid step, cocking our heads.

Deep rumbling, low and resonant. Elephant. It is not their stomachs digesting their food as was thought till just recently, it is their language. Elephant song, land song, at the deep end of whale song.

Leon feels for the wind direction, and then we move, as softly as shod humans are able to in this environment that is not ours, till we see them. A small herd, tearing the bark from young trees, rumbling their morning communions over breakfast.

It is soon hot and the animals, wiser than we are, stay hidden, but as we curve back toward camp Leon stops again and holds up his hand. In the distance a family of rhinos is grazing among the thorn trees. He feels again for the wind's direction and leads us in a semicircle until we are well downwind of the animals; then we quietly approach until we are within danger of being heard. Rhinos are quite shortsighted but have an acute sense of hearing.

We stand as still as possible while they graze, the silence broken only by the click every now and then of a camera. Then as the rhinos nose among the grasses they change direction and their course begins to take them directly toward us. There may have been a moment during which we could have backed away without their hearing us, but that moment has quickly passed and the distance between ourselves and them steadily decreases. Soon we can hear the sound of their chewing. Leon begins looking around, and soon we are all doing the same, looking for a tree, something to climb or hide behind.

Suddenly the largest of the rhinos lifts his head and seems to look directly at us. We freeze. For a long moment we stare at each other, then in a movement almost frolicsome, he kicks up his heels and trots away, followed by the others. There is a moment of silence followed by a long exhalation of combined breath. And another tale of a close encounter joins the stories that become fireside reminiscences.

One night a lioness comes through the camp; we wake as we hear her first short, deep coughs from far off. Later, when she is closer, I get up and roll down the reed door, aware that its flimsiness is no barrier. Back in bed, I sleep easily, feeling quite safe under the tall white tent of netting. (I wonder whether this is because we slept so, under netting, when we were babies and the world was still safe.)

Still later, we hear her again, and again we doze; then suddenly she is outside, and her roar erupts, spewing sound around like fireworks. In the morning we laugh and compare awakenings, and are entranced by her broad pad prints on the path outside the reed door. But our laughter also has an edge to it. Only recently a woman was taken by a lion in just such a setting as she went at night to the toilet. It is easy to forget, as Marco often reminds us, that this is not a zoo, that here we are the interlopers.

During one of our earlier visits to the bush, driving in the Land Rover one evening we had come across a group of lion stretched slim and careless in sleep. Every now and then the large male lifted his head and leveled a long look at us, then unhinged a wide yawn and returned to his slumberings.

Back around the fire, we commented on how relaxed they had been even with our vehicle close by. "What would have happened," I asked, "if one of us had climbed out?"

"Then," replied Leon laconically, "you would have seen a kill."

On the last night, a night when the moon will rise, full, three of us, all women, sit naked in a cool black pool of water, watching the eastern sky, waiting for the amber eyelid to lift. And as she rises clear of the horizon, so do we, our wet breasts mirroring moonlight, and we bay our greeting primeval. What a theater of grand passion Africa is.

17

Killings and Drummings

While we are gone, the city has been a place of killing.

We come back to a political murder: Chris Hani, charismatic leader in the Communist Party, has been shot by right-wing radicals. And the people react violently.

Mehlo calls and says I shouldn't come to Zulu lessons this week, it's better to stay away from the university. Over in Bordeaux, Sylvia arrives late because transport has been disrupted. She is without her usual smile; people are dying. "Our driver that always used to drive us back to Bryanston was killed this weekend," she says, her voice heavy with sadness.

Tomorrow is a stay-away day, a day of mourning for the death of the political leader.

"Are you going to stay away?" I ask Sylvia.

"Yes," she answers, "it won't be safe to be out. I'm just going to sleep at my friend's place." Then she shakes her head. "Innocent people are just dying now for nothing. This is not going to bring things right. *Aaiiee*," she wails, "they are really, really stupid; really, really stupid."

Mandela calls for calm. At a gathering in a sports arena near Soweto the police lose theirs.

Friends who had invited Ron for dinner call to reschedule, saying he shouldn't be out on the streets after dark.

It is always interesting after such events to watch the television news, both international and local, to compare the reporting. Inevitably CNN International focuses on the violent, and in an immense simplification casts players in roles of villains and victims; Sky News (the English international news) and the South African versions inevitably present a rounder picture, including those gatherings that remained peaceful, and seem less inclined to create starkly oppositional frameworks.

Sylvia has made herself a dance skirt to wear at Madota's graduation, which is quickly approaching. She models it now, and we talk about Madota's final test.

"I pray that she finds everything," says Joyce, rolling her eyes.

"What does she have to find?" I ask.

"She has to find the goats and the chickens we will hide."

"What happens if she can't find something?" I ask.

"Oohoo," says Joyce, rolling her eyes even more. "Then the people will laugh."

They are all nervous. Madota, Miriam, her teacher, and Joyce. I had spoken to Madota when they came over to the flat to dance, I'd asked her how she felt. "I'm so frightened I can't do my work properly," she said. "It is always in my head."

To fail would bring great shame to the teachers. Joyce and Miriam have been preparing for weeks. Both have made the beaded necklaces with the herbs sewn into small fabric packets, the long blue and white beads with the thorn tree roots in between that she will wear across her chest.

The ceremony will be in Balfour, Miriam's hometown, and everyone will be traveling down by bus. I worry because of the recent violence; bus stonings have again become all too common.

"No," says Miriam, "no one can hurt you because you have taken the spirit and the spirits will protect you."

I look at her sideways.

"You see, I was once on a bus and some bad people started to stone it, and everybody just crawled under the seats, but I just sat straight because I am a *sangoma* and I know they can't hurt me."

"And you weren't hit?" I ask.

"No."

And I can picture her, straight-backed and long-necked, proud head high.

It's time now that you must buy your drum," Joyce says to me one day. Each of the *sangomas* has her own drum, which they will be taking with them to Balfour. So one day, on her lunch hour, we drive again down to Diagonal Street and go into the dark, crowded, *muti* shop. Ghostly mélanges of dried animal parts, beaked heads, whole monkeys, mouths frozen wide in death, hang from poles, crammed one upon the other. Skulls, skeletons, and pelts crowd the ceiling, hanging so low that we have to weave and duck and are still brushed by things we don't look up at. The walls, floor to ceiling, are deep with cubbyholes of dark brown roots, woods, sticks. On the floor newspapers are spread with more dark bark. Two men on stools pound wearily, reducing woody knots to medicinal pulp. The smell closes around us, thick with decay.

The drums are lined up beneath the roots and bark, hides pulled over tin canisters. We move down the row testing for sound, listening for depth, for clarity. We finally settle on one that has a deep resonance and is covered with brown and white goat hide, a tuft down one side. When we carry it out into the street, the smell of deceased matter follows us.

I hold the drum protectively; people look at it, then at me; a couple stop and say, "*Hau*, are you *sangoma*?"

"I'm in training," I answer, and Joyce sails on with her head held just a little higher.

Both Ron and I feel seedy, as though we've picked up a bug. I notice, on my hip, first a slight discomfort, then a reddening mound; Ron finds a smaller mound behind his knee. We wonder if we were bitten by a spider while in the bush. Since Ron has workshops to give, he puts himself on an antibiotic to be safe.

The mound darkens in the center, then the darkening turns green black. Every joint in my body begins to ache, then every organ. Glands spring up like Ping-Pong balls in the groin, neck, under the arms. It is tick-bite fever.

There is nothing to do but go to bed. The body craves sleep; sometimes I get up to fetch water or go to the toilet and seem to fall asleep even before I can reach the bed again. Once I dream that I stop breathing and wake up hearing myself calling "Mommy."

It will be a week before I'm up again, and two weeks before I feel human. And I will miss Madota's graduation.

When Joyce comes back from Balfour, I am eager to hear how it went. "No," she says, "it was very good. There were so many people, Miriam's place was full, full of people. But when they saw that you're not there, many of them went home."

"Oh," I say, "so they came to see the white *thwasa*, not Madota do her work?"

"Yes," Joyce answers, "they wanted to see you."

And I am glad that I wasn't there because this was Madota's time.

"Did she find her things quickly?"

"Yes, she found her goats and chickens quickly, but the next morning, when she was looking for the gallbladder from the goat, she just looked and looked and looked and couldn't see it."

"Where did you hide it?" I asked.

"We put it in a tree, and she did say when she did her *'shaya ngikutshele'* that it was in the tree, but she just walked around and around, just looking up at the leaves, and she couldn't see it. 'Woo-hoo,' Miriam was shouting at her. 'What's wrong with you, are you stupid!' And Madota, she begins to cry, and we leave her there, standing under the tree."

"So did she find it?"

"Yes, after about two hours she did find it."

Although I'm glad that Madota was the central figure in her graduation, I was sorry to have missed seeing it because the cere-mony is something that I, too, will be going through. And I'm beginning to understand that it won't be simple.

Several times now, when I tell black people that I'm becoming a *sangoma*, they look at me and shake their heads. "Will you be able to do this?" they ask. "It is very heavy, very heavy."

So now I tell Joyce what people have been saying to me and ask her why. "No," she answers, "we will talk about it later." And I'm left with a slightly ominous feeling.

18

Madota Thanks the Spirits

❡

I sit wedged between the ample bodies of Agnes and Joyce. There is still trouble in the country since Chris Hani's killing: rioting, shootings, rock throwing. I do not allow myself to think about shooting.

Madota had rented the red minibus taxi to take us to Kestel, her hometown, to her parents' house for her graduation party. This is an important event, the celebration of the completion of her training. It is the time when the ancestors will be thanked by the killing of a cow and a goat; and the ancestors must be thanked because it is through them that the power to divine comes.

Madota is now a *sangoma*. On her wrists the multilayered beaded bands; on the right wrist a knuckle from one of the goats she had to find, and in her hair the gallbladder that she had such difficulty finding. She will use a traditional spear for the killing of the cow, plunging it between the animal's shoulders. Death, thanksgiving, and rejoicing are made one.

By now the people of the township have been told that this daughter of theirs has completed her training, and they will be present and preparing for a feast. And other *sangomas* will be there, ready to drum and dance and accept this new graduate as one of them.

The singing begins as soon as we pull away in the taxi. I know most of the songs; I have learned to dance to them. Now there are nine voices, playing with point and counterpoint, sending the song high and low, back and forth, beginning each song with one sending out the first note, then the others answering, and the drum sound moving through the minibus like a wind.

The big drum, four feet wide, with its white-and-black cowhide, sits on top of the blankets on the seat in front of me, and every now and then I lean forward to drum on it and fill the car with its deep resonance.

For five hours we drive, heading east, out of the Transvaal into the Orange Free State. The six *sangomas*: Sylvia and Melita, the smokers, who have been relegated to the back of the minibus; toothless Miriam, who trained Madota; and Agnes and Joyce, who cushion me. I'd not met Agnes before; she is a *sangoma* who lives in Lenz, where Miriam has her little house.

Also in the taxi is Jeanett, who is thinking about becoming a *thwasa* and, if she does, will study with Sylvia, and two family friends whom we do not know. Every other bit of space is filled with our overnight bags, two blankets apiece, the drums.

We arrive in Kestel, a small town with white homes and a church spire, in the late afternoon. In the distance is the Golden Gate, the Drakensberg Mountains, from which the evening cold sweeps across the land.

We drive first through the town where the white people live, then into the dirt road township where Madota's brother waits for us.

He will take Joyce and Miriam to Madota's house ahead of us so that they can prepare for her arrival.

We climb out of the taxi and stretch. Across the dirt road there is a red-brick general store, and all around small houses of tin. Little black children in scraggly clothes and unlaced shoes play in the road, kicking soccer balls, rolling metal hoops with a stick. Little girls with torn panties sit on their haunches, talking. A drunk man staggers across the road and trips into a ditch. The *sangomas* laugh.

We need to change into our ceremonial clothes, and a plump woman washing clothes in a blue bucket offers her home to us. We change in the kitchen, the first room we walk into; it is the only room, large and separated in the middle by a curtain that almost hides the bed.

The *sangomas* put on their red skirts and the shorter, pleated overskirts fringed with beads. On top, white T-shirts, then the beads, mostly red, white, and black, some green, some blue, several strands around the neck, others crossing the chest, and a wide white band circling the head. Around her shoulders and chest Madota wears the goatskin that has not been properly cured and trails a strong, rancid smell.

Joyce and Miriam go on ahead to the house. They are to hide the cow and the goat that Madota will kill, and make sure that the house is safe and free from evil spirits. The rest of us wait on the dirt road, Melita holding a drum. Madota is crouching on the side of the road with a blanket pulled over her head. She is not to be seen yet.

People begin to gather, first a few, and, as we keep waiting, more. Whenever I am out with the *sangomas* I try to be as much a part of them as possible. It is enough that my whiteness, of which I am sometimes shy, makes me different. Even so, I catch the wide eyes of the children, staring at me.

As we wait, Sylvia begins to sing, Melita joins her with the drum-beat, and we dance. There are stones in the dirt road that dig into my bare feet, but I am eager to show that I know how to do this, and so even though I still tire easily, I dance and dance. First the *umdawu* style that I do with Joyce and Sylvia, then the Zulu style that echoes so in my bones; and slowly the audience joins in, all except the children, who cannot take their eyes off me.

Eventually the notice comes that it is time to move. Madota stands, still holding the blanket over her head. Melita takes her by the arm and leads us, still singing, in single file down the road at a methodical, low-footed trot. Stones stab into my feet and I keep my eyes fixed on the road's sandy surface, looking for clear places to step. When I fall out of line trying to avoid large stones, Sylvia grabs my arm and pulls me back. By the time we reach the house, the soles of my feet are throbbing.

We stop in the driveway of Madota's parents' home, a brick house that seems to be larger than the rest we passed on the way. Joyce and Miriam are waiting in the driveway with two white-feathered chickens. They have made a small fire in the middle of the driveway entrance and they now sprinkle herbs into the fire. This, Joyce has told me, is to invite the spirits in.

They begin to sing, and Sylvia, Melita, and Jeanett dance, so I join them. The ground here is softer and there are fewer stones; my feet are grateful.

Still singing, Joyce picks up one of the chickens and with a small knife slits its throat and throws it to one side. It lands among the gathered crowd and flops around squawking, wings flailing.

In horror, I stop dancing, my eyes fixed on the flailing hen, then notice that the *sangomas* are all down on their knees. I quickly drop to mine and remember what my desert friend Jenice once said after I went down the big water slide in Palm Springs and thought I would die.

"Did you scream?" she asked.

"No," I replied, "I was too busy straining against death."

"Oh," she said, "you've got to scream."

So scream I did, both then and now, the sound mingling with the singing.

The second chicken's neck is slit, and it, too, is tossed to the side.

Later we will eat the chickens, except for the one half that will join us in the living room as a sacrifice, an offering to the ancestral spirits.

There is so much sound, so much happening, and I am determined that nothing other than my whiteness shall set me apart, so I am focused on doing the right thing. I concentrate on the others: Sylvia, Melita, Agnes, Jeanett. What they do, I do, not even a half step behind. As their feet dance, so do mine, as their song soars, so does mine.

Suddenly Madota stands and sprints up the driveway into the front door of the house. All the *sangomas* except Joyce and Miriam chase after her and I, bewildered, after them. She, and we, race through the small living room, into the kitchen, the sandy back-yard, around the square orange tarpaulin tent there, the small, many-branched tree, back into the kitchen, out the front door, and all the way around again.

In and out, through the rooms, around the yard, in and out we run like foxes before some invisible hounds and then come to a stop in the living room, where we all stand, panting, and only I am totally confused. Later I learn that this is to make sure that any residual evil spirits have been chased away.

Joyce and Miriam join us in the living room, and several young men follow, bringing in our overnight bags, our blankets, the drums. We make piles of our things in the corners, unroll a couple of reed mats, and settle down on the floor, leaning against the bags, the blankets. Madota comes in carrying a basin half filled with warm water and a hand towel.

Like a Passover ritual she moves around the room allowing each of us to wash and dry our hands. Then she and her mother carry in bowls of steaming sour porridge. They had decided that I wouldn't like this ethnic delicacy and so I am brought tea. I ask Joyce for a taste; it is like porridge laced with yogurt, and I pass.

The *sangomas* chatter in Zulu; I lean back against the pile of blankets in the corner, sipping my tea and feeling the soles of my feet hum after their encounters with the stones. I am still not totally recovered from the tick-bite fever, so it feels good just to lie back in the corner and relax.

It is a small room, maybe ten by fourteen feet. The walls are painted in white enamel. Part of the floor is covered with an off-white furry rug. There are two or three wooden dining-room chairs, a polished wooden sideboard with sliding glass doors holding tea-cups and a few porcelain figures, and, against the far wall, a large wooden chest.

On the wall facing me is a calendar dominated by the ANC logo and pictures of the representatives for this area. On the adjacent wall hangs a framed collage of the Zulu chiefs from Shaka on, opposite that a reproduction of the Last Supper. All bets are hedged.

There are two doors; one goes into the main bedroom, which we don't enter. The other leads to the kitchen, as large again as the living room and dominated by an old iron range. The kitchen seems always filled with people, chattering, chopping, cutting, mixing.

Madota goes around the room making sure everyone has eaten enough, trailing the putrescent pungency of the goatskin vest. Whenever she passes me, I hold my breath.

•

It is close to seven, still light outside, as the *sangomas* rise. I follow them back out to the driveway. It is time for Madota to find the hidden cow and the goat. This, apart from the dancing and feasting, is the highlight of this thanksgiving ceremony and will show her family and the township people that she can "see," that she can divine.

She goes down on one knee in the driveway and starts her chant of *"shaya ngikutchela"*: Clap your hands and I will tell you. The *sangomas* chorus *"Yezwake"* after each chant.

A large crowd has gathered and they quieten and close in tightly. In between her chants of *shaya ngikutshele*, Madota has begun narrowing down the location of the cow and the goat. The *sangomas* answer loudly, excitedly: *"Yezwake, yez, yez, yezwake,"* their voices rising and falling.

Suddenly she has it, the *sangomas* clap their hands, chorusing *"Yezwake, yezwake,"* their voices rising high in joy and relief.

Madota tears a passage through the crowd and is off, down the sandy road like a hare, her bare feet pounding. We all take off in pursuit, I more cautiously watching for stones.

As I run an old woman draws alongside me and whips the back of my legs with her skirt. "Hurry up, hurry up," she shouts. She is all bone and empty skin but pulls steadily ahead.

I join the crowd in an empty lot. There stands the cow. She is large and black, and if cows may be majestic, she is majestic. Bull-large, full-shouldered, with horns. But what horns! Not small calf horns, but horns that make a half halo around her head.

She is tied to a post, the long rope wound around her horns and extending for several feet on either side. She swings her body this way and that. Several young men untie her, and five or six to a side they hold her, but she heaves her head and they are tossed around, sprawling in the dirt.

The goat is hidden behind a group of old cars, and it is quickly untied and led back to the house. In the meantime the young men have been up on their feet and down again in the dirt several times and the cow still stands where she started. Finally they maneuver her into the dirt road. She shrugs and twists, turning her body sideways, first one way and then the other.

Young boys, laughing, run up and smack her rump, the older ones, looking determined, take the place of the fallen. Slowly, as she is pulled, pushed, and coaxed, distance is gained and when we think it safe to pass, we circle her and her cloud of sand-covered pilots and return to our places in the living room.

It is getting cool now and I reach for a blanket. Joyce, who is sitting next to me, tucks it around my legs. "You mustn't catch cold," she says, and fusses for a moment longer. I watch her face as she rejoins the conversation, softer now, gentler than when I first began, when her chin seemed dourly ever thrust at the world.

⊖⊬⊝

$\mathcal{S}$oon we eat dinner. Again Madota brings in the bowl and cloth, and circles from one to the other as we wash our hands. She is still wearing the goatskin vest, and again I hold my breath as she passes.

We eat mealie pap and the chickens, those late of the white feathers. We eat with our fingers, with our right hands, holding our metal bowls in our left. I cannot eat the chicken and give it to Joyce.

"You must eat so you get nice and fat," she says. She comes from a culture in which plumpness is preferred and is always admonishing me for being too thin, but she nevertheless takes the chicken. When we are through Madota again comes around with water and a cloth and we wash the grease off of our fingers.

Again the *sangomas* chatter. I catch a word here and there and sometimes get the gist of their conversation. Sometimes I know they are talking about me; I hear my name, Melisande; sometimes Joyce leans across and wraps her plump, soft-skinned arms around me. "I love you," she says. Then they all look at me: "You won't forget us when you go?" they ask and touch me softly, and I say that I won't.

They touch me so often now, sometimes without words, just reaching out and catching my hand or stroking my face. And I feel myself unfolding, like a flower to the sun.

Someone begins to sing. The lone notes sift through the room, then others join in. Melita, ever the showman, gets up and dances, her arms stretched forward, her rear pushed out. Miriam joins her, glasses flashing. Her feet are older than Melita's and not as nimble. And where Melita bends and wraps her body this way and that through space, Miriam holds her back straight, bending only sometimes from her hips.

The drums are pulled out from under the blankets, and Joyce and Sylvia drum. I sit in the corner against the blankets, soaking in the sound, drowning in the sharp hoofbeats of the drum.

"Melisande," they call, "come and dance."

I am heavy with sound. "No, my spirits just want me to sit here."

But they urge, "Come on, come on," and I join them.

There is little room in the living room with all of us and our bags and blankets, and we dance in tight formation and laugh when we jostle each other, but mostly we are in the spirit of the dance, turned in on it, not out, until Miriam ululates high and loud and we push our bottoms out farther, hold our arms out higher, push our feet faster and then collapse onto the floor gasping, reaching out to each other.

Again they take up their conversations. Now and then Joyce leans across to me and strokes my arm or puts her arm around me. "My darling," she croons, "I'm going to miss you so much."

*M*uch later, when I am back in San Diego, I will find that of all the things I learned in those months, it will have been their love that created a new pattern in my being.

For reasons engraved deep in my youth, the act of being loved had always carried with it elements of danger. Often, in a women's group I had joined, when one of us would weep wretchedly, Valdene, the therapist, would hold the weeper to her; "Let it out," she would murmur, "let it out."

I couldn't weep, I was afraid to weep in case she came close. Not even with D., a fellow group member whose wonderfully ample body made for the safest cushioning, could I relax into closeness. And it was in that group that I had said, "I need to learn to be loved."

And now, from these brown African mothers, it is the lesson I am learning.

*I*t is dark when Madota kills the cow. Dark and cold. "Bring your camera," says Joyce, and I run back in, my bare feet already numb.

The night is moonless. Someone brings out a lantern, but its gold halo is quickly eaten and I can just make out the cow, tied tightly against the small tree, her head firmly against the branches, her horns circling it. Then Madota approaches, holding the spear and, close by, Joyce and Miriam gesticulate in silhouette.

The three move cautiously toward the cow, who groans and swings her hindquarters around toward us. The fifteen or twenty of us watching scatter backward, barefoot in the dark sand.

The cow's head is turned toward them now; I can see Joyce showing Madota where to put the spear, below the head, in the back where the spine begins. The lantern is held high as Madota moves in. I focus the camera and click as she plunges the spear between the cow's shoulders. The animal bellows and stays on her feet. Again she plunges and again I click. Again the animal bellows and stays on her feet.

The two *sangomas* come in close, conferring. We all watch in silence, I, lowering the camera. Then once again the spear is lifted high and plunged between the broad black shoulders. This time there is no distancing lens, and the full dark horror hits me. I quickly lift the camera back up to my eye and with the merciful distancing the horror recedes. The cow, trumpeting and snorting, drooling from the mouth and the nose, remains standing.

Now several men gather around, holding a long length of chain. Having learned my lesson that a camera creates objectivity, I watch everything through its lens. One end is thrown over the cow's body, and as the cow moves it is dropped beneath her and pulled up on the other side. Suddenly she is pulled tight. Again she trumpets and bellows.

Someone sends for knives from the kitchen. They cut her throat, sawing through her jugular, her breathing coming in loud, wet snorts.

When we go back into the house she is still standing.

The small living room is warm after the cold night air. We sit back on the floor, part linoleum, part carpet. While the women chatter in

Zulu, my mind skitters around, hearing again the awful bellowing, the rattling snorts as her throat was cut. Oh God, I think, I will never be able to do this.

Madota brings in tea and scones. Tea and scones! We drink the tea and eat the scones while my skittering mind shakes itself as though it has run into a wall.

A short while after tea we go out for the killing of the goat. Again Joyce says to bring my camera. I have learned my lesson and watch through the lens. The goat is small, her curly coat gray. This time no repeated stabbings are required, and she is quieter in her dying. Still, I drift away earlier than the others, through the hot, bustling kitchen, back into the house.

I sit on the floor in the living room, surrounded by the drums, the blankets, woolly bright with pinks, blues, and greens. For the first time, a small doubt has crept into a corner of my mind. Am I really willing to kill something as part of this exercise? I, who walk carefully around ants? During this training I have done things, been a part of things I never thought I would, but taking life?

I remember the people who said, "This is very heavy, very heavy." Is this what they meant? Or is there more? I must talk with Joyce.

Later in the evening, after more tea and scones, two young men come into the living room and begin to move our bags and blankets from the corner between the ANC calendar and the lineage of Zulu chiefs. They fold back the rug and walk out.

A few minutes later they return carrying the late cow's hide, which they stretch out on the floor, the inside up. I feel my eyes grow large in their sockets, but the *sangomas* are paying this no attention. The young men straighten the hide so that it fits squarely in the corner and lies flat. It glistens, red, white, wet in the candlelight.

With the hide organized, they go out and return with the cow's left haunch. Walking carefully around the skin, they maneuver the heavy haunch so that it leans against the corner, the hoof sticking up high.

Then again they go out and return with the second haunch and maneuver it next to the first. The two rear hooves, dark and still dusty with life, the legs hide-encased from knee to ankle, thrust upward like some demented offerings.

Throughout this maneuver I dart quick looks at the *sangomas*, but not one has so much as blinked. It is clear that not one of them thinks this odd, there is hardly a break in their conversation. Only I seem transfixed, my mind floating in a vacuum of disbelief.

Soon the ribs: large and bowing, cleanly cleft through, showing small bone-hugging meaty semicircles against a sudden thick whiteness of fat. They lay the front quarters lengthwise so that the horizontal hooves and legs seem to emerge from some sleeping animal. A black curl, the tuft of the tail, protrudes nearby.

Two large, baby-blue metal bowls are carried in, one filled with the udder, buttery, floating in a halo of milk, the other with the kidneys, pancreas, and stomach. A small, darker blue bowl holds the liver.

Finally the head is slowly lowered. They hold it by the horns and try to balance it on the open neck. It slides a few times down the slippery meat surface before settling only slightly askew.

I feel caught in some Kafkaesque play where everyone knows the script but me. My eyes are riveted to her head; her eyes, her nose, her ears; I watch, convinced that there will be a blink, a twitch. Her still-bright eyes glint, not far enough from life to have clouded. Her nostrils are damp and flared, her mouth drawn in, closed. She fills a third of the room. Down the white wall behind her run a few red rivulets.

A little later she is joined by the goat, its peltless body intact.

Sacrifice is something that is commonly found throughout Africa, and the animals of choice are usually ox, cow, goat, or chicken. Depending on the circumstances, these offerings may be made in the spirit of gift giving, as a means of communion, or a means of giving thanks. During the home celebration of a just-graduated *sangoma*, the sacrifice is an opportunity to give thanks to the spirits of the ancestors who have successfully guided the trainee through to this happy occasion.

While God is most often a remote figure in African belief systems, having withdrawn once the job of creation was over, the spirits are the accessible agents. They form the link between the living and the Creator. But there is clearly also an intermingling of new and old beliefs in a bypassing of the spiritual messengers. Joyce often tells me to pray to God "that the spirits may come to you."

Precisely at eleven the formal dancing begins. We pull our wraps around us and Miriam and Joyce lead the way out, through the kitchen filled with family, hot with its steam horse of a range, into the cold, cold dark.

Single file, the *sangomas* singing softly, we slowly trot into the tarpaulin tent. Blanketed forms, washed gray in the light of a single lantern, sit, some on benches, some on the sand; blanketed children are massed together for warmth. The drums stand at the far end of the reed mats that are unrolled and waiting.

Still trotting, we cross the length of the tent to the mats; Joyce sits and motions to me to sit beside her. Our blankets are waiting, and it is soon clear why. The cold seeps from the ground like unseen clouds of dry ice, into my feet, my legs, my rear.

The *sangomas* settle themselves on the mats, and drums are brought between bare feet, their hide faces leaning toward the drummers. Then the first notes uncoil, are echoed back, one small, tight drum picks out the beat, the others join, the big drum sounding deep into the darkness.

Madota runs in, the soda-can tops wrapped around her calves rattling. She comes to a stop in front of the mats, holds her stick in front of her, and begins the short side steps and gallops of *umdawu* dancing. She dances through several songs until her eyes are squeezed shut in fatigue and even in the freezing tent she is dripping with sweat; then she crosses to Miriam and drops to her knee.

"*Shaya ngikutshele, shaya ngikutshele,*" she begins. Family members, friends, have hidden coins, in their pockets, under their head scarves. She is quick; only a few times do the *sangomas* say "*Yez*" with the voice lowering, and then "*Yezwake,*" voices filled with delight, and off she runs to one of the blanketed women and pulls from under a scarf, from out of a pocket, a coin. Four times she dances, drops to her knee, chants, and four times she finds the coins that have been hidden.

As she dances her last dance and then thanks the spirits for their guidance, Joyce nudges me. "You will dance next," she says. Madota finishes and runs back into the house. Joyce pushes me, and I run after her into the living room, where we quickly transfer the clappers from her legs to mine.

I run back out, carefully, across the cold, dark sand, back into the tent. Again the *sangomas* sing, Joyce beginning the melody, the others joining, the drums beating, and I dance.

Oh how I've grown to love this dancing of Africa, this dancing to invoke the spirits, for the spirits. What freedom it has brought me, what sweet deliverance from old constraints.

I stretch out my arms, my stick clasped between my hands, arch my back, and bend into the song. I dance with my heart, with joy in my heart. I bend and sway and turn and circle, reveling in the movement, in the freedom, in the ancient remembrance deep in my bones. I hear Miriam's soaring ululating and an answering *yayayayayaya* from somewhere deep in the shadows, and as my feet pound the sand, my soul flies on its African wings.

When I am finished, I kneel in front of Joyce and in acknowledgment I address her, as I've been taught, as my father and chief teacher. Then I turn to Miriam, Sylvia, and Melita, whom I refer to as my brothers, all trained by Joyce. Then my brother Madota, now also a *sangoma*; and finally Jeanett, regal Jeanett of the high cheekbones, who is deciding whether to begin the journey of the *thwasa*.

She will dance next, and we run into the house and transfer the clappers to her legs.

Back in the tent, I sit down on the reed mat, next to Joyce. She takes my hand and strokes it. "Oh, you dance so nicely," she says, "you make me so proud." And she makes sure the blanket is tucked around me.

After a while, when it seems that there is no warmth left in our bodies, several of us wander back into the living room. Six white-saucered candles have been lit beside the cow. Agnes, who remained with the cow so that no evil spell could be cast upon it, has rolled up in her blanket and is snoring on the floor. Not much of a guardian.

Madota brings in more tea and scones. The room fills, and condensation drips from the tin ceiling. Jeanett and I go back out into the tent. Ghostly forms lie, blanketed rolls on the sand, the children now making a small hillock, all one upon another. A small group is still singing and dancing.

Jeanett and I talk, low-voiced, our breath wisping in the cold. I ask her where she works. She is working in Johannesburg, she says, as a maid to a German couple. They are very dear, she says, and support her in her effort to be a *sangoma*. I ask her why she wants to do this training.

"I was sick," she says, "all the time. I would go to the doctors, they tried all kinds of things, but I never got better."

"What kind of sick?" I ask.

"Everything," she answers. "My head, my stomach, my legs. And I am sad all the time. They did X rays, and a CAT scan, and tried different pills, and eventually they told me they couldn't help me. So I know I must do this. I must take the spirit to be well. And I can feel it, when I am with you, with the others, dancing, I am so happy.

"But," she pauses for a moment, "it's so hard. I have three children, and they are all going to school. I have to buy clothes for them, and books, and things that they need, and I'm only earning three hundred rand a month. I don't know if I can afford this, but I need to be well, I need to be happy." She pauses. "Life is so hard," she whispers. Her eyes fill, and I put my arms around her and we stand together in the cold, dark tent.

•

I have since wondered whether many of the women who experience these strange symptoms for which no cure can be found are not suffering from long-term depression. Circumstances in South Africa certainly foster the condition. All the years of repression, the high unemployment rate and low wages, the breakdown of the old traditions, the lack of support systems as people leave their villages to look for work in the city, all take their toll.

And if indeed deep depression is what these women are experiencing, then certainly they would feel better once they began training. There is something meaningful to do: The role of *sangoma* is a respected one, something that is culturally significant; there is an instant support group, and the comfort of being taken under the teacher's wing. Whose spirits would not fly while dancing to that most ancient beat, the African drum? Was this any less true for me?

•

It is after three in the morning when two of the young men come into the living room to carve meat out of the cow for the feast. They work with knives and an ax, throwing the cut chunks into a large blue basin. Chips of bone, flecks of blood flick away and speckle the walls.

The *sangomas* talk softly, sometimes directing where a knife or the ax should be placed. When the basin is filled, they tidy the carcass and replace the head. I notice that the cow's eyes have begun to glaze over.

Miriam has dozed off, leaning against the sideboard. Agnes still snores in front of the chest, Sylvia now blanketed tightly up against her. Joyce rolls up in her blanket and lies down, clearing a small space next to her. I roll up in my blanket and lie down in the space. Next to me, Melita rolls up, and Jeanett wedges in behind her. We keep our knees bent to avoid the cow. Even sausaged between the two, it is cold. Joyce feels around and finds another blanket and throws it on me. It is five-thirty; soon it will be light.

Every now and then the condensation from the tin ceiling drips on my head. I listen to the chatter from the kitchen, where the feast food is being prepared. The sound washes in and out.

•

It is almost seven when Madota comes in, carrying first one large basin filled with hot water and then another. Two by two, beginning with Miriam and Joyce, we strip and bathe. I watch as they undress, soap their washcloths, and then wash every part of their bodies. Face, neck, ears, arms, armpits, breasts, back, stomach, legs, then, stepping into the basin and crouching, crotch and bottom, and finally feet. Once dry, they spread themselves liberally with lotions and creams, leaving their full brown bodies shining.

Dressed in clean wraps I wander out the back door and blink at the sharp morning sun. The drums have been moved out of the tent, and a couple of men drunkenly slow-dance. I greet the older women sitting on a wooden bench against the sunlit brick wall, and they make space for me.

The children keep their distance, wide-eyed. I close my eyes and soak in the still-young warmth. When I open them, the children have crept closer, and for a while I play finger games with them. Most are in well-worn hand-me-downs, a couple of little girls in pink, ruffled party dresses and always the torn panties.

The old woman sitting next to me asks, in broken English, how I like the township. I answer, kindly, that it's very pretty.

She smiles and nods. "Yes, it is," she says, her voice rich with pride, "isn't it."

And suddenly I think how arrogant my kindness is; how presumptuous of me to feel sorry for people because they possess less than I do. Or do they? They who bathe in small basins filled with water while I waste gallons soaking in large tubs; whose candles never create pollution; who still eat what they kill and leave offerings to the spirits; whose delight lies so close to the surface. I am ashamed, but the thoughts have been mine, and there are no words that cross the divide.

Inside Miriam is cutting up the rest of the cow, the head now sitting atop the milk-rimmed udder basin. Large sections, bones hacked through with the ax, are set aside, then wrapped in plastic bags. Each *sangoma* will take home a section and the rest will be distributed to the people of the township. Nothing of the animals will be wasted: Everything that can be eaten will be eaten, shared by the people of the township. The hide will be used to make shields and drums.

At ten, just when my stomach yearns for a strong cup of coffee and a slice of toast, we are served the cow. Not only the cow, but the feast. Meat, mashed potatoes, mealie pap, rice, two kinds of beets, cabbage, pumpkin, and the cow's liver and stomach are laid out on the living-room floor on large platters.

Joyce nudges me to eat some liver. "It is good for you," she says, but I can't, not with the head still sitting a few feet from me atop the udder. In a half circle around what remains of the cow, the *sangomas* feast and feast.

On the way back home there is less singing; we are all tired. Agnes leans her head against the window and is quickly asleep. I look out at the road ahead, the thin thread of tarmac rising and falling between cornfields yellowing into winter.

Joyce looks out of the window, her chin thrust forward; from her head a hundred dark strands of woolly hair roll loose to her shoulders. In front of her, Miriam's straight back, arched neck. There may be much said about this tradition of healing: that it allows some ailments to perpetuate when they might be more swiftly cured; that it is bound up in superstition and ritual killing; but it has also conferred dignity on these women and given their lives a value and purpose beyond the endless sameness of their days.

And it is not an imagined value. So often have I seen clients sit and talk with Joyce long after the divining and prescribing are done. This is when the *sangoma* becomes both priest and counselor. Who else, after all, do these people have to talk with? A white doctor who no longer spends time with his same-color, same-language patients, let alone his black ones? Their clan, their families, their elders are usually elsewhere, across the country in another town or village. And so there is the familiar figure of the *sangoma*, the connector, providing the role that is surrounded by trappings comfortable in their traditional constancy, offering concern, solace, advice.

It is warm in the car; the tires drone and lull. For a strange moment, the I-ness that is me diffuses, my cells drifting out, not those protoplasmic membrane-enclosed units, but some incorporeal essence that is the being of me floats away, merges with the others, and becomes one, becomes us.

Soon we are among the slanting, rectangular gold-mine dumps of Johannesburg and one by one we drop off the *sangomas*. Agnes and Miriam's friends in Lenz, Sylvia and her son in Potch, Miriam where she works, and finally, in Hyde Park, Melita and I climb out together with our belongings.

As she goes off toward the maids' quarters, two young African men come out. Their eyes widen at the sight of me in my red skirt, beads, and wraps. "Are you *sangoma*?" they ask. "Not yet," I answer, "I'm still training." But the leap has been made and, with smiles of clear delight, they clasp my hand in a shake of African kinship, little knowing what precious absolution they confer.

19

Spirit-Speak

❧

U*landa induku,"* says Joyce. Fetch your stick. I kneel in front of
her spirit corner and clap three times, then take the stick. I light
the *imphepho* and breathe its fumes. I feel heavy this evening,
reluctant, and come slowly to my feet. Sylvia and Joyce begin to
sing, and I move my feet in the first side steps. The song, the
rhythm, seem to lighten my body, I can feel a buoyancy float from
my feet upward, my cells filling with air.

Suddenly my head is jerked up and back, my knees buckle, and
I almost collapse. In slow motion now, as though in a dream, I see
Joyce's hand reach out to steady me, growing larger as it reaches
forward. Their singing has been replaced with a roaring sound; I
cannot tell if it surrounds me or is only in my ears. Then again my
head is jerked back and deep in my gut the muscles contract.

A growl, cavernous and dark, is pushed up seemingly from the ground under me, through the soles of my feet, is pushed up from my contracting diaphragm; and as it rumbles across my vocal cords and out my mouth, my head comes forward and I see, in the same slow motion, Joyce's hand go to her mouth, which has made an O shape. Still the air around me roars; again my diaphragm contracts, pushing the deep sound up and out of my mouth.

My awareness comes in flickers like an old movie: my feet now, moving faster, faster into the gallop, the growl coming shorter and sharper as my breath quickens, quick flashes of Joyce's and Sylvia's hands clapping. My eyes squeeze shut and once again my head jerks back, the dark sounds rasping now, until I drop onto my knees.

"Shaya ngikutshele, shaya ngikutshele." The words come out in the same rasping growl. Sweat drips from my chin.

"Yezwake," says Joyce and Sylvia, *"yezwake."* Their voices come from somewhere else. Power prowls through me, squeezing sound from me, energy absorbs me, pushing me up from the ground, driving my legs, my arms, throwing my head back, until I collapse and begin the round of incantation.

And when we are done, and I have found the things they have hidden, Joyce takes my shaking hands in hers. "It is your spirit," she says softly, "it is your spirit."

What is this—this spirit thing that comes and invades my being so? It is as though I have become connected to some deep energy, or perhaps some deep energy field. Questions that were only partially roused after the experience of the snake and the leopard now leap out fully formed.

"Joyce."

"Yes?"

"What happened when my spirit voice came?"

"It just came to you because it was time."

"But it felt as though it was coming from the ground, through me."

"Yes, because it was not your voice, it was from your spirits."

She wasn't helping me get at some root question that I hadn't quite formulated yet. "Then where are the spirits?"

She laughs. "No, you are asking too many questions now."

Later we talk about the man with the pains around his middle and the itchy face who is still coming to see Joyce. "Why wouldn't he go and see a doctor?" I ask.

"No," she says, "he knows it's for black people, this sickness. Maybe for the pain in his stomach he will go and see a doctor, but for the itching and for hearing somebody knocking on the door, he knows it's not for a doctor."

"So," I say, "there are some things that people will go to a doctor about, and there are things people will go to a *sangoma* about."

"Yes, because if you go to the doctor, they won't see the itching and they won't know what it's about."

"And if you would say to them 'I'm itchy all over?'" I ask.

She laughs. "Maybe if you say that, they will give you something, but it won't help."

"Why?"

"Because it's not for the white people, this thing."

Lying on the mattress, my nose tingling from the dreaded snuff, I can't still the thoughts scurrying like mice in my head. Thoughts of those strange things that are so infused in that other world for which reason cannot be applied. And, filling the spaces, pictures of energy fields, like swirling galaxies, and we, as moths, on the edge.

Perhaps Joyce is right: I ask too many questions. Or perhaps it is that reason should not be applied; for I remember the story of the man who, in wanting to know how the Polynesians of old had navigated the oceans in their flimsy rafts, had traveled with them. In so doing he had unraveled the mystery. But in that act of investigation and analysis, in the unraveling, so had each strand of the magic been lost.

So are passages of wonder made arid. Perhaps that is why the *sangomas* always laugh when I ask them why we do this or that—so that the magic may be preserved.

Joyce is snoring softly in her bed, and I hunker down under my blanket.

20

Clients and Lessons

ᖳᖴ

When I arrive at Joyce's this evening she tells me that someone is coming to be fortuned and that I will do it.

"Are you nervous?" she asks.

"No," I say, then catch her looking at me sideways. "Well, just a little, maybe."

The woman arrives. She is young, with a gentle brown face. I watch her for signs, but she gives nothing away. Her movements are fluid, her face reposed.

As we sit in the little hallway, a headache begins over my eyes. My forehead pulls tight, my eyes ache. Along my cheekbones, under my eyes, sinuses echo the ache. My neck tightens and my left shoulder joins the chorus. My hands begin to feel hot and heavy and the heat creeps up my arms.

I pay attention to my body and think of what Sylvia said: If you wake in the morning with a pain, it's your pain. If it comes to you when you're with somebody, you're picking up their pain.

Joyce stands, and we take off our shoes and go into her room. She unrolls the reed mat and tells the young woman to sit on it. I wrap the *ibayi* around me and, in the spirit corner, light the *imphepho*. I kneel over it, blowing softly to keep it smoldering, taking in the sweet smoke, holding my mind open. Deep in my diaphragm I feel the muscles again contracting, and the spirit sound once again rumbles as a train, through my chest, my throat, the cavern of my mouth, emerging as a growl, low and resonant. My eyes smart and tear and I wait till they have cleared. Then I take the candle in its blue tin holder and turn to the young woman, telling her to light it.

I sit for a moment looking into the flame and then I start. "You are having headaches here over your eyes that are very painful, and they are going into your eyes so that they hurt." I pause and in Zulu Joyce asks if this is so. The woman nods a yes.

"The pain goes into your neck in the back here," I say and point to the back of my neck, "and moves down into your shoulder." Again I pause, and again Joyce checks. She answers yes and nods.

"And your shoulders sometimes feel very heavy; and sometimes your hands feel hot and heavy, and then your arms also feel hot and heavy." Again Joyce checks. Again she answers yes and nods.

I feel quite assured as I speak; I feel no doubt about what I'm saying. "And sometimes your body feels very tired, like it wants to rest." "Yes," she answers.

"And sometimes your legs around here"—I massage the lower parts of my legs—"are heavy and tired." "Yes," she answers.

She says something to Joyce and Joyce says, "She wants to know about her boyfriend." I pause for a moment, allowing the question to settle and my mind to stay open.

"Your boyfriend comes and goes," I say, and Joyce asks her if this is so.

"Yes," she answers.

"She wants to know if she will get married," Joyce says.

Again I pause and allow the question to settle. For the first time my mind seems to hang without answer. I open my mouth and allow myself to speak. "Yes, you will get married, but not to this man who comes and goes."

Again she talks to Joyce. "She wants to know about her house."

And now I draw on what I have seen and heard from other for-tunings, for this is the part that my western mind cannot seem to incorporate. "You need to make your house safe," I say. "There are people who are jealous of you because you are working and you must make your house safe from these people. You must also make yourself safe. There are other people in the house." She nods. "They must also be made safe. You must all steam and *phalaza*, and you must take the herbs from Joyce and take them to your house and do what Joyce tells you to do to make it safe."

I don't know; I don't know whether I have invented this last piece about her house based on what I've heard, or whether this is some-thing that has come out of the same recesses as the other things I have said.

For a while she and Joyce converse in Zulu, then she takes out a twenty-rand bill and lays it on the floor between us. Joyce rolls up the reed mat and sees her out. When she comes back into the room she throws her arms around me. She is beaming. "You were so good. You got everything, everything. I can't believe it."

Again and again she touches me, holding my hand, stroking my arm, glowing. I worry about feeling smug. It seemed to come so easily, the reality of what my body felt and the leap into their real-ity. Both rolled out of my mouth with assurance.

For a long while we sit on the two wooden chairs on either side of the little table and talk, going over the session again and again. And again and again she shakes her head, smiling as broadly as her small mouth allows, saying, you were so good; and I say it's because I have a good teacher, and we hold hands.

There is something I have become aware of, staying with Joyce, being with this circle of women: It is the replaying, resaying, retelling of an event. I don't understand enough Zulu to hear it in those conversations, but when we speak in English, the talk will meander around and around an issue, repeating itself, pausing, restating, pausing, in no hurry to move on to something else. Even when they are speaking in Zulu, how often have I been surprised when I've asked what they're talking about only to find that it is the same thing they were talking about half an hour before.

Sometimes when I listen I am reminded of the time in the bush when we watched the giraffe make its way down to the dam, taking perhaps half an hour to cover the short distance between the bushes and the water. It was being cautious, but it also had the time to spare, not having meetings, deadlines, things to do and places to go. There was no sense of hurry. And with these women, too, there is no sense of hurry. There is time to take out an event and chew on the pieces of it again and again, time to stop on the way there, time to amble.

And their actions often reflect that speech pattern. When Joyce and I go downtown, the visit is pockmarked with previously unannounced stops she decides on en route: here, to pay the furniture installment, there, at the supermarket.

"You're dealing with African time now," Harry will say when sometimes Ron and I fume over deliveries that never happen when they're promised, return calls that are seldom returned within the same week, or even month. And while we might fume, I wonder if it isn't healthier, this amble through life.

The days are becoming shorter, the nights cooler, the long African summer giving way to fall. A short fall here, where the days will stay warm. There are fewer late-afternoon showers now, and the red trumpets of the bignonia vine have turned to deep coral and drop slowly into the garden below.

The ground under the mulberry tree is dark with the summer's droppings; the mousebirds that had dashed through its branches in small groups are fewer. But the woodhoopoes, with their mad cacklings, still visit the old jacaranda, tearing at its bark, picking at the insects they uncover.

A man has come to Joyce to have his car made safe; he is portly, with silver hair, and wears a navy-blue security suit. In the driveway sits a BMW, shining silver, newly painted. It seems that people are jealous now because he has this car.

"They don't see," says Joyce, "that he worked hard to get it. And when he goes home, he's noticing that people just stop talking when they see him. So he's worried now for the car."

Joyce brings out the horn filled with the black, tarry *muti* that is used in making things safe and asks him to pop the hood. She walks around to the front of the car and looks long and thoughtfully into the engine well, then walks first to one side and then the other, looking for all the world like a judge at a dog show, assessing a canine candidate first from this angle, then that. Finally she seems to reach a conclusion and with her fingers pulls from the horn a dollop of the tarry substance.

She reaches into the well and makes a cross, first inside to the left of the radiator, then she walks around to the right and again makes her cross. Next she walks around to the front, where again she reaches in and makes the cross. Then she opens the driver's-side door, leans into the car, and under the dashboard makes the last cross. Finally she hangs from the rearview mirror a small loop of red and white beads and two pieces of porcupine quill filled with *muti*.

Later, when I tell Ron about the safe-making exercise, he suggests that since we don't have insurance maybe we should consider doing likewise. But when I speak to Joyce about fixing our cars, I realize that this is not an inexpensive procedure. Normally Joyce charges one hundred rand to do it, but, in deference to our relationship, the cost was reduced to sixty rand for each car.

We were reassured, however, when one evening we went through to Pretoria to visit with Mario, the Jungian playwright, and Margaret, the earth mother; Marco, who was in town from the bush, leaned into the car to look at the small loop.

"Nobody will mess with your car now," he said, speaking with the authority of one who knows African superstition. "They'll be too frightened." And indeed, up to the time of this writing it has not been touched.

Again they are singing, this time a new song, and again I dance, first slowly and then faster into the gallop. It is not every time when I dance now that the spirit voice rises from my belly; sometimes it comes without warning, erupting like some slow volcano of sound, possessing me. Sometimes it does not rise at all, and then I push the sound out, contracting my stomach, my diaphragm.

But it is not the same, for when it rises naturally I am absorbed in its power, enveloped in a force that isolates. Joyce, Sylvia, the room and its contents become removed, and I, with no real self left, become a focused point of growling energy. Sometimes I begin by pushing the sound out from my belly and then am suddenly sucked into its power as its force whirls me away.

"Yezwake," says Joyce, and I drop onto my knee.

"What am I hiding?" Joyce asks.

"Shaya ngikutshele, shaya ngikutshele. People made this thing," I say.

"Yezwake!" they shout.

"Shaya ngikutshele. It is this long." I motion about a foot in length.

"Yez," they answer; it is wrong.

"You are using this thing," I say.

"Yezwake," they chorus.

"Shaya ngikutshele, shaya ngikutshele."

"What color is this thing?" asks Joyce.

"Brown."

"Yez."

"White?"

"You are guessing," says Joyce. "You mustn't guess."

"I'm going to dance." My head is empty, no vision, no picture.

They sing and clap, and I dance. And as I dance the image of something small and silvery comes.

"Yezwake," says Joyce, and I drop to my knees and click my fingers again.

"It is silver."

"Yezwake!"

"It is round."

"Yezwake!"

"You put it on your body."

"Yezwake."

"Where on my body?"

"On your arm."

"Yezwake!"

"What part of my arm?"

"Around your wrist."

"Yezwake!"

I am sure that this is either a bracelet or a watch, until . . .

"Is this thing alive or not?" asks Joyce.

"No," I answer, "it is not alive."

"Yez," they respond.

"It's alive!" I say in surprise.

"Yezwake," they chorus.

In my head my brain spins. "I'm going to dance."

As they sing and clap I try to think of what could be made by people, be silver, be worn around the wrist, and be alive. Thoughts of mice and rabbit pelts, goat bones track through my mind.

"Shaya ngikutshele, shaya ngikutshele, shaya ngikutshele." I repeat it over and over, but I am totally confused.

"It is alive when you wear it," I say, feeling around.

"Yezwake," they chorus, but I am only more confused.

"*Shaya ngikutshele, shaya ngikutshele,*" over and over I pant the words, my brain spinning.

"What is alive when you wear it?" asks Joyce.

My breath is coming now in deep grunts.

"When you say it is built by people, it is true, and when you say it is alive, it is true," says Sylvia. "What is it?"

"It's not soft," I say, "it's hard." This is more for something to say rather than a realization.

"This thing, can you hear any sound when you bring it close to you?" asks Sylvia.

"A shell!" I explode suddenly in exuberance.

"*Yez,*" they answer. It is wrong.

"Does this thing have numbers on it?" asks Joyce.

"I'm going to dance," I say, and while I dance I try to put the pieces together: it's small, it's alive, it must have numbers on it or else Joyce wouldn't have asked the question, it makes a sound, it goes around the wrist, it is silver, and suddenly I stop and it the quiet of the room I hear the wall clock tick, tick, tick.

"Your watch," I say quietly.

"*Yezwake!*" they shout. I start to laugh.

"Don't laugh," they say sternly.

"Where is that watch?" says Joyce. I stretch out my hand and feel around the room, my eyes closed. As I come to the area that feels warm I stop. "Here," I say.

"Take it," says Joyce. It is in her lap under her apron.

As I take it from her I give her leg a quick slap. She laughs, and they begin to sing, and I stand and dance. I dance the dance of the relieved.

"O.K.," says Joyce, "give thanks to your parents," and I drop onto my knees, exhausted.

"I give thanks to my parents." "*Thokoza.*" "To my grandparents." "*Thokoza.*" "To the spirits of my parents." "*Thokoza.*" "To the spirits of my grandparents." "*Thokoza.*" "To the spirits of my great-grandparents." "*Thokoza.*" "To all the spirits of Africa I give thanks

and I ask that you keep my head open that I may see, in goodness."
"*Thokoza.*"

"*Bongani emabongweni wena . . . ,*" they say, and I stand again
and dance as they sing and clap.

"Sit down now and stretch quickly," says Joyce. I sit facing the
sacred corner, legs straight out in front, and stretch my arms out in
front of me, pushing them out one at a time, then reach across
each leg for my toes, stretching and pulling on the toes, telling the
spirits that they can leave me now.

When I am finished I look at them. "About the watch, you say
that a watch is alive?"

"Of course it's alive," says Sylvia, "it's working, yes? So it's alive."

"So then, do you call anything that is working alive?" I ask.

"Yes," they answer.

"So the radio." I point to it.

"It's alive," they answer.

"And the television?"

"It's alive."

"And the hot plate?"

"It's alive. And your car, it's alive," Sylvia says, "and when it isn't
working, then it's dead."

A lesson in different perceptions, different perceptions of aliveness. Thank goodness, I think, that I learned it.

Later, as we eat our pap sitting on the floor, they talk about how
it was for them when I began.

"I was so frightened," says Joyce, "that I called Sylvia and said
she must come and do this with me. Because we didn't know how
it would be."

"Because I am white?"

"Yes, because you are white. You see, we can see that you have
the spirit, but we don't know how you would be with us, staying
with us."

I nod. I, too, hadn't known how it would be with them, staying with them. "Has it been difficult for you with me being white?" I ask.

"No," says Joyce, shaking her head firmly. "It's been easy. But there are other people, white people, who have the spirit, who wouldn't do this."

"They wouldn't take the spirit?"

"No, they wouldn't be here with us, because," she shrugs her shoulders, "they think they are better than us."

Agnes is bringing her daughter to be fortuned," says Joyce. "You will do it."

I am nervous. I did so well the last time that I am sure I can't do it again. I sit on the wooden chair and take some long breaths and try to pay attention to my body. I develop a headache, but I'm sure it's stress.

Joyce finishes the washing up. Before she is through, Agnes and her daughter arrive. The girl is plump, with a stomach that looks distended—or is it that the dress is too tight across her belly? She walks as though her body is in pain and she doesn't want to move it. She talks as though her throat is immensely painful.

Joyce and I take off our shoes and go into her room. She takes out the yellow plastic bag and separates out a chunk of *imphepho*. She puts it into the old, blackened shoe polish tin and puts a new candle in the holder while I wrap the shawl around me. Then she calls in the two women.

The daughter lowers herself to the floor in slow lurches. There is sweat on her legs, or is it oil? She pants in short, rasping gasps. Every now and then her face puckers with pain.

All I experience is turmoil. Every pore shouts out to stop—this woman should be seeing a doctor. But I start.

"You often get headaches that go across your head like this, and your face hurts and your mouth, and down into your neck, and your shoulders hurt, and your joints are painful, and your stomach becomes full and pushes out and hurts . . ." on and on. Everything is apparent in the way she holds her head, her mouth, her eyes, her arms, her hands, her legs. Yes, she keeps nodding, yes, it is right.

"You must steam," I say, feeling traitorous, feeling that I am leading her to her doom, "you must steam and *phalaza*. Joyce will give you *muti*."

"And her mouth?" Joyce asks.

"You are having problems with your teeth," I say, having seen it in the hold of her head and her speech.

"Yes." She nods. She recently had a tooth removed, she says, and now the other side is very painful. I notice that one side of her face is swollen. I am sure that she has an abscess and is running a fever. Oh, God, help me, I think. "Joyce will give you *muti* for this," I say, and quickly add, "but if your mouth doesn't feel better by Monday, you must see a doctor." She nods and I feel a slight relief.

Joyce goes out and prepares the pot for steaming while I worry that if she has a fever she shouldn't be steaming.

"You will not steam for long," I say.

"No." She shakes her head. I want to reach out to her, to tell her that what I'm saying is wrong, that she really needs the intervention of western medicine. But I can't do it and sit mute with the shawl around my shoulders.

When Joyce calls her to steam she looks anxious, but she undresses and sits on the little stool, leaning over the pot, red water bubbling, the long strands of root floating near the surface. I lower first the pink blanket, tucking it around her ankles, then the blue blanket, and then the old worn fawn blanket. I look at the clock; it is 7:10.

"Tell us when you've had enough," I say. After five minutes she calls out, but Joyce only unplugs the hot plate. In my anxiety, another five minutes seems to drag. She calls again and Joyce nods at me. I lift off the blankets one by one.

I look at her dull, brown body. She is bone dry, there's not a drop of sweat. For a moment I am speechless. "She didn't sweat," I finally say to Joyce.

"No," says Joyce, unsurprised, "because she is afraid of the steam."

"But how can you shut off your sweating because you are afraid?" I ask.

"No, you can do it," says Joyce.

The daughter pulls her skirt and top back on and starts to put on her sweater. I stop her. "No, it's cold outside; wait until you go out and then put it on." I am now convinced that she'll come down with pneumonia.

Joyce calls me into her room and hands me a slim bottle. "She must eat this; you must put it in her hand."

I call the girl, and holding her hand palm up shake a little of the black powder into her palm. "Now lick it," I say, and she does. Then Joyce unwraps a tablet of charcoal from its silver wrapping. She holds its edge to the candle until it begins to shoot sparks. Then she lays it on the old shoe polish lid and drops a few incense crystals onto it.

She beckons the girl over and tells her to kneel and lean over the incense and breathe through her mouth, then covers her with a blanket. Eerily, as though her back is smoking, plumes begin to rise from the blanket. The sight seems to quicken my fears. It is not long before Joyce lifts the blanket and they take their leave, the daughter shuffling out the door after her mother.

I feel awful. I want to run out after her and seek absolution; I want to pay penance. "We must burn some incense tonight," says Joyce as though she has read my mind. And we do, dropping crystal after crystal into the smoldering charcoal until the small room is filled with a smoke, a strange mix of lemon, lime, and rose fumes, and thus engulfed, I feel released.

The next evening the girl is back. Tonight Joyce heats water and adds herbs for her to gargle, and when she is through, Joyce takes a length of cloth and dips it into the hot herb mixture and holds it to either side of her neck.

When they have left, to soothe (or, God forbid, add to) my worry, I ask Joyce how the man is doing who had come to her with the itching face and body, and the pain around his middle.

"No, the itching is all gone," says Joyce, "just a little bit around the eyes."

"And the pain," I ask.

"The pain is all gone," says Joyce.

I feel reassured. I was convinced that it was his gallbladder and that by now all his other organs would be infected.

Is it because he believed? Is it because the *muti* works? Oh how I wish I could suspend these quarrels with my western mind. Strange that it is easier when I am held in an experience, say, of the snake moving through me or in the grip of the spirit growl; here I can say, "Allow, do not analyze." Perhaps, I, too, need to believe that a treatment will work before it will. Perhaps, in Agnes's daughter's case, Joyce's belief will be enough; perhaps she will survive.

21

Farewell, for Now

❧

It is not long now before Ron and I are due to go back to the States. Joyce is becoming visibly sadder by the day.

One evening we are sitting on the floor of her little room, Joyce's short, plump legs stretched out in front of her. "You remember that thing you asked me, that people were telling you that becoming a *sangoma* is very heavy," she says, and I nod. "It is because you will have to drink the blood from a goat." She looks hard at me.

I look back at her, feeling a little startled, then think about how my blood tastes when I cut my finger and suck on it. Sort of metallic. Then the next thought. "How much blood?"

"It's not too much."

"How much?" I ask again, still thinking of sucking on my finger.

"Maybe one cup."

"A cup!" It seems an enormous amount.

"Yes, and then you must drink some water and *muti*, and *phalaza* it all out again. You must drink and *phalaza* until there is no blood left inside you."

I sit, trying to accommodate the thought. A cup of blood. "How do I drink it?"

"I'm going to cut the goat here with a spear," and she points to under her right arm, "and then you will put your mouth there and drink."

"Is the goat alive or dead?"

"No, it's alive."

My brain wobbles and bobbles around in my head. "Is this what Madota did?"

"Yes, but if you were there, then we would just put you in the bedroom so you wouldn't see it, because we don't let the *thwasas* see this. But I'm telling you now because people have been saying these things to you and you must know."

We sit quietly. I am aware that she has broken with tradition to tell me this, and I don't know what to say.

"You must also eat the poop from the goat."

"The poop!" I exclaim so hard that she laughs.

"*Aayy,*" she says, wiping her hand over her face, "maybe this will be too hard for you."

"How?" My throat contracts and I shudder at the merest thought of taking it directly from the animal.

"No." She laughs, reading my thoughts. "When we kill the other goat, then we take out the insides, those long things where the food is, and we squeeze it out."

"Does it taste like poop?"

"No, it's not bad. We mix it with some herbs and then we pull it along the ground and you must follow it on your knees and eat it." She sees my face. "But it won't stay inside you; you will drink and *phalaza* again until it's all out."

Now it's my turn. "*Aayy,*" I say, dropping my face into my hands, "this will be hard."

"Can you do it?" she asks, looking at me sideways.

"When will I have to do it?"

"When you finish; when you find your goats and chickens."

When I lie on my mattress that night I begin to wonder whether I can really do this. Can I put my face up against a living animal and drink its blood? My brain bounces away; I can't even conceive of it.

I remember Madota killing her cow; that is something else I will have to do that I just can't see myself doing. I turn on my side, facing into the musky aroma from the corner with the herbs and potions. Perhaps, I think, I can ask a veterinarian to come along and give the cow a heavy dose of tranquilizers before I spear it. The thought comforts me, and I doze off.

The Saturday before we leave, the *sangomas* and Jeanett come over to the flat once more to drum and dance. It will be the last time we all get together until I return. We are all sad.

Dear Miriam loops me in her arms and rocks from side to side with me. "Oh, my *nu-nu*," she says, "I am going to miss you so much."

And Joyce makes sure I'm always sitting close to her, and she holds my hand and strokes my face. *"Ngizokhalela wena ngoba uyahamba,"* I will cry when you leave, she says.

"Woooo," says Melita, "we will all cry."

Joyce hides things for me to find, and then we drum and sing and dance. And between each dance, as their words spill across and overlap one another, I know they're talking about me, I'm picking up words I understand: *pesheya*, overseas, *khaya*, home.

"I am going to fly with you," says Sylvia. "I'm going to jump on a broom and *vvvrrrmmm*." She mimes flying off on a broom and they all laugh.

And Ron is again the perfect host and brings around glasses of wine and tea and cookies. After we've had our drinks and eaten, I kneel in front of Joyce with my head low and begin saying my farewells formally, as they would.

"I want to thank you," I say, and they clap and say, *"Thokoza."*

"I want to thank you for sharing your life with me."

"Thokoza."

"For teaching me the things you know."

"Thokoza."

"For teaching me about your people and your past."

"Thokoza."

"And making them my people and my present."

"Thokoza."

"For teaching me things about myself that I will never forget."

"Thokoza."

"I will remember you every day."

"Thokoza."

"Particularly at six o'clock in the evening."

"Thokoza."

Then I turn to Miriam. "I want to thank you."

"Thokoza."

"For sharing your house with me."

"Thokoza."

"And for dancing next to me so I could watch your feet."

"Thokoza."

"And for taking me into your circle."

"Thokoza."

Then, to Sylvia for teaching me to dance, for allowing me to tease her, for telling me to keep going even when I felt down. And then Melita and Madota.

Then, to all of them, the most important acknowledgment. "I thank you for sharing your love with me, because what you give me is something more than learning to be a *sangoma*. You taught me how it feels to be loved and that was something important for me to learn."

And even though I am not sure they understand, all our eyes are misty as they answer, *"Thokoza."*

Then they, in turn, to me, tell me to go well, to remember what I've been taught, to do my herbs every day, to practice "seeing" with Ron, to remember them, and to eat well so that I come back nice and plump, not skinny like when I arrived.

And as they speak I look at them—this circle of *sangomas*. I have been so happy working with these women, being with them, dancing with them. Perhaps what they say is true: that when you take the spirit, you become well, your happiness returns. The thought brings echoes of Joseph Campbell saying "follow your bliss."

I know that I have behaved differently toward the *sangomas* and they toward me than Madota when she was a *thwasa*. Sometimes I forgot to get down on my knees when I was in the room with them; I was playful in a way that an African *thwasa* would never be. I teased Sylvia endlessly about her smoking, but she just shook her head and laughed. "You are so naughty," she would say, but her eyes would twinkle.

And they did not prod me as they would have a black woman, to cook, to clean, to fetch and carry. Yet they are proud, proud that a white person is interested in their tradition, proud of my affiliation with them. When I, in my red skirt, trailed Joyce into a supermarket, and every black head turned to stare, her walk down the aisles became a regal procession.

And yet I am one of them, accepted as one of them; maybe different, but not separate. Their love is real, and since I cannot be both black and white, I cannot say whether or not this love has to do with my whiteness, with my difference. I experienced this love as I imagine a young chick would when under the wing of its mother, drawn close to the downy warmth of her body, safely to her softness. It is not a thing to think about, these women's love just is.

In this they have become my teachers in a greater sense. In taking me to their hearts they have, with their quiet, soft brown fingers, unknowingly peeled away layers of defense, hardened old layers so carefully constructed long ago, and taught me a lesson far more basic and essential than those which I had come here to learn.

Fifteen years ago, at my mother's funeral, in a fury driven from deep within, I jabbed at her stiff, coffined body. "You never taught

me nurturing," I screamed at her, much to the horror of the offici-
ating rabbi, "you never taught me love."

And it was true, for there was such danger in her loving, the danger of invasion, the dangers of her unexpected attacks, that the
doorways that should have opened—to love and be loved, and love
myself—remained forever barred. It is only now, in this circle of
sangomas, that seeds so long dormant that I never knew of their
being slowly grow.

And even in the dancing there was a lesson. For there was such
sweet delivery from the embarrassment of all those years when my
large, flat feet would never point, my legs would never lift. When I
danced now, oh when I danced now, there was such deep joy that
had I owned wings I would have lifted skyward with all the bril-
liance of a sunbird. So while their love watered the dryness in my
soul, the dancing gave wings to my spirit.

This journey of the *thwasa*, this pilgrimage after the African
grail, is the journey toward my own liberation. Strange that it
should occur here, in this country that I so long ago fled, at the soft
brown hands of those who were our nannies, our other mothers, at
a time when they are reaching toward their own liberation.

Perhaps not so strange at all; for all along has there not been an
element of design in this passage? "I need to learn to be loved," I'd
said once, before this passage ever began.

The one who weaves had already long spun the web. Had created the answer long before I knew what I needed to ask.

22

Back into the
Motherland

ৡৢ

The mail is two feet deep, as it usually is when we return; the garden lusciously, horrendously overgrown. I pound into it, obsessed with beating it back into submission and feel guilty about doing away with all that vibrant growth. But it grounds me, getting my fingers into the earth.

Then the other grounding, and I'm off; heading north, driving too fast on the freeway, through Escondido, past Fallbrook with orchards curling around green hills; then north again on Route 79, winding through rich farmland, small towns: Winchester, Hemet; then a right turn onto 10 East, the San Bernardino range green-sloped on either side. The colors changing now to dun, through Banning, past the turnoff to Palm Springs. Now it's yellowing desert scrub. On the left, riding the ridges, white windmills, stiffly three-pronged, wait at attention for the wind that swoops through this valley from west to east. Sweeping northeast from 10 onto 62, the last stretch. Cholla now, and embracing creosote arms. To the south, the hills curling purple, in front, the hills beckoning, the black tarred strip pointing.

Pushing it, pushing it, the needle goes to 90, to 100, and then into the hills, the winding turns, the crest, the little sign: MORONGO VALLEY, ELEVATION 2500, POPULATION 1300.

Slowing as the road divide ends, edging left; then up Juniper and the car windows come down so I can smell it. Palo Verde Street, Ash Street, up the last bumping dirt roads. And when I stop and open the car door, the quail sounds hang in the air like mobiles.

As always, the black guardian angels, the dogs, come with smiling eyes. The wall-eyed Australian shepherd, her head low in submission, the younger Australian shepherd with laughing mouth, then the old black Lab and the Rottweiler, nudging and slobbering. I fill the birdbath twice, the first filling wetly lapped away by the dogs. Then the scratch in broad swathes and the seed for the birds. And the air as soft and warm as a womb.

And when the sun dips behind still-snow-rivered San Jacinto and the eastern hills slide into shadow, I take my offerings and climb up to the small circles that enclose my meditations.

A strange offering this time: lion hair, brought from one beloved land to another. Lion hair, which we found in small balled tufts among the hard crunch of the bush grass. From long-ago lion droppings; caught on a rough tongue as, like a cat, it cleaned. Now sunburned and rain-washed free of its casing, the fawn-colored hair smells warmly of game, of life.

I stop and greet the old manzanita, small jade leaves elegant on red-skinned branches. In beauty she reaches her crown to the sky; in determination her roots snake through the sandstone hillside. I will leave an offering on the way back.

On the top of the small hill, to the lip of the ridge, the length of the valley like a belly stretched thin between its hipped enclosure.

I face, as always, first the east, the place of illumination, and slowly bring my mind to quiet. And after mind has stilled, after time has stilled, and self and space have become one, then slow comes the humming, the circuit, the communion.

Sometimes it is from the east that the message comes, sometimes from the north where the woman shape rests, or the southeast where the ancients reside. Sometimes it rides with the wind's wailing song. And always home is the west, the mother, the earth; here, the bosoms of the Bernadinos.

Before we went to Africa I had set myself a goal: to reach the top of the mountain behind the house. I almost made it, reaching the old tree, blackened by lightning, close to where the eagles nest. This seemed poetic enough to compensate for not reaching the crest. Now I tried again with four dark angels milling, mostly in the lead, the young Australian shepherd with smiling mouth keeping close. And of course, as in life, there was no top, but finally, after an hour or so, a small river, a waterfall and pine trees in a craggy crevice between mountain crests.

In the morning, in the silver slant of the early sun, the quail are quickly out and bickering; the little ones, tiny as mice, scuttle by, single file. On an old juniper stump, a black-collared lizard lies, a foot long, with iridescent blue throat.

It is the time of year again when the orioles pass through on their journey from Mexico to Canada, and I stick orange halves on the yucca tips, where they look like misplaced mallows. But, as usual, it is the red-breasted finches who discover them and flurry about, chattering.

Still, even here in this valley of the spirits, I miss the fine, dancing shadows of the jacaranda in the morning, filtering across the wall, across the streaming mane of the gilt-framed green horse we have hanging over the dresser. She is all movement, head arched, feet flying. I loved seeing her there; she symbolized the growing freedom I felt—the gift of the women with the soft brown skin.

23

Return to Africa

ॐ

It is only four months before we return to Africa and the time passes quickly. How strange it is to be looking forward to returning when for so long this waiting had been filled with dread. So much has changed since the old one with the milky eye spoke her words. So many things have fallen into place, no, not only into place, for that they would have done anyway as the ball will tumble into a slot when the wheel is turned. But there is such harmony to these places, such flair, such beauty.

Here now the sweetness of anticipation where before there was fear; here now something to share with Ron where before the pleasure of return was his alone. Here, in this slot, the lesson of love; in that, deliverance. Ah, this wheel, this whorl, this elegant, exuberant dance, surely this beauty is not the work of chance?

Coming off the plane in Johannesburg, we wait and wait in the passport-checking line, grinning at each other because of the snail-paced inefficiency. "We're in Africa now," I mouth at Ron.

At the counter, the grim-faced computer operator punching one-fingered shakes her head over numerous incorrect entries, but finally, having checked the passports, looks up with a sweet smile, and thickly accented says, "Have a lovely time here, and happy birthday, sir." She has noticed the date, and our irritation is immediately salved.

On the drive in from the airport, the streets seem emptier than before; Harry says it's because business is nonexistent, the recession joining the sanctions impact with a deadening thud. And when I finally go across to Woolworth's to get some basic food items, the shelves, too, are emptier than usual.

With not a container of margarine in sight, I ask a member of the staff when they'll be in. "I don't know," he answers, "we're having trouble getting them from the distributor."

Is this how it will end up, I wonder, stores with empty shelves. Is this the Third World creeping in?

Ah, but when I cross the road back with my bag of milk, bread, and butter, Elias, in his blue coveralls, is out sweeping up droppings from the trees in front of the building; his face creased into the broadest smile possible wipes away any thoughts of shortages.

"My man," I almost shout as I put down the bag and go over to him, ready to hug him. But hugging wouldn't have been proper, and so we clasp hands in the longest exchange of African handshakes, going back and forth between thumb hold and hand hold, grinning our heads off.

I am nervous about seeing Joyce again, nervous because toward the end I began to slack off in doing the work I should have done in the States and I'm afraid I won't be able to "see," or divine.

Also because once out of the African context I had come to doubt whether I really could carry through with the graduating exercises and their bloodletting and blood drinking. Could I drink the blood from an animal that had been speared for this purpose, for my purpose? That the goat would then be eaten somehow didn't lessen the ugliness of it. Could I really crawl around on the ground eating its shit?

As for killing the cow, once in America that had become so foreign a thought that when I talked about it, it was as though I was describing someone else's story. When people asked, "Will you really be able to do that?" I would shrug and say, "I don't know, we'll see." They could have been asking me if I would fly to the moon.

I drive over on a Wednesday evening at our usual time, six o'clock. It was strange putting on the red skirt and white T-shirt again, it felt more like a costume than the clothes I'd been wearing for so many months before.

She is standing in the doorway to her little rooms in her light-blue maid's outfit, her plump legs bowed beneath her. "Oh, my darling," she says as she hugs me tight, her frame even more ample than I'd remembered, "I missed you so much."

We sit in the little kitchen area on the two white wooden chairs and she reaches across the table and strokes my arm, my hand, my shoulder, my face as though touching will confirm that I am really here. Over and over she tells me how she had missed me, how she had read my letters again and again, how, after she'd written, she would count the days till my reply arrived.

When we finally go into her room, the warm, musky aromas of all those roots, bulbs, tendrils, and animal fats wrap around me like a mantle of belonging and I feel myself settling slowly back.

There are new faces now. Mercia has hired a gardener, July, and in exchange for his services, he is living in the shed among the gardening tools. Living with him, and unknown to Mercia, is his lady friend, Alvis. They come around, most evenings, either to cook something on Joyce's little hot plate or to get hot water to wash, and we all sit and chat in the little kitchen area.

July is short, taut-muscled, hair tight to his head. He is a traditional African male: dominant and determined to be the one who is right. With me he feels his way, at first deferential, then becoming more assured. Occasionally when he is noisily imposing his will on Alvis he looks to me, as though I in my whiteness will confirm his superior position. I don't.

Alvis, with the face of a brown Botticelli angel, flirts and rolls her eyes, and gives back as good as she gets. She is as playful as a puppy and I am quickly drawn to her. She neither speaks nor understands English, but with hand signals, exchanged eye signals, or Joyce translating, we banter, tease July, and play simple games, ingenuous and unsophisticated.

It is spring, and everyone waits for the first of the summer rains. When we were young, those first rains brought us out, shrieking like parrots, with arms stretched to the sky, heads thrown back so we could catch the fat warm drops in our mouths.

The mothers did not allow us to swim until after the first rains, and now it seems this waiting, this anticipation, has become part of the common psyche. Perhaps it is also the always pervasive fear of drought; but we all talk of it. Soon, we say, soon the first rains will be here.

They came on a Friday. We had watched the gathering together of darkness in the southern sky, smelled dampness from the cement sidewalk as though it, too, like the land, was opening its pores in readiness. Then the wind, driven before, swirled a sheet of newspaper into a pas de deux. An empty cardboard box scurried, turning slowly. Then lightning, in long whips, cracked across the darkness, followed by dark kettle-drum rolls and cell-splitting rifle shots.

The rain came, dancing so hard one could not tell whether it was rain or hail. It beat, pummeled, frightening children and young dogs. In the gardens around Johannesburg, frogs would come to life, gargling wetly, leaping from puddle to puddle. Gutters became raging rivers. People trapped in doorways took their shoes off to wade. "Ah," everyone agreed, "it was truly a marvelous thing."

Even Joyce, who had previously clucked like a worried hen when the wind had blown promising clouds away to the north, even now when her little kitchen carpet puddled a leak, was happy. But she kept a piece of special bark in her pocket to protect her from the lightning.

The veldt, still winter yellow, will begin to green now. Outside, the jacaranda tree is beginning to fuzz; soon the blossoms, like small lilac trumpets, will follow. And always the birds chortle and whistle. Indian mynahs, flashing orange-eyed, bicker in the old, overfronded palm trees out back, filling the hallways with riotous bird chatter. In the mornings the bulbuls call their liquid song from tree to tree, or the woodhoopoes crack the air with their demented cackle. And everywhere the yellow weavers with their swizzling sound.

As soon as we can all come together, the clan of the *sangoma* women gathers again in our apartment to sing and dance and celebrate the return of the *pesheya thwasa*, the trainee from overseas. What a joyful troupe we are, drumming and singing together once again.

There are two other red-wrapped *thwasas* now: Jeanett of the regal cheekbones has begun working with Sylvia, and Cynthia, a *sangoma* I'd met at Madota's party, is training Myna, a pretty young woman who works in a travel agency. We now sit together, like three hens, on our haunches with our heads down and speak only when we are spoken to.

The *sangomas* drum and sing, the *thwasas* dance and find those things they have hidden, beginning with the newest inductee, Myna, then Jeanett, then me. I am suddenly terrified that I'll make a fool of myself, but I am no slower in finding what has been hidden than the other two.

Ah, the joy of dancing again, of hearing the drums and the singing and the ululating. The heady richness of this and the tender care of my fathers and brothers leaves me limply smiling.

After the dancing and the singing is done, and we've had tea and cake, I drive Jeanett and Myna up Jan Smuts Avenue to the Randburg taxi station. There is a small crowd there, maybe twenty or so, waiting. And when we get out of the car, to hug and to say goodbye, the crowd stirs and stares and buzzes.

A young man separates himself from the crowd and walks toward me. As he reaches for my hand I feel panicky, but he raises my arm up high, turns to the crowd, and proclaims, "Praise be to God and the New South Africa!"

"*Yebo*," I answer, making a high fist, and leap back into the car feeling both heady and relieved.

24

Passages

Although the New South Africa is on everybody's lips, although the date for the elections will soon be announced, grief still stretches like a net across the land. Killings escalate as political rivalries intensify, and it seems that there will be no end to the ugliness. And in addition to the slaughter, to that fear and grief, there are yet other fears and other losses.

"The saddest thing," Zac De Beer had said three, even four years ago, "is the rate at which young people are leaving the country." That was then. Now the trickle has become a torrent.

Two of Harry's children have already left, leaving quiet the dinner table that had been the court for their rages. "It was people like you," Shaun had screamed at his father, "people like you who got us here."

And Harry howling back, "What do you know?" Stuffing food into his already ailing body as though to block it all out—the disintegrating universe.

"The kids really liked Australia, so they'll probably be leaving," said Joan and Ivor, still flushed with the blessing of their first grandchild, "They've said they'd like us to join them if it works out," says Ivor. "It's very sweet of them, but I'm too old to start over, what would I do? I don't have the money to support myself, and if I did I wouldn't be able to get it out of the country."

They talk about the things they had planned to do with their grandson, the trips to the zoo that will now never be taken, the stories unread, the closeness, all about to be lost.

There are other passages. Kiki, an old Greek friend, talks about how all those things that had made her life meaningful will probably not be there when her grandchildren grow up: the symphonies at City Hall, the cultural evenings, the events at Wits University. "You know," she says in her whispering voice, "in the States you know that you will be able to take your grandchildren to the museums you went to, the opera houses, the places that enriched you; you know that they will be there for the next generation and the next; but here we don't know. There is nothing that is sure anymore."

And no matter how much I say that with black rule will come a different culture—new avenues to explore, new traditions to learn—there is no salve for their mourning. For mourning is indeed what they are doing.

And at Wits, which increasingly looks as though it's being trashed, Mehlo, always so calm, so controlled, has tears in her eyes. "He wants to go," she says of her son who is waiting for the ever-striking teachers to return to school so that he can finish his studies, "he wants to go overseas."

And in the white suburbs, after the walls had gone up and the electric wiring, after the three, four, five dogs were bought, after the electronic gates were put in, there is still murder.

"I was sitting in the car waiting for the gate to open, and I felt the gun against the side of my head. 'Get out,' he said. I reached for my bag—that was stupid—and he slapped my hand away. I was lucky, he could have killed me then. I got out. As I stood there I thought 'now, now he's going to do it,' and I closed my eyes. But he got into the car and drove away."

"Do you have nightmares?" I asked.

"No, not really. I felt I was fortunate. My best friend was murdered."

"He just got his driver's license," says another of her son. "Normally I would worry about him drinking and driving, now I worry that he will be hijacked and murdered." As soon as he matriculates he will leave for England.

Then there is poor Sandra, she who was once the front end of a dancing donkey while I was the rear, wailing, "What am I going to do? I'm so afraid there's going to be a revolution and I hate the sight of blood."

With Joyce I discuss what to say if someone threatens me. She thinks a while. "Say, '*Uma ungangithinta uzobona amehlo esibungu.*'"

"What is that?" I ask.

"It means, If you touch me, you will see the eyes of the worms."

I ponder on it. It doesn't seem strong enough.

"How about: If you touch me your peepee will disappear up into your tummy?"

"*Hau!*" She claps her hand to her mouth, her eyes horrified, then laughs. "Wooo, you are so naughty!"

When Alvis and July come around that night to fetch their bucket of hot water for washing I test out the two sentences. "July, if some *tsotsie* comes up to me and wants to make trouble, what do you think would make him stop and run away. If I say *Uma ungangithinta uzobona amehlo esibungu*, or if I say *Uma ungangithinta umpipi wakho uzobuyela phakati esiswini*?"

July's mouth falls open and Alvis collapses into the bucket. "That one," he says.

∾

There is a murder in our building. It is one of the old men who does maintenance and some gardening. He is found with his throat axed. The young man with whom he shared a room has run away. The police find the bloodied ax in the bushes.

"Why?" we ask. The women say it was because the old one was a *sangoma* and the young one was having a lot of pain and thought the old one, Willie, was putting bad *muti* in his bed to kill him.

Ron says, "Now you see how powerful this thing is."

I feel a chill.

One day Joyce says, "It is time to get your beads, we must start making your things for when you finish," and my stomach lurches. So on a Wednesday we go back downtown to Diagonal Street to the shops.

The beads hang in clusters, fill drawers, spill across the counter. Joyce, with serious hands, fingers them, pushing this red strand away for that one, holding up this blue, that yellow loop. Red beads, green beads, black beads, small beads, large beads, four hundred rands' worth of beads, and I wonder how those who have so much less than I do can afford this.

Now the evenings are filled with sewing as well as dancing and divining. There are beaded bandoliers to be made—the *umukaxo*, six of them, they will cross the chest, each with its own packet of herbs; the beaded necklace—*izimfiso*, with the little bag containing herbs that will go around my neck; the red pleated skirt and over-skirt both beaded around the hem.

The date is set for Saturday, November 13, six weeks away, in Madadeni, which is Joyce's hometown. The final exercise is always held in the home village of the *thwasa's* teacher.

We begin mixing the herbs that go into the *umukaxo* and the *izimfiso*. Joyce calls out their names and tells me to write them down: *umlomonandi, madlozini, munandi, manono, iphengula*, and *ubububu*; I will have to find out what they are in English.

Ten different roots, barks, and bulbs that are crushed, grated, and pounded into powders that are mixed according to an old formula that is nowhere written and are then rolled into little red fabric pouches. The beads pass through the pouches, which are then sewn tightly around with thread.

We sit on the floor, the flat stone between our legs, the small round stone or the old metal grater in our hands. We pound, crush, and grate, pound, crush, and grate till small, gray, powdery mounds surround us and my arms and back ache.

"Why don't I run home and get my food processor?" I say to Joyce. "It'll be much easier."

"No," she says firmly, grimly, "we must do it this way." There's clearly to be no modernization here.

We need roots from the doringboom—the thorn tree—to make the blue and white beaded necklace with the middle coil of *indorro*. Joyce says she knows where some trees are across the river and we'll go to dig some out.

So one lunchtime, Joyce, Alvis, and I, carrying pick, shovel, and plastic bags, walk down to the Jukskei, the river that meanders through much of Johannesburg and after heavy rains sometimes washes away the street children who sleep on its banks.

Alvis leaps as nimbly as a goat from stone to stone, Joyce takes off her shoes and wades. I balance the pick across my shoulders and follow Alvis's route, worrying about that dreaded fluke, the flatworm bilharzia, which is carried through South Africa's rivers by snails and which can infect the liver, bladder, lungs, or central nervous system.

On the opposite bank a wide, grassy knoll follows the contours of the river. We walk a while, a strange trio: round Joyce with her rolling gait, Alvis, as sprightly as a nymph in hand-me-down clothing, and the gangly white one, red-wrapped.

Joyce points out the tree, the thorns green-leafed, subdued. She circles the perimeter, testing the give of the earth with the pick, then finds a spot she likes and begins long, arcing swings that slowly expose the top roots. She kneels and pulls them out with her fingers and then tosses them away.

"What's wrong?" I ask.

"No, they're too small, we must get bigger ones."

Off we go to find another tree, and again she circles, then begins the rhythmical swinging of the pick. Dogs in the neighboring homes begin to bark. I idly wonder if we're on public property. If someone happens to look out of their window and sees two black women and one strange white one desecrating a tree, would they call the police?

I begin to rehearse a speech should the law descend. "Well, you see, officer, we need the roots for a graduation necklace." Somehow I don't think the law would understand, and for the rest of the time that Joyce digs I maintain a nervous lookout.

This tree, too, only reveals roots too thin to be useful. "No," says Joyce, "July must come and do this." With his muscles he will be able to dig lower and get to the larger roots. I am relieved, saved from the possible ravages of the law.

I am "fortuning" more regularly now. Often the deep growl arises from some unknown place. Sometimes my body feels that it's no longer mine but is rather a reflection of those whom I read. Many of the symptoms are similar: pain in the back of the neck, headaches, sometimes sore joints and pain from indigestion. I know their diets are high in starch and low in vegetables and fruits, and I urge them to include more of the latter.

Their madams will buy, for those who work as maids, stewing meat, pap, and bread, but seldom fruits and vegetables. And seldom will the maids buy those things for themselves. Joyce, when she makes salad for her madam, will sometimes save a little for herself, or take an orange from the large ornate bowl in the kitchen, but other than cabbage, I have never seen her buy fruits or vegetables.

Cabbage is a favorite, and this she stews all day on her little hot plate until the house smells and Mercia complains. And when, in the spring, the wild spinach grows, the maids will slowly amble off to the veldt with plastic shopping bags and come back with bags ballooning with spinach.

They earn little, these women who take care of our homes and our children. Maybe three, four hundred rand a month. Ah, but it's all found money, the white madams will say, forgetting that these caretakers have homes of their own, children of their own.

Your heart is very heavy," I say to one who is not so young.

"Yes."

"You have children who are away from you."

"Yes."

"You are worried because your mother is taking care of them, and she is getting old herself."

"*Yebo.*"

"And your husband was drinking and is gone now."

"*Yebo.*"

"And it is hard for you to send them money every month."

"*Yebo.*"

If I did not know it, I would still know it.

I cannot tell her to *phalaza* or *spuyt*, no steaming will fix this. This is the time to be the therapist, but I miss the language and instead massage her neck and her feet.

A young girl, maybe eighteen, comes. Her boyfriend no longer cares for her, but she loves him and wants to hold him. I talk about wet hands and holding soap too tightly. But she wants a fix, and Joyce mixes the *intando* with its snake fat and thumbs it into the small nicks she has made with a razor above her vaginal hair and on her lips.

While Joyce is mixing I ask her if she knows about AIDS. Yes, she has heard, she says. If her boyfriend comes back, I ask, will she use a condom? No, she answers, if he comes back, then she wants to get pregnant so he will stay. But you don't know who he has been with, I say. No, she shakes her head, if he knows she can get pregnant he will stay. I want to shake her.

25

Visiting Balfour

It is a glorious spring in South Africa, with trees, bushes, and shrubs bursting into bud everywhere. Wisteria, gardenia, bignonia, large pink, yellow, and white clusters that bow slender branches and cascade over walls. And the scent lingers around bushes, beneath trees, invisible fields of soft sweetness to walk through.

Outside the balcony, the jacaranda is billowing great clouds of lavender. Later, as gently as snow, the flowers fall and lace the rain-greened grass with lilac.

One Sunday we take the day off from sewing, and Joyce, Madota, Miriam, and I drive out to Balfour to visit Miriam's mother. It was at Balfour that Madota had done her graduating exercises the last time we were here, the time I was felled by tick-bite fever.

"My mother was so sad," Miriam had said when they came back,

"she is old, old, old, and she said, 'Now I will never see Melisande.' " I promised then that we would visit this time.

We set off, my little car with its shot shocks groaning as Miriam,
who travels home only by taxi, takes us on the route the taxis
take—the most circuitous route imaginable. But finally we are
on the freeway, green fields and small koppies stretching away,
and I always wonder to whom they belong, these vast tracts of
fenced land.

Her mother lives in the township of Balfour. The same tin homes
we see in Lenz, some sudden solid brick homes. The streets here
are a quagmire of boulders, trash, potholes, chickens. At a wire
fence curling like the hump of a sea monster, Miriam tells me to
stop. There is a span of buckling gate hanging crippled from
one hinge.

Even before she climbs out of the car, Miriam's mouth is wide in
joyful ululating. As I drive in, children come running, chickens
scatter, and a tall-combed rooster crows in ownership. It is not a
yard but rather a square of dark earth, creased with tires, bricks; a
rambling bush spreads bleakly, as sunless as an octopus.

Miriam sweeps up the littlest one and covers his face and his
head with kisses. The older ones stand around, cross their legs in
shyness, find her skirt with their hands, look at me sideways.

We walk in through the dining room with its linoleum floor and
formal dining-room suite. Through the large kitchen into the bedroom where Mother, Mama, lies in bed wrapped in sweaters even
though it is quite warm. As we troop in, Miriam, Joyce, Madota,
and I, the six or eight children and assorted adults, her lips spread
wide in almost toothless ecstasy.

We line up to give her hugs. She takes my hand as though to
shake it, but I bend down and hug her sweatered body, and everyone cheers. Then we settle down around her, on the floor, on stools,
on the other bed, the children and the other relatives crowding
around.

They begin speaking in Zulu, Miriam's voice loud, Joyce sometimes translating. After an hour or so the children and the relatives

have filtered out, and when Madota wanders into the kitchen I join her. We talk about politics; I say that I could never understand how the governing Afrikaners could have been so stupid as to not see that they were painting themselves into a corner. She says if you want to see stupid, try the Zulus. I adroitly deduce that she is not Zulu.

Before we left Johannesburg, Joyce and I had stopped at a bakery and I had bought a cake for Miriam's mom. Now, when Madota and I finish our comparisons of degrees of stupid, Joyce comes out and suggests that I bring in the cake.

I carry it into the bedroom in its large pink box as though it were a crown. The children, the relatives, come after, crowding behind, spilling from the doorway into the small room, the children poking each other in the ribs.

When Mama opens the box, and the large white-iced carrot cake emerges, with its icing-orange miniature carrot topknot, there is an ovation of cheering and ululating that almost brings down the walls.

Mama clasps my hands, hugs me, wipes her eyes, and then slowly pushes aside the bedspread. Stiffly, slippered feet emerge, swollen legs move reluctantly off the mattress and onto the floor. We are hushed as she straightens to a slightly wobbling stand, then begins to move her body slowly, creakingly, from side to side. And suddenly the silence is broken, and while everyone sings and claps, she slowly picks up first one foot and then the other and dances.

Oh, the excitement! The cheering and whistling and ululating bounce from the walls, doubling in volume. Her gray-haired son takes her hands and dances a few steps with her, then helps her back onto the bed while the family shouts hallelujahs and praise be to God.

There is so much contained in her gesture of dance. This was not just an old lady taking some shaky steps—this was an enactment of something far deeper. This was a salute that transcended the mundane and called the very spirits into being.

I feel the fullness of tears prodding at my eyelids. For in that room, the room of Miriam's mother, with its sacred corner of wraps, clay bowls, and bottles of *muti*, with three, four generations making a daisy chain of continuity, the loop of tradition, solid as amber, shone as a light that linked all in the solidness of its embrace. And I, for a moment in time, felt illuminated within the richness of the weave.

Taking our leave is difficult. There are so many people Miriam would like me to meet and my carefully constructed schedule has to give way to African time. But as the afternoon winds down I am content that we have more than made up for the missed weekend of Madota's graduation.

26

Prayers, Transmigrations, and Strange Happenings

❦

Joyce is getting nervous now; while we sew she looks sideways at me every now and then.

"What?" I ask.

"Are you going to find your goats and chickens?"

Someone has given her a long stick and she has started notching it at regular intervals.

"Is that to hit me with if I don't?"

"Yes, Ron and me, we'll hit you." And she waves the stick at me.

"Oh, I better start praying," I say.

"Yes," she answers, "pray to God that you find your things or I'm going to run away and leave you there."

July is listening. "No," he says, "pray to me first because God is farther away."

"How about if I pray to Alvis first?"

"Alvis! No, she's not going to help you."

ᛟ

Sometimes they sit in the doorway while I dance and divine. If the spirit sound has arisen and consumed me, I'm no longer aware of them, if not, then I notice Alvis singing and clapping, July watching intently as though it is important that I do this well.

One evening when I arrive, July and Alvis are bickering—she has bought more at the market then he told her to. He appeals to me: "Isn't it correct that I should be cross?" he asks, and adds, "If she can't do what I tell her, then I must hit her." He is unsmiling, serious.

"Hit her!" I exclaim. "That's, that's . . ." I want to say barbaric, but I know he won't understand the word.

But before I can complete the thought, he's up off his seat, voice emphatic, finger wagging. "You see, a man must control a woman, otherwise he's not a man. It's like a horse, isn't that right? The horse must know you are the rider, and if the horse wants to go his way, then you must hit it; and a woman, too, she must know you are the rider."

"But a woman is not a horse, and that's not the way I see a relationship," I answer, my voice becoming just as emphatic, "I see it as a partnership, where no one is the horse or the rider."

"No, you are wrong." He has sat down again but is leaning hard forward and punching out each word. "You are wrong, because it is the man who is the boss and the woman must know that it is the man who is the boss."

"Woooeee," I say and look over at Alvis, who has been watching all of this with a slightly quizzical smile. "If he wants to hit you like a horse, maybe you should say no more boom-boom." And I thump my palms together.

While Alvis may not have understood the sentence, she has certainly understood the intent and claps her hands to her mouth while her eyes widen with glee. July laughs and catches hold of my hands.

He and I will have many such encounters as time goes by. Sometimes I wonder if he provokes them to test what must be a new experience for him—going toe to toe with a woman, particularly a white woman.

One day I notice that Alvis is getting quite a tummy on her. I pat it and make baby rocking motions with my arms. "Uh-uh," she answers, shaking her head. She grabs the plumpness between her fingers. "Fat," she says, "fat."

But July would like her to have a baby.

"But you've got a wife and children in Zimbabwe," I say.

"Yes," he answers, "but that is in Zimbabwe. Now I must put my seed here."

*O*ne day while meditating over the herbs, I feel again the strange pulling around my cheeks; my mouth and nose seem to draw forward. Again my shoulders begin rotating one after the other, rolling forward as though following the motion of legs. Once again I am walking as though four-legged, slim-muscled. Shoulders slope with each loose step. Each footfall is sure, absorbed in each shoulder.

My eyes are closed. I am aware, and yet not; I am present, and yet not; space exists, and yet not. All is consumed in the motion, all is concentrated in the motion.

Then at some point movement slows. Face draws back; sound surrounds; body settles, room settles; fingers feel, legs return; gradual, gradual, the return to myself. It has been well over an hour.

That night I tell Joyce.

"What animal were you?" she asks.

"The same as last time," I say, "a leopard, I think."

She takes so long to answer that I think she's not going to speak at all. Then she begins slowly. "The leopard is a very strong animal, and it's very lucky that this thing has come to you. It means you are strong like the leopard. In the village the king will wear the skin of a leopard. Now this thing has come to you."

She sits quietly, thinking, then she looks up. "Maybe you will find your things easily now."

❦

"Saturday morning," says Joyce, "someone is coming to take us to her house."

"What for?" I ask.

"No, you will see."

She comes to fetch us on Saturday morning, a young white woman in a Ranger. We drive to Sandton, to her two-million-rand home with green gardens sloping away to a columned pool and a summerhouse. On the way she talks continuously about her maid. She's had her for many years; the children don't like her, in fact, she doesn't like her. She's lost three gardeners because of her, because they think she's a witch.

Around the house the walls are high, the gates towering. The entryway is tall and marbled. She allows us to stand a moment and look around. The air is cool.

We cross the marbled floor to the formal living room. The room is light, airy, and cold, much colder than the marbled entryway. The cold seems discontinuous, in pockets. We step into it and out of it, then back into it. At the far end of the room is a fireplace, it is white-tiled, decorative, unused. As I move in front of it, all over my body the hairs stand up.

"Do you feel something?" asks Joyce, watching me.

"Yes," I answer, "all my hairs are standing up."

"We found something here," says the woman, "in the fireplace, a heap of something like reddish powder."

"Do you have it?" asks Joyce.

"No, it frightened me and I got rid of it."

We walk back through the hallway.

"This is the kitchen," she says. It is sunny and large, with an island in the middle. We walk around it, and as we pass a large white freezer, I feel a pull. I stop, they walk on, I begin to go after them. The pull stops me again. "Wait."

"What do you feel?" Joyce asks.

"I feel a pull."

The woman opens the freezer. It is filled with ice-furred cuts of meats, boxes of frozen food.

"Will you empty this out?" the woman asks her mother.

"I want you to see the main bedroom," she says. As we walk down the long hallway, Joyce seems to lose her sense of balance. I notice her wobble. "What's wrong?"

"I'm feeling dizzy," she says. Her voice has grown husky.

Between the Roman-tubbed master bathroom and the bedroom there is an entry way. Here chill hangs in the air as in a morgue. My skin prickles; I rub my arms to keep warm.

"It is bad in here," says Joyce.

"Last night," says the woman, "I was lying in bed reading, my husband was asleep. Suddenly I saw a figure come around the corner into that little area," she points to the entryway.

"What kind of figure?" asks Joyce.

"I couldn't tell because it was dark, but it was like a small person. He put his hands up on either side of his face and spread his fingers." She looks at us. "I'm not making this up, I don't believe in this sort of thing."

"It was a *tokoloshe*," says Joyce. She shakes her head. "There are bad things in this house."

"I want to get out of here." The woman shudders, and we follow her across the green lawn to the summerhouse.

As we walk, Joyce fills me in. "She wants to sell her house, but nobody is buying it. Always they come close to buying it and then just go away. She is worried that her maid is doing bad things."

The summerhouse is furnished with wrought iron and cool greens.

"Do you think it's my maid?" the woman asks.

"Yes," says Joyce, "it's your maid. She doesn't want you to sell the house, so she's doing bad things."

"What must I do?" she asks.

"You must tell her to go, and then we must come back and make the house safe again."

"Must I fire her?"

"Yes, you must fire her." Joyce is firm.

Later, on the way back, the woman anguishes over the need to fire the maid. "Maybe it isn't anything she's doing; I would feel terrible if I fired her and she isn't involved."

"Perhaps," I say, "you should separate her out of what's happening. Do you like her as a maid, does she give you what you need, does she get on with your children and they with her? Ask yourself those questions first." She nods.

When we pull up to Mercia's house I ask the woman if her mother found anything in the freezer.

"Yes," she answers, "she found a little bottle with some kind of powder in it."

For the rest of the day Joyce has trouble with her voice, and my skin prickles. Hysteria? I didn't have an answer.

That woman never does call us back, but instead a friend of mine from school days calls; she would like her home to be made safe.

We had begun standard two together at End Street Convent when we were eight. The old polished wooden desks were made for two, side by side. She sat next to me and needed a pencil. I had two; I gave her the blunt one.

Her name was Pamela Small, her parents two tiny immigrants from Wales. She grew to tower over them, drawing from some older genetic pattern. They lived in Bez Valley, a middle-class community of small family homes in the dip between Athlone and Kensington. Often on weekends I slept over.

We would lie awake till we were sure her parents were asleep, then climb out the small square bedroom window and creep across the dark street to the park made haunted by night. The hard-edged frames of the swings, the swift curve of the slide, the poles and bars of the merry-go-round, silver touched by moonlight, alien in their stillness.

We walked around them, laying a light hand here on a rail, there on a bar, as silent as the swings, our bare feet wet in the grass, our pajamas softly fluorescent.

On Sunday mornings, while the faithful prayed, we walked up the south hill to Kensington. Past the quiet stores, across Kitchener Street, double-lined with trolley tracks, to climb the koppie, or rocky hillside, above the valley. This had to be done barefoot. It was our secret tempering, as today climbing into the mountains behind the house in the desert is for me. She was a far better climber than I, but we both developed tough, resilient soles.

She lives today in a meandering thatch-roofed home on eleven acres out in the country, where she runs a kennel. At fifty-five she still looks like a tomboy, her short, dark hair standing straight out in spikes, but her frame is rounder and she wears a hearing aid in one ear.

These homes out in the country are always vulnerable. There is no cushioning from close neighbors. She obsesses about hearing strange noises at night, and on one occasion the telephone wires were cut. From her years of breeding Alsatians, she has ten or twelve dogs, but still she is afraid.

During the last week, Joyce and I had sharpened to a point twenty-five four-inch sticks and coated them with the thick black *muti*. We had gone down to the river and collected thirty river stones and crossed them with the tarry mix.

And now we drive out into the country, Joyce with her brown leather briefcase looking for all the world like a visiting doctor.

We spend three hours working in the still, afternoon heat. We dig holes around the property periphery and bury the sticks, then more holes closer in around the structures, burying the stones. We say the words that need to be said. Then again we circle, making black crosses above the windows and the doors.

I had been curious as to what the response would be when we circled the servants' quarters with our sticks and stones. But they had been unperturbed, as though there was nothing uncommon about this practice. They, too, would be shielded by this safety net.

"You think this will work, Joyce?" Pam asks, anxiety making her voice breathy.

"Yes," Joyce answers solemnly, "it will work."

Making a home safe is not cheap. To make an average-size home safe, Joyce charges twelve hundred rand. Normally, to do a property the size of Pam's she would charge two thousand. And it seems that there are people willing to pay it, who either believe enough in the old traditions or see it as yet another form of insurance—the version that appeals to the spirits.

27

Dreadlocked and Oiled

❦

It is time for my hair to be dreadlocked, this in preparation for the graduation exercise. Once it is all rolled, it will be colored red with a combination of oxide and car oil. And it will stay that way for six months, after which it will be unrolled and washed out with special herbs.

We start on a Thursday during Joyce's lunch break. She begins at the back, above the neck, taking a strand of hair, separating it into two, rolling each strand, then rolling both around one another.

She has taken a chair out into the garden, and I sit on the grass at her feet. After about an hour, a two-inch-square section has been done. That evening we continue, and for another five hours she rolls. By the time she is done my scalp feels as though my hair has been trapped in a wringer. When it is time to go to bed I sit on my mattress and gently put my hand against my head to see how it will feel to lie on it. And I discover it hurts. It hurts a lot. I contemplate sitting up all night, but then decide to heck with primitive practices and take a painkiller and a sleeping pill. But I don't tell Joyce.

The next morning when I arrive at the flat, I first stand outside the door and warn Ron. His mouth drops a little when he sees me, but he manages to slide by without laughing. "Maybe it'll start a new fashion," he says.

My head, which was never the shapeliest part of my body, being too small for the rest of me and burdened with overlarge ears, is now inescapably exposed. Going into the shopping center is difficult.

First I try putting a scarf around my head, but that hurts, so off it comes. I look at myself in the mirror. There is a lesson here, I think. It is time to come to terms with my head. It took me only thirty years to come to terms with my breasts, pulling them up as though wishing would lift them higher. So it will have taken me a little longer to come to terms with my head.

Elias is sweeping the hallway when I go out. "See," I say to him, "my hair's been done."

"Yes, I see," he says, and then he smiles proudly. "I'm so happy you are doing this. I, too, I am a *sangoma*."

Dear Elias. Did the gods put him here on this day at this time to say these words, just the right words? Oh sublime serendipity! I sail across the street with my head high.

The next morning Joyce mixes red oxide and the car oil in a small bowl. The mix is deep red. She dips her hand into the bowl and coats each dreadlock, smoothing the mix around the rolls and into my scalp. I smell like a car engine.

Now the looks that I get turn into stares. Children, who are of course the most unabashed, gape. White people, knowing that it's rude to stare, go through an elaborate series of eye flicks, quick enough not to be impolite but enough of them to get a good look. Before I get together with friends I warn them, and strangely enough, many of them, once over the shock, even seem to like it. "The color is definitely you," says my husky-voiced sister-in-law.

"I'd keep it." She looks at me with hand on hip. "Turn around." I do. "Mmm," she says, she of the high heels and earrings, "it's not bad, not bad at all."

Saturday and Sunday we are going out once again to Lenz. Miriam has a new *thwasa*, and it is time for her initiation. We go in that miracle of public transport, the minibus taxi.

It is already hot as we walk from the house to the taxi stop, and my oiled head begins to fry in the sun. While Joyce lopes in her rolling gait, I run from tree to tree, from shade spot to shade spot, trailing the odor of car oil like a cloud of flies.

We take the taxi first downtown where we will meet Miriam and Emily, her *thwasa*. Then a second taxi, radio blaring the latest in rock, takes us through to Lenz and drops us off at that same Indian store where we had bought the chickens for my initiation.

By now it is midday and the sun is baking. The *sangomas* amble slowly down the red-earth roads, I follow within my cloud of oil fumes. After five minutes an egg could be fried on my head.

Finally I recognize the morning-gloried fence that surrounds Miriam's house, but there is to be no relief from the heat. The tin house has been closed up all day with four chickens inside. The heat is tangible. One can hold it and squeeze liquid from it. The smell is also tangible, and it would not be liquid one would squeeze from it; the floor is covered in chicken shit.

As we walk in, the chickens make flapping runs around the room before crowding into a corner, their long-toed feet slipping, scrabbling on the linoleum. Miriam unrolls the reed mats and we sit down. No one pays attention to the shit. It is only later when Sylvia and Cynthia come with Jeanett and Myna, and they clean it up, that I realize how spoiled I've been because I am white and that it's the *thwasa's* duty to do such things. Had I been black I have no doubt Joyce or Miriam would have told me to clean the floor.

Till four we sit in the heat-heavy room, the four *sangomas* and Emily with their brown legs stretched forward toward the center, the three *thwasas* hunched on our haunches side by side, heads lowered, the four chickens, three hens and a rooster, crowding in the corner.

The streaks left on the linoleum from the quick swipes the *thwasas* made at the chicken poop hypnotize me, as do the flies that hover quizzically over them. I watch their progression from streak to kitchen counter and back to streak. Later we will eat on the same shit-streaked floor. Oh woe, my western eyes!

At four o'clock, as before, the initiation begins. The mats and drums are taken outside, Emily is wrapped in shawls, and we three *thwasas* wait with her in the driveway. When she runs into the yard Joyce signals for me to sit next to her and I watch as the ceremony unfolds, a tradition so old that these women no longer hold the threads, the stories, to its beginnings. Only the actions remain.

Later, when it is time for the chickens to be slaughtered, Jeanett offers me the knife. I shake my head. I can't do it. Oh, God, I think, and I will have to kill a cow.

Myna holds the chicken, extending the neck, and Jeanett deftly saws with the knife until the head is removed. The decapitated body is held neck down over a small metal bowl until the blood has drained, then laid in a larger baby-blue bowl. Reflex arc, reflex arc I say to myself over and over as the body jerks and the wings flap. And on the ground the decapitated head, mouth opening and closing, opening and closing.

Later the *thwasas* clean and cook the birds. How strange it is, after fifty-four years of life, to be cleaning a chicken for the first time; how inured I've become—we've all become—to the living thing that what we eat once was. It comes now cleanly wrapped in plastic, allowing us to reach guilt-free into its interior, which smells of little more than stale refrigeration.

Ah, but to reach into that which has been freshly slain, still smelling of aliveness, succulently warm, almost hot. Fingering deep, find the delicate connecting tissue, then gently pulling down, withdrawing a hand redly wet with heart, with liver, with stomach, fat the rich yellow of marigolds.

And eggs, not yet eggs but yolks, webbed with fine blood vessels, some the size of a nickel, some larger, one already calcium-coated but still soft, which we lay gently on the shelf in the kitchen.

For these occasions, for all ceremonial occasions, the chicken or goat or cow is neither seasoned nor fried or stewed, rather it is cut up and boiled, then eaten plain with pap.

When the chickens have been cooked, with half left for the spirits, the *thwasas* dish it out, handing breast, back, legs around to the *sangomas*, to the guests. For us, the wings, so our spirits might fly, and the feet, so that we may be fleet of foot.

We take our tin plates outside and sit under the stars, on the narrow, red-polished ledge, the small stoep that runs around the house. These birds were not the youngest of souls, and the wing is tough and fatty. When it comes to the foot, however, it is all yellow skin, fat, and bones. I gag on the first mouthful and, in the darkness, mush it between my fingers until the bones and fatty stuff are separated, then hide the skin and fat under the pap.

This time it is not as late when we go to bed and Miriam gives me a towel to put on the pillow so the oil and oxide won't mess the pillowcase.

The stuff on my hair will become an enormous nuisance. The oxide-oil mix will come off on everything. Clothes, towels, facecloths, sheets, blanket, the carpet, even the bathroom curtains get their share of red oil stain. Ron begins to grit his teeth. "How long did you say you have to keep this stuff on?" he asks.

"Six months," I answer.

"We'll see," he says.

Even I will begin to wonder how long I can deal with it.

28

A Meeting about Children

ॐ

One morning Alina calls. There's to be a meeting in Alexandra, a brainstorming session around the issue of marginalized kids, those kids already running wild and those on the brink. She asks if I would like to go.

When I pick her up she shakes her head and laughs at the sight of me in my oiled dreadlocks. "Look at you," she says. "I can't believe it." But she sounds intrigued and before we drive off she calls out to her neighbor. "I just want her to meet you," she says, "she is a *sangoma*." And when the wizened old woman approaches, we both bow and clap our hands. *"Thokoza,"* we say.

The center is solid brick, large. Its goal is to create young leaders among the children of Alexandra. We tramp up the stairs to a long, tabled room where three of the recent graduates, young men in sports shirts and slacks, lead us to our seats. Alina introduces me with an interesting interplay of emotions: while on the one hand she is firmly grounded in her faith as a born-again Christian and has long turned her back on traditional practice, there is a clear delight that dances in her eyes as she moves me around the room.

There are forty people at the meeting, community leaders, teachers, psychologists; maybe 10 percent are white. The issues are presented by one of the young program graduates. He is self-assured and speaks with authority. A national survey of both black and white youngsters, he says, shows that of the youth in South Africa, 5 percent are considered lost, 27 percent marginalized, 43 percent at risk, and 25 percent O.K. Although it is not spoken, we all understand that these figures reflect the status of black children rather than white.

In Alexandra, someone points out, youths number 48 percent of the population, almost half. Which means, rather frighteningly, that over 35 percent of the population of Alexandra is either lost, marginalized, or at risk.

The talk moves on to the conditions that create the statistics: whole families living in a one-room house; half a dozen, a dozen families camped in a small backyard. The rate of incest is high; girls are pushed into prostitution to earn money. There is a need for sex education. In the old days, in the villages, kids used to be taught sex education and clean habits during the time of circumcision, but the old ways are no longer being followed.

Unemployment among men is at 50 percent, and with unemployment that high and without anything meaningful to do, they have turned to drink and sex. HIV has become an even greater factor.

Boys are packing guns, and both parents and teachers are becoming afraid of them. Parents have abdicated their roles to teachers. There is a lack of communication in the homes; homes are dysfunctional, homes are broken, and the kids have lost trust. There is no sense of community anymore.

On and on the dirge continues. And the story is not unfamiliar, even to an American, perhaps particularly to an American. At this stage the only difference is in the numbers. But then, after each visit to South Africa I realize that what is different between the two countries is only so by manner of degree.

"We are lost as a black people," says one, "we must go back to our roots. We were always so welcoming, we always greeted one another; in Malawi we would put food out in the pathway for travelers. And look at us now, we are killing each other; look at our children, should we be surprised?"

And I am reminded of one of the women who stood in a small group talking the day after Willie was murdered with an ax: "Soon there will be nothing left of us," she said, "nothing but the birds."

29

Whisks, Warps, and Visions

❦

The elections have been set for next April. The excitement is palpable. The talk of the New South Africa doubles; more bumper stickers, more billboards extolling peace. The bloody rampages in the townships and out in the country escalate.

Newspapers are filled with advertisements offering emigration assistance. "If you want to emigrate to the United States we can help . . ." or Australia, or New Zealand. Millions of rands flood out of the country. In the newspaper, the smalls, or personal ads, are filled with headings: WHOLE HOUSEHOLD OF FURNITURE FOR SALE. The ANC go on the radio, on television, trying to reassure the whites. "We need you . . . we need your expertise. . . ."

Harry sits in front of his television set watching the news, watching the ANC. "Come on," he shouts, gesturing at the set, "come on, I'm ready for you."

There is a little skirmish over the government's approval of cellular telephones without consent from the ANC. This has to do with the fact that it is anticipated that once the ANC gets in, telephone service will be hopelessly inept, so the message is "Get those cellulars while you can."

I meet Joyce's older son and his wife. She is svelte and sophisticated. "I guess I'm not supposed to wear my ANC colors when I go and vote," she says. "You're right," I say, "who you support is your business." Particularly in a country where different affiliations are dealt with by murder.

I ask Joyce if she will vote. "No," she answers with great emphasis.

"Why?" I ask. "This is your chance."

"No," she says, "the spirits are my chance."

We have finished all the necklaces and bandoliers and they hang now in Joyce's corner. There are only the two red skirts to be beaded, the long one that goes to my knees and the short pleated overskirt that comes down to my thighs. For these we use small white beads and make intricate loops around the hems.

There is also the whisk to be bought and beaded, and one lunchtime we drive downtown, this time not to Diagonal Street but to Jeppe Street under the overpass, where there are small market stalls selling herbs. I ask Joyce why we come here rather than go to Diagonal Street. "No," she says, "it must be made of buffalo hair, not horse hair, and here I know it's the right thing." We choose a whisk from the six or so hanging from the ceiling in one of the little stalls. It must have been hanging for years, it is tacky with grime.

We drive home past the city hall, sordid now in its begrimed stolidness, the streets surrounding it laced with squalid stalls of sweets, cigarettes, and shoelaces. It had long ago been the scene of those dreaded competitions, where my lack of dancing talent was annually put to public viewing and my mother tried to charm the judges into recognizing some deeply latent gift, which, of course, they never did.

As we pass I am signaled over by a traffic cop. I pull over and he walks around to the driver's side. "Can I see your identification?" he asks, his Afrikaans accent as thick as lard.

I pull out my driver's license. "It's from California," I say apologetically. This seems to confuse him thoroughly and he walks with it over to a second traffic cop, where they huddle over the license and engage in long conversation. Finally he comes back and hands the little card back to me.

"O.K." he says, "you can go. But you should be wearing your safety belt."

Aha, I think, a reprieve at that place of previous torment.

Joyce rolls down her window. "Thank you," she says, reaching out her hand, "thank you and thank God." And I am struck by the degree of her gratitude.

"Woooo," she says when we've pulled away, her little mouth all smiles, "the spirits are with you today. They are looking after you." And for the next five minutes she shakes her head, repeating again and again, "Wooo, you are so lucky, the spirits are with you."

As we drive through Rosebank I ask if she's had lunch. "No," she says.

"Well, how about we go to Mr. Crusty and pick up a couple of meat pies, take them back to the flat and sit on the balcony and eat them?"

Of course we end up not only with meat pies but also with a couple of their wonderful muffins and, as I open my purse, the woman at the cash register asks, "Are you a *sangoma*?"

"Soon," I reply.

The manager waves away my hand extended to pay. "No, no," he says, "it's a present."

Well now, once back in the car Joyce claps her hand to her mouth and rolls her head. "You are so lucky," she says over and over, "the spirits are very happy with you, very happy!"

"Maybe you won't have to bring your big stick to Madadeni," I say, looking at her sideways.

"No," she answers, "I'm bringing the stick so I can hit you if you don't find your goats."

Since Madota told me that she had seen in a dream where her goats and chickens were hidden, I have been waiting for some kind of sign. I ask Joyce for some of the powder to sprinkle on my pillow so that I can remember my dreams, but nothing emerges.

But one midday, when bent over the *imphepho*, I see a small tin shed beside a large green tree, and when I see it day after day, again and again, I know that something will be hidden there.

Strangely, I am not nervous. "Don't worry," I keep telling Joyce.

"No, I'm worried," she answers. "You must find your things, otherwise everyone will laugh. There are lots of people coming to watch you." But I stay unruffled. There has been too much of a guiding hand to this journey for me to doubt the spirits now.

There is a formal greeting we give to the *sangomas* before we begin our work, either dancing or divining, and for the last two weeks I've been working on the Zulu version of the greeting. I walk around with my piece of paper reciting, *"Thokozisa. U baba wami ngingu Melisande . . ."* "Greetings. To my father I am Melisande . . ." There are four short paragraphs that seem, at first, impossible to keep in my head, to hold in my aging brain.

We give Joyce four hundred rand to send home to buy the goats and the chickens. They will be held for us. We begin making lists of the things we'll need, what we'll buy here and what we'll buy in Madadeni.

And there is something strange happening: the nearer the graduating exercise draws, the more I seem absorbed into a larger African community. In the shops, women who are also *sangoma* greet me easily with the formal greeting and then enquire with true solicitousness how my work is going; the women who work as maids in the building ask when they can come and see me so I can "fortune" them. The guards, the gardeners, gently ask how it's going. Even those I pass on the street each day as I walk. "It's the *thwasa*," I hear them say to one another. And to me they say, "*Amakhosi*," and bow their heads, and young black men lift their thumbs to me.

It is as though there is some unseen line that I have crossed, some silent threshold. It is no longer only the tight circle of *sangomas* and *thwasas* who encompass me now; they have all become my community, those who hold and honor the old traditions.

Has the great wheel turned again? Is there yet another healing? Is it my African-ness, that which was lost in the shame and the pain and the guilt of being white? Can I say now how wounding it was? The hate with no resolution, the guilt with no absolution; the acid bath of humiliation.

And in this surround of community am I now being reabsorbed? Absolved? Are new roots reaching down into the earth? Is my African soul being sung alive once again?

•

It is only a few days now to the thirteenth, and we make the final arrangements. Joyce, Alvis, and I will travel down in my car on the Friday. Ron and Dennis will follow on Saturday with Joyce's son and his wife.

The skirts are crisply ironed. Joyce smooths them, lays them on the bed, and rolls her eyes. "Wooo, I'm so nervous," she says, "I can't sleep anymore."

I have been sleeping like a log.

I shampoo the whisk twice, until it smells of freshly washed hair, and then we slide beads onto the coarse strands and knot them in place.

On Thursday Joyce, Alvis, and I drive up to Randburg, to the OK Bazaar to do the shopping. We will need three grocery carts. Thirty pounds of cornmeal, twenty pounds of potatoes, ten large cabbages, twenty pounds of flour, six pounds of butter, dozens of eggs, baking powder, pounds of sugar, twenty rolls of toilet paper, soaps for hands and for dishes, juices, sodas, stewing meat, a few chickens, and whiskey for the men. The back end of the car dips as we load it all into the trunk.

By Thursday evening all my new personal trappings are laid out on the bed: the bandoliers, necklaces, the whisk, bags of the beads that will be sewn onto my wrists when I'm finished, the shells for my hair, my new white bra and T-shirt, the drums.

And when it is time, after I have danced, to give thanks to the spirits, there is a joy so sweet, so breathtaking, that my arms lift high and my eyes fill.

"Are you O.K.?" asks Joyce. I cannot answer. I am so swept into the electricity of the joy that my breath catches in my throat.

And while my arms stretch high to the heavens, through my feet my roots reach deep into the African soil, and around their tendrils closes the earth, like a dark mother, embracing, nourishing.

"Are you all right?" Joyce asks again.

My breathing returns, my arms lower, but between my feet and the earth the current still hums. It is a while before I can answer. "Yes, I am very O.K."

30

A New *Sangoma*

❦

On Friday morning the sky is gray, the clouds high, not yet threatening. The car is so loaded that Alvis hangs back. No, I say to her, if you don't come, we won't leave. She has, after all, become part of the family, been a part of our nervousness and the games about Joyce hitting me with the big stick. So she crowds in with the food, the drums, the red, white, and black carpet Ron and I have given Joyce as a graduation gift.

We take the M 1, looping around the city, and then the N 1 out of Johannesburg toward Durban. Joyce and Alvis are quiet, Joyce turned in with nervousness. I wonder how it must be for her, going home, bringing with her a white *thwasa* who may make her look foolish in front of her family and her friends.

As we make the long sweep west off the N1 toward Volksrust, the rain begins, slow at first, then building, closing in, tighter and tighter, until the fields, the trees, the road are all drowned in a lake of gray drumming. We slow to a crawl.

It had rained so on the day I began this training; it was, I felt, the spirits blessing. How fitting that they should offer this benediction now as I finish. The tires plane and I grip the wheel. Aside from the intensity of driving through this pounding shroud, I am quite calm. Did I think I would end feeling such calm? Did I think I would end? Perhaps not from the remove of San Diego, but once back, once in Africa again, this passage seemed as inexorable as the unfolding of day to night. It is, after all, my life's unfolding; it is the dance with the Other, the gift of the Other.

A particular gift, for is not all of it really a gift? This miraculous universe; this enchanted planet, spinning blues and golds, shimmering greens, mystical browns. Its song drifting through undulating seas, round hillsides, through trees, carried on throats, leaves, rocks. We have only to slow to hear it, to slow and listen. And when we feel its rhythm and let loose our will, then indeed the dance may begin.

The rain drums on. By Volksrust it has slowed to a mist, and we stop to use a gas station toilet. A white farmer with a truck bed filled high with sheep pelts stops us.

"Are you *sangoma*?" he asks in Zulu.

"*Yebo*," Joyce answers.

His sheep, he explains in flawless Zulu, are being stolen. His farm is not far from here. Could we please come and make the farm safe? Joyce explains that we are on our way to Madadeni, perhaps when she next comes this way, and they exchange phone numbers.

Once through the flat dullness of Volksrust, we cross into Natal. One can sense that crossing, from the Transvaal into Natal. The countryside begins to undulate, flatlands giving way to green rolling hills; the feminine face of Africa. Here and there guinea fowl suddenly materialize, emerging out of the mist, and dash in dotted clusters across the road.

At Newcastle we leave the main road, but we don't head into the town, the white area, instead we head toward Madadeni, the township where Joyce's mother lived, where her house is.

This is part of KwaZulu, the sometime killing fields of South Africa. Now it is quiet as we make our way past a few squat official buildings, the new Tecknikon, or trade school, and onto the dirt roads lined with small brick or tin homes.

Her house, small, brick, a front door at its center framed by two windows, sits on one of those roads, rutted earth lined with debris. Again I wonder why nobody cares enough to clean it up, but I don't say anything for fear of offending Joyce. We pull into the driveway alongside the house.

We enter a dining room furnished with a formal dark wood table and six chairs, the seats still wrapped in plastic. Leading from the dining room are two bedrooms, one stripped of furniture except for a large wardrobe, and the kitchen dominated by the same sort of large, hardworking, iron range I've seen several times now in these small homes.

We troop, without words, through the dining room into the empty bedroom. In one corner hang the wraps, whisks, and beads of the *sangoma*. In all African homes where a member of the family is a traditional healer, we find such a corner. It is the sacred corner, where the *imphepho* is lit and in front of which offerings to the spirits are placed.

As soon as we put down our things, reed mats are laid on the floor, the drums pulled out, Joyce sings and I begin to dance. This is custom, this practice of drumming and dancing as soon as the house is entered, and is done to bring alive the spirits. The doorway is soon stacked with curious brown faces of all ages. I dance three, four, five dances, until my legs are shaking and I finally collapse on the reed mat. Only then do we acknowledge the others.

There are nine people who live in this house. Joyce's daughter, her eighteen-month-old twins and older son, Joyce's niece and her three children, and the neighbor's daughter. Later in the afternoon the first of the *sangomas* from out of town begin to arrive, and the house continues to fill until late that night. Many of the faces are unfamiliar; some join us on the reed mats in the empty bedroom, some simply put their heads around the door to look at me.

In the early evening several men arrive, young men, older men, and Joyce tells me they want to meet me. One of the older men takes my hand between his and speaks with great emotion. Unfortunately his mix of Zulu and broken English is difficult to understand, and when his eyes fill with tears I can only hold his hands gently and then put my arm around his shoulders. Later he presses some money into my hand. I shake my head and try to give it back, but Joyce intervenes. "No, you must keep it," she says, "it's for luck."

While the men sit around the dining-room table, the women are busy in the kitchen, beginning the rounds of cooking that will continue for three days. The littlest children run, laughing and diaperless, from brown arms to brown arms, occasionally piddling like puppies, a fact that only I seem to notice. With me they are shy, approaching cautiously, coming only so close, then off they run, giggling with the deliciousness of their daring, their round buttock cheeks dancing.

With each new arrival the ritual of drumming and dancing begins once again, the new arrivals dancing first and then the others joining in. Miriam and Emily are the last to arrive, close to midnight, and I am delighted that some more familiar faces are appearing.

It isn't until the early hours of the morning that mountains of blankets are pulled out of the large wardrobe and laid over the reed mats (which I eye carefully for piddle spots), and we roll up, ten, maybe twelve of us, tight against one another. In the dining room, the children lie, as tightly rolled as we are, under the large wooden dining-room table.

A word about blankets. When a new *sangoma* completes her training, she buys, for each of the other *sangomas* in her group, a Bantu blanket that is thick, warm, and colorful. So with each graduation, the stack of blankets a *sangoma* possesses grows. It is not unusual to see, as in Joyce's wardrobe, blankets from top to bottom, side to side.

As we lie, we still talk softly among ourselves for another hour. Constance, rolled up next to me, had been the first *sangoma* to arrive earlier that afternoon. She had appeared, a sudden chic apparition in a deep-rose suit, lacy white blouse, pert beret, and high heels, so elegant that she seemed to have landed in the wrong story. But when later she slowly stripped first her skirt, and then her blouse, shoes, hat, and petticoat, and wrapped herself in the beaded skirt, shawl, and beaded bandoliers of the *sangoma*, in a slow morph she had dissolved one culture into another, one time period into another. And when she danced, oh when she danced, her head high, chest forward, switch flying, she was Africa regal, Africa bold, Africa unvanquished.

Now she talked about being a black servant, the undervaluing she felt as a human being. I had had this discussion before, with Sylvia. "They think we are dogs," she had said, "just to order around. If they want to go away, they just tell me to be there to take care of the animals. They don't care if there is something I want to do."

"But why," I had asked, "don't you tell them if you have other plans? You needn't get angry, you can negotiate something that might work for both of you."

"No," she answered, "there are too many people looking for work."

And now I am lying next to Constance hearing much the same complaint and once again I try to explain the relationship between employee and employer as I have experienced it, as it should be, and get much the same response as I did from Sylvia. And I reach my arm out from under its blanketed wrapping and touch her— this elegant, articulate woman made less by history and her unquestioning acceptance of it.

Some of the *sangomas* are still chatting quietly as I roll over onto my side and try to sleep. In the kitchen I hear the women's voices, comforting sounds, as they cook through the night. My mind drifts to finding the goats and the chickens.

Even now, as I hover between sleep and waking, even now with it so close, some deep trust keeps me calm. "Don't worry," I had kept saying to Joyce in the car.

"No, I'm worried," she would reply. And she was; she didn't even bother to joke about the big stick anymore.

Saturday dawned warm and sunny, and after tea and scones, baked during the night in the big iron range, I told Joyce I was going out for a walk. This prompted much discussion in Zulu among the *sangomas* and it was proposed that Constance accompany me.

I wanted to head left, but she steered me right, saying that she wanted to see the newly built Tecknikon. And, of course, I suspected that there was something to the left she did not want me to see, or hear. But the Tecknikon was indeed a building worth taking a look at, large, and among these little houses, imposing.

We walked on farther to the brick home in which Joyce's cousin lives. This is where Ron and Dennis will spend the night, since it has a proper bathroom with bath and indoor toilet. She was a schoolteacher; her husband, who died a year ago, owned a chain of taxis. The house is elegantly furnished by any standards, with rich, deep sofas, wall-to-wall carpeting, and a modern kitchen. We are given tea and cookies and talk, as ever, about South Africa. "I don't know," she says, "I don't know what's going to happen. We seem to have gone mad."

It is surprising to walk into such a home after dodging the potholes and debris on the dirt roads. I remember once asking Alina why she didn't move out of Alexandra, which, more often than not, had become a Little Beirut. Well, she answered, she wouldn't mind moving, but her husband had put so much into the house, and besides, he was old now, too old to want to change.

After the tea, we walk slowly in the warm sun, along the red-dirt roads, until we hear the sounds of women ululating and turn back to find that the last of the *sangomas* and their students have arrived from Johannesburg.

Once again the round of dancing and drumming begins, starting with the new arrivals. And when it came time for me to dance, I remembered Constance, back erect, head high, switch flying, engaged in not just a dance, but a glorious African anthem, and my feet found her song, my head her grandeur and I danced as I had never danced, feeling myself joyously letting go of some last anchoring control, my spirit voice joining the whisk flying in high arcs, while the room filled with shouts and cheers and Joyce ran from *sangoma* to *sangoma* taking their hands, accepting their salutes.

In the early afternoon, Ron and Dennis arrive. Immediately the drums are moved outside and we all, in a semicircle, our red skirts flying, dance a greeting to them. Then they are led inside, seated at the dining-room table and fed while the children stare goggle-eyed and the *sangomas* and the *thwasas* settle back down in the reed-matted room.

I will see little of Ron during the next twenty-four hours. Occasionally he will put his head around the door and ask, "Are you all right?" or just look in without saying anything.

I know from previous ceremonies that this one will begin at four, the time the spirits arise, and so at three o'clock I ask for an hour alone in the room. I light the *imphepho* and sit over it a while, inhaling its sweet green fragrance, allowing it, as it always does, to transport me to another realm.

Then I stretch out on a reed mat and begin deep yogic breathing, watching my breath as it rises slowly from my belly, through my diaphragm, into my chest, and then back down again. Slow, slow, bringing my mind to stillness. And somewhere in that stillness comes the vision of a goat's head and the number four. I hold the picture no longer than it wishes to stay, then go back again to my breath, following it as it moves up through my body and back down.

Then again the picture of a small shed, light in color with a tin roof, beside a green leafy tree, and the number one seems to hover with the image. And I know again that it is a place where something has been hidden. And it is with those two pictures in my mind that I slowly stretch and bring myself back to the room where I lie.

Joyce comes in. "Are you finished?"

"Yes, I'm finished."

"We must start."

It is four o'clock.

Joyce and Miriam are in the room. They have both changed into their ceremonial garb.

"Stand up," says Joyce, and she takes a porcupine quill out of its horned container. She pricks me—light, quick pricks, starting with my head, down my arms, body, legs, my feet. The pricks are light enough that I feel them as pinpricks.

Then she opens the pack of fresh razor blades I had insisted we buy, and makes small cuts: on my head, forehead, neck, chest, down each arm and each leg. She squeezes each cut, making sure blood appears, then quickly rubs *muti* into the cuts. I stand holding up my skirt with my eyes tightly closed, expecting the cuts to hurt, to burn when the *muti* is rubbed in, but Joyce has been gentle and I feel nothing.

Now I am left alone in the room again and I sit on my haunches, hands cupped in front of me, head low to the ground, the way we sit while we are *thwasas*. Ron peeks around the corner.

"Are you all right?" he asks.

"I'm fine," I answer.

"What's happening?"

"I don't know. I've just been cut."

I wait, hanging in the unknowing.

Hanging in the unknowing. So much time I had spent in a cloud of unknowing while my peers moved their lives purposefully onward. And I, seeking my touchstone.

And so here I am now, made safe from evil interference with the prick of the porcupine quill, made safe by the quick slits in my skin, dancing the dance of the silent partner. The sacred dance. Guided by a hand unseen and yet made manifest in the falling of a feather, the streaking of a star, the shell that rolled three times to stop before me. "This means you must study to be a *sangoma*": the old gnarled woman with one eye milky in blindness.

I sit hunched on the reed mat and wait.

Miriam comes in and I look up. "You must come out now," she says. I begin to stand, but she stops me. "On your knees," she says.

I get down on all fours and follow her, through the kitchen where the floor is a rough cement, down the steps into the back-yard. The red-dirt surface is filled with small stones that dig and jar. A reed mat is laid out not far from the kitchen steps, and here she tells me to sit and stretch my legs in front of me. Joyce is wait-ing next to the mat, and in a circle around the small yard a small crowd of men, women, and children.

Joyce is holding a small pot and she tells me to close my eyes. Beginning with my face, she works an oily reddish-brown mixture into my skin, moving down my body, my arms and hands, down my legs to my toes. When she is finished I crawl back into the room, hunker down on my haunches, and wait.

This time the wait is shorter. Connie comes to get me. "You must come out."

"On my knees?"

"Yes, on your knees."

Again I crawl through the kitchen, down the steps and out into the yard. Joyce is waiting, holding a piece of bamboo about a foot long. A small fire has been lit, and on it sits a large piece of clay shard. Joyce signals me over. When I am kneeling in front of it, she hands me the bamboo. On the shard something is smoldering.

"You must take this," says Joyce, handing me the bamboo, "and suck in all of this." She points to the red, smoldering embers. I take the bamboo and suck hesitantly, afraid that whatever it is will burn my mouth. "Suck," Joyce repeats, and suddenly I feel charred bits fill my mouth, and stop. "All of it," says Joyce, and I inhale again. More charred pieces fill my mouth, but they don't burn and so I suck until the shard is emptied of its contents. Connie gestures "Go back now," and I crawl back into the room.

Before I have time to think, to register how I feel, the *thwasas* run in and they tie the ankle clappers around each leg. "Come," they shout, and all four of us run out.

The reed mats have been set up along the width of the yard opposite the house and the *sangomas*, drums between their legs, are sitting on them. Around each side, thirty, forty people crowd. "Run," Jeanett shouts, and I run with them and kneel in front of the mats. Together we greet our teachers, each *thwasa* saying her particular greeting, then in turn, we greet the additional *sangomas*. Quickly then we are up on our feet and we dance until we are panting and sweating and then back into the house, running through the kitchen and into the bedroom where we collapse onto the floor.

For the rest of the day now, the *thwasas* will stay inside the house, in the other bedroom, so that they do not see any of what will follow. It is not allowed for them to know what happens next. That is why it had been such a break with tradition when Joyce had told me about drinking the blood from the goat, about eating its poop.

Now once again I am called and once again crawl out on my knees. Again I chant the greeting: *"Thokozisa, U baba wami ngigingu Melisande . . . ,"* first to Joyce then to the other *sangomas*. Then still on my knees I begin. *"Shaya ngikutshele, shaya ngikutshele"*: Clap your hands and I will tell you . . .

"What is it?" Joyce asks.

"It is the goats," I answer.

"Yezwake!"

"How many?" Joyce asks.

"Two goats."

"*Yezwake!*"

"Where are they?"

"*Shaya ngikutshele, shaya ngikutshele.*" They are not far.

"*Yezwake!*"

"They are this way." I point to the left, the direction Constance had not wanted to go.

"*Yezwake!*"

"They are four houses this way."

"*Yez,*" they answer, voices low, denoting a wrong answer.

I am so surprised that for a moment I stop dead.

"How many houses counting this one?" asks Joyce, filling the sudden silence.

"Five counting this one."

"*Yezwake! Yezwake!*"

But I hardly hear them as I streak, far faster than my legs have ever carried me, across the red earth pockmarked with stones. I feel nothing, experience nothing other than the air, the wind created by my running. I fly down the dirt road as though through air, up the fifth driveway and there they are, white and brown, tied to a tree.

I have outstripped everyone, but now they are here also, helping me untie the ropes and pull and push the goats back toward Joyce's house. The goat I pull strains backward, but my push is forward, hard forward. Then the men take the goats from us and once again I dance.

"*Shaya ngikutshele, shaya ngikutshele,*" I chant again as I drop to my knees.

"What is it?" asks Joyce.

"It's the chickens."

"*Yezwake.*"

"How many chickens?"

"Two chickens."

"*Yezwake!*"

"They are near."

"*Yezwake!*"

"They are in a shed."

"*Yezwake!*"

"*Shaya ngikutshele, shaya ngikutshele.*" They are this way. I point to the right.

"*Yezwake!*"

"How many houses?" asks Joyce.

"One house."

"*Yezwake!!!*" And again I'm off, feet pounding; one house down, up the driveway, and there sits the shed with the tin roof and next to it a tree just as I'd seen. I run into the shed. If the chickens are startled I don't notice. I scoop one up under each arm and race back.

Once again I dance, then give thanks to my spirits, sit and stretch my arms and legs, reach down to my toes, sending the spirits back, and run back inside. I hunch on my haunches, breathing hard, my heart pounding. The wait is not long.

Again the crawl through the kitchen, down the steps and out into the yard. Joyce is walking ahead of me, leading me forward. She is holding a spear. It has a long haft and a tulip-shaped head.

One of the goats has been tied upright to a tree. It is standing on its hind legs, chest forward. From my position on all fours, I see only its hind legs and chest, and the legs of the men holding its forelegs high.

Joyce lifts the spear, places the tip under the goat's right armpit, and pushes it in. The wound is clean, no blood emerges.

"Drink," says Joyce.

I put my mouth to the wound and suck. Nothing happens. "Nothing's coming out," I say.

Joyce places the tip of the spear back into the wound and pushes. Once again I put my mouth to the wound and suck. This time blood runs into my mouth. I swallow quickly. It has little taste.

"More," Joyce says.

Again my mouth goes to the wound, again I suck, and as I suck there is a moment of strange awakening. I am suddenly aware. Aware of her warmth under my lips, of her fur—sandy-colored, soft, not coarse, of the ropes holding her. And then the moment is gone.

Later, when they brought her into the room, stripped of her coat, her head thrown back in this death she had strained against, I knelt and blew softly into her mouth and asked her forgiveness. But her dead eye stared wildly at me, evoking only horror.

I suck and swallow until Joyce says, "That's enough." I begin to stand but Joyce says, "Stay on your knees and come this way." Her voice is sharp, abrupt.

I follow her, crawling, across the yard, around the house. There a hole has been dug in the ground, maybe two feet deep. Beside the hole stands a basin of water with herbs floating in it.

"Drink," says Joyce. I lift my hands off the ground.

"No!" says Joyce, "just your mouth."

I put my face in the basin and take a few mouthfuls.

"More," says Joyce.

Again and again I dip my face into the basin and drink, until the gorge rises in my throat and I begin to gag.

"More," says Joyce, but I drink only two more mouthfuls before I begin to vomit.

Later when I look at the pictures, I see the other *sangomas*, the drums they must have been beating, the wrap they passed under my stomach and which they must have pulled up on to help me vomit. But now I see and hear nothing of that. There is only the basin, the drinking and the vomiting.

I vomit until my head swims and the liquid runs clear, then back on my hands and knees, back through the yard, the kitchen, and into the empty bedroom.

My nose runs, I search for tissues and collapse back into my crouch. The blood thuds in my temples, my breath comes in gasps. My eyes are closed against sight, sound, against thought.

I don't know how long it is before Miriam comes to get me. My knees are now scraped raw and when I reach the kitchen I slow.

"Come on, come on," shouts Miriam as I lower myself cautiously down the steps and into the yard.

On the ground is a basket covered in plastic. In the center is what looks like a cupful of bile-green blancmange. A rope is attached to the basket and Joyce is holding the other end.

"You must eat," she says. I move my hands forward to hold the basket, to scoop up the mixture. "No," she says, "not with your hands."

I lean forward and dip my face into the greenness. As I do so Joyce pulls on the rope and the basket leaps forward. I follow slowly on my raw knees and again dip my face. Again the basket is pulled away. Instinctively I try to grab it with my hands. "No hands," Joyce shouts.

Again I hobble slowly after. Again she pulls. Finally I catch up with the basket and take a mouthful. Immediately the taste hits; I retch. "Swallow it," says Joyce firmly.

I battle to hold on, to keep it in my mouth, then squeeze it down my throat. "Again," says Joyce, walking backward, pulling the basket after her. My eyes are watering, my nose running, my throat contracting in gags.

I crawl slowly after the basket, each small stone cutting into my knees. "Eat it," shouts Joyce, and pushing myself, pushing myself, I reach the basket and take a mouthful. I squeeze my eyes shut and fight to get it down.

In three mouthfuls, mouthfuls that seem the longest ever held, the hardest ever swallowed, it is done. I hobble on my knees to the hole, drink the herbed liquid, and vomit that dreadful bile out until what comes up is clear. Then back into the house. I am trembling, exhausted, my innards bruised.

That night I sat alone, with only the peltless goat, while, in the dining room, now cleared of furniture, the *sangomas* and *thwasas* danced and fortuned.

For a long time I sit on the reed mat, legs stretched out, leaning back against the wall, too tired to move. After a while I am given a little pap, and eat it slowly with my fingers.

My eye is drawn, again and again, to the goat, to her wildly staring eye. Each glance is a quick one, as I will the eye to glaze, to lose its link to life.

From the dining room the sounds of drumming and singing. I can hear the other *thwasas* as they begin their divining exercises: *"Shaya ngikutshele, shaya ngikutshele,"* and then the *sangomas* answering *"Yezwake"* or *"Yez."* But it is all background sound. I am too numb to hear, too tired to listen.

For an hour, two hours, I sit, back against the wall, my legs stretched out in front of me. Then slowly, as I sit so, I notice my brownness. First my brown thighs, the skin glowing in the candlelight, the hairs smoothed silky gold. Then, stretching away into the shadow, my slim calves, the darker shadow beneath the anklebone, my strange long feet. I trace my fingers across my skin; the color awakens me, arouses me.

I stroke my arms, turn my palms up and back over again, spread my fingers. The color seems to sit not on my skin but in my skin, not as a phenomenon apart but as part of my being.

Again and again I stroke my thighs, my arms, my slim calves, all unburdened of their whiteness. How strange, this sense of unburdening.

"I want to stay this color," I say to Joyce when she comes in to see how I am.

"Why?" she asks. I can't put words to it and she laughs. I laugh with her.

As a baby will find its foot or a finger and be wrapped in the discovery, so that night I sat wrapped in the wonder of my brownness, in the arousal of it, in the unburdening I felt.

From this distance now, the distance of writing this tale, I am still not sure what it was that occurred there in Madadeni that night when I was loosed from whiteness.

So much has been said, so much written of the anguish of black South Africans. Yet we were all, white as well as black, cast members in the apartheid play. Where could we turn, those of us white-skinned shamed, who were too cowardly to throw ourselves among the brave, the unsung who offered themselves to the cause. Too shredded by guilt to stay, we fled.

And even at a distance we kept our eyes and ears stopped, like a child who covers her ears and sings to drown out sound. And when people asked where we were from, we hung our heads and mumbled. For distance never lessened the shame. And always lurked the traitor's shadow. For Africa is not a host; Africa is possessor. Her talons lie tight in our souls.

So as I sat that night on the reed mat, deep in the circle of an ancient African act, was the color yet another manifestation of acceptance? Was this the moment when in my brownness I felt finally forgiven? It felt so; in the quickening flickers of delight, in the lightness that filled each cell, it seemed so.

In the early morning hours, while the night is still dark and the *sangomas* still dance, Joyce and Miriam come into the room. They unroll a couple of reed mats and sit on them, pulling the drums between their legs. They tell me to cross my legs and turn my palms up.

They begin to drum. "You must shake your hands," Miriam says, and I move them in quick short shakes. "You must make your spirit sound." And the growling sound comes from deep inside.

They drum for ten, maybe fifteen minutes while I shake and growl, and then stop. "Stretch your legs," they say, and I stretch for a minute or so, and then they begin once again.

After ten such drummings, it is not my hands that shake but my whole body, beginning with my shoulders and moving down to my legs. After each ten or fifteen minutes there is a one-minute break while I stretch and then again the drumming starts, the deep spirit sounds, my body shakes. And so we go, on and on, until finally, body convulsing, I howl out the sound and the sky grows light.

⚭

In the morning, when the goat's eye has become milky, the *sangomas* circle around and wash me clean of my brownness. None of us have slept through this night; the *sangomas* and *thwasas* have danced and fortuned till morning and we all look bleary-eyed.

But now, as I am washed and dried they gather around as though readying a bride. Joyce unfolds the white-beaded, two-layered skirt of the *sangoma*, the one we had stitched and beaded for so many weeks, and slowly brings it around my waist. Over it, like a sash, she ties the new black, red, and white wrap. Around my wrists, slim circles of still-wet goat pelt.

I had asked Joyce, while we were still preparing, what I should wear on top. She had said that people either wear nothing or a bra. I'd said that I would wear nothing. But now she shakes her head. "Put on your bra," she says. Perhaps she is worried that the sight of white breasts may not be as familiar as brown ones.

Finally she hands me the beaded buffalo-hair whisk. The *thwasas* crowd around. "You look so pretty!" they say, and stroke my skirts. Ron's head appears around the door, looking anxiously to see if I'm all right. He and Dennis are back from their two hours of sleep at the house of the cousin.

While I am being readied, I hear the reed mats and drums being moved outside again. Soon *sangomas* will be lined up, sitting, legs stretched forward on the mats, drums held between their feet. Now there is only the goat's gallbladder to be found and the bandoliers.

Through the small window I see the village people gathering, the *sangomas* settling; Joyce goes out to join them. For the last time the *thwasas* tie the clappers around my ankles and we run out. Again we kneel and give the greeting to our "fathers"—our main teachers—then to all the *sangomas*, and we dance.

Then I am alone.

"*Shaya ngikutshele, shaya ngikutshele,*" I chant.

And they answer, "*Yezwake, yezwake.*"

"What is it?" asks Joyce.

"It is the gallbladder," I answer.

"Yezwake," they chorus.

"Where is it?"

"Up in a tree."

"Yezwake! Yezwake!"

"Where is the tree?"

"It is in front."

"Yezwake!"

"Which side in front?"

"The right side."

"Yezwake!" The chorus is loud and joyous, and off I dash, down the little alley by the side of the house where yesterday I had vomited.

There indeed is a tree, and there it hangs, like a dun-colored semi-filled balloon. The *thwasas* help me get it down and I run back. After I have danced, I kneel and Sylvia ties it to a loop of hair on the back of my head at the crown.

Now there is only one more.

"Shaya ngikutshele, shaya ngikutshele." This is for the bandoliers and necklaces. I sense that they are high up but have no clear picture. It is as though they are hidden beneath something.

"What is it?"

"The necklaces."

"Yezwake!"

"Where are they."

"They are high."

"Yezwake!"

"To this side." I gesture left.

"Yez."

"This way." I gesture right.

"Yezwake."

And then I notice the shed. "They are there by the shed."

"*Yezwake! Yezwake!* Where?"

"High up."

"Yezwake."

My mind falters, no picture other than one of height.

"Where?" Joyce asks again.

"On top," I blurt out without quite understanding.

"*YEZWAKE!*" they shout. "Go fetch them."

And as I run over, I see on top of the shed my old wrap, stained red brown from yesterday's oiling, and as I pull it down I feel the beaded bandoliers inside.

Again it is Sylvia who loops them over my head and arranges them so that the little pouches with *muti* sit at my waist. Finally I am draped with the goat's pelt. It is warm and wet and sits like a small bolero. The drums begin to sound for my final dance, and the voices rise.

There is so much I feel: joy, triumph, gratitude, elation, I want to pour it all into the dance, and for a few moments I do, snapping my whisk high, but I am so tired that soon there is nothing left. My unflagging spirit cannot move my flagging legs and finally I collapse. On the reed mat I lean my forehead against Joyce's and for a quiet moment we savor what we have done.

Much later, when looking at the photographs, I notice that Joyce had wept when I had been quick to find the things that had been hidden. That picture stays with me: the white handkerchief against her dark skin, up against her eyes. It moves me, so my eyes also tear. I reach down for the reason I am moved. The word "love" comes into my mind. She wept because I had done well; because she had been afraid I might not; because she loved me—loves me.

And I think about life spirals—circling, coming back, almost to the point of beginning, and yet not, for while the whorls of the spiral seem to cross and connect, they are layered.

And so we have spiraled, the silent partner and I, to arrive again where I started. I have come not to the same beginning, yet to a beginning of the same lesson, that old lesson of love that I did not, could not learn during that other, earlier passage when I was young. She loves me, and she weeps with joy, with relief, with love.

Strangely, or perhaps given this journey not so strangely, a few days earlier I'd been browsing in the bookstore across the road from the flat and my eye had fallen on a slim volume of T. S. Eliot's poetry. I eased it out and cracked it open. The page was from "Little Gidding." And these were the words:

> *We shall not cease from exploration*
> *And the end of all our exploring*
> *Will be to arrive where we started*
> *And know the place for the first time.*

Now, here, in this small backyard, in this land where I began, I sit among these women with whom I have journeyed to that knowledge. Knowledge not only of the place as in this land, but also of place as in where I began, where my story is rooted.

One by one the teachers dance: Joyce, Sylvia, Miriam, Cynthia, but they too are tired and it is not long before the drumming stops, the reed mats are rolled up, and the people slowly disperse.

31

Interlude

❧

After the goats and the chickens have been eaten, after we have held high our plates and given thanks to the spirits, Joyce and Sylvia thread around my wrists the red and white beads of the *sangoma*: on my left wrist, seven bands, on my right, four, and in the center, a knuckle of the goat from which I drank the blood.

When those are done, they tie the four cowrie shells in my hair, centered in their brass rings: one in front, just above my forehead; one at the back, just below the goat's gallbladder; and two on either side, just above my ears.

They are so tired that as they work they occasionally nod off and I nudge them awake. It has been a trying time for these women. It is always so when one of their students graduates, but harder still now; with a white woman, it seemed, more was on the line.

Dorkus, Joyce's daughter, had said earlier, "We have never seen this before—a white person doing this; it is very important for us." No wonder Joyce had been so nervous.

Much later, at a gathering in Los Angeles, when I described this graduating ceremony, someone suggested laughingly that I'd been had, that it was the revenge of black Africans on a gullible white; but while I chuckled with him at the thought, I knew it wasn't so. I sensed that it had to do with endurance, descent and rebirth.

I am somehow reminded of when my son was born. There was a point during the birth, when the pain coiled around and within me so tightly that nothing else existed; when all that was ego, all that was self-aware was gone, and what was left was animal, stripped bare and basic.

And so also had I been reduced during this event. Here, too, I had been stripped of all that was trapping, all that was rational and self-aware, reducing and descending to only the essential elements of the ritual. And then the hours alone, no contact, no moorings, until finally the last of any still-clinging selfhood is torn away in three early-morning hours of pounding drumbeat and orchestrated hysteria.

Ah, but then comes the renewal, then the resurrection begins. By handmaidens the body is gently washed; by soft brown hands it is wrapped and adorned, and, as a bride, the initiate emerges to join the other, elder brides of the ancient lineage. As a snake in shedding her skin embodies the cycle of death and rebirth, so was I symbolically stripped, not only of ego and the darkened skin of the previous day and night, but also of all that had gone before, all that I had been before, and was reborn anew, now as a *sangoma*.

Usually a new sangoma gives thanks to the spirits by killing the cow soon after her graduating ceremony, but Ron needed to get back to the States, so with Joyce's blessings we decided to wait on the cow until we returned the next time to South Africa. I was relieved. Even now, even after all that I had done, I still couldn't comprehend doing that last act of killing.

So it was not long after the ceremony in Madadeni that we boarded the plane, I with the merciful reprieve like a soft mantle around me, and a small dark towel in hand to prevent the oil and oxide mix from messing up the airplane seats.

In the airport, as had been the case almost everywhere we went in the days since the final exercise, my presence creates a stir. I hear the whisperings as we walk through the concourse, the *ss* sibilance of the word "*sangoma*."

In the restaurant we had dined at the night before we left, the manager had come to our table to say that there had been chaos in the kitchen as the waiters spread the news of a white *sangoma*. "Would you please just come and let them all meet you?" Some were shy, some bold, but all had eyes as wide as saucers.

Now, in the international departure area, behind the recessed counters of the duty-free stores, salesladies' heads come chattering together as they notice my hair, my beads. Clusters of them wander over.

"Are you a *sangoma*?" they ask shyly.

"Yes," I say and nod.

"Oh, we have never seen a white *sangoma*," they say.

One wants to know whether she should marry the man she is currently seeing; another what lies in her future.

"I'd love to spend some time with you," I say, "but this is not really a good place to do it. I will be in the country again soon," and I give them my phone number.

"Oh, please," implores one with long brown hair and dark eyes, "what do you see for me?"

I look into her eyes, soft as velvet. "I can tell you what I see in you."

"Please."

"I see beauty."

Her smile lights candles in her eyes.

Back at home the dreadlocks do not effect the same responses as they had in South Africa, although I receive quite a few thumbs-up signs from African Americans. However, the goat's gallbladder dangling from the back of my head is beginning to take on the aspects of a used condom and this definitely provokes interest.

"Excuse me, what is that on the back of your head?" This question usually occurs in supermarket lines and usually comes from men.

"It's a goat's gallbladder," I reply.

There is a moment of stunned silence, then, "Pardon me?"

"It's a goat's gallbladder."

"Oh," the questioner would respond and that would be it. I wondered why they never asked why; maybe, I decided, they would rather not know.

As time goes by the oil and oxide mix in my hair dries out and less and less comes off on everything my head touches. My scalp, however, prickles and itches and I take to carrying around a porcupine quill with which to scratch it.

One evening as I sit on the floor at Ron's feet he leans forward to hug me and stops, suddenly lifting his nose. "What's that smell?" he asks. It is my long-unwashed hair.

As in times of yore when perfume was used to disguise unwashed bodies, I have taken to spraying my head with "fragrance of the fields" or whatever else carries intimations of freshness. Either it works, or people become polite. The goat's gallbladder turns a dull brown, begins to dry, crack, and loose bits of itself. Men in check-out lines still ask what it is and still don't ask the obvious follow-up why.

Children and babies become absorbed in the beads around my wrists, fingering them again and again. Dogs become absorbed in the goat's knuckle centered between the beads, forgoing my crotch and returning their noses to it again and again in seeming perplexity.

A question I'm frequently asked in America is why I was allowed to become a part of what is, after all, an ancient African tradition; why a white person was allowed entry. I can only answer that the circle of *sangomas* with whom I worked seemed to find it an honor that I was interested in their tradition. And it was not only the women with whom I worked. As time went by, those Africans that I came across again and again, in the shopping center across the road, in the supermarket or in the streets where I walked, greeted me warmly. And more important, they greeted me the way they would greet a black *thwasa* or *sangoma*.

I remember, early in the training, browsing in the rather elegant design store across the road from our flat. After a while, the black saleswoman who was watching me came over. She looked at me suspiciously.

"Are you a *sangoma*?"

"No, I'm a *thwasa*."

"Who is teaching you?"

"Her name is Joyce. She lives in Bordeaux, where she works."

"Is she a black woman?"

"Yes."

She still looks at me suspiciously. "What are you doing with her?"

"Well, I'm learning to dance and divine. I have to eat the foam from the *isitundu* and light *imphepho* three times a day, and I steam and *phalaza*."

"What kind of dancing are you learning?"

"*Umdawu* dancing." And I put my bag down on the floor, and in the aisle between the glassware and candles, begin the steps of *umdawu* dancing while I sing the words that Joyce and Sylvia sing.

She watches me for a while, then says, "Yes, she is teaching you right," and from then on whenever I am in the store she greets me with two hand claps and bends her head. *"Thokoza,"* she says.

There were many such encounters, each one becoming a small gem in the net of community.

⚭

While I try to keep the thought of killing the cow out of my head, it prods like an insistent thing at the circle of my mind. In my meditations, again and again I see the cow Madota killed, blood drooling from her mouth, hear again her dreadful bellowing. And my mind recoils in horror.

Ron, as though sensing what is happening, reaches out every now and then as though to soothe the horror away.

"I don't know that I can do it," I say.

"There is plenty of time," he answers, "there is so much you thought you wouldn't be able to do."

"Yes but—"

"Uh-uh," he says, stroking my arm, "you'll see when the time comes."

Although neither Ron nor I can vote, we had been planning to return to South Africa in time for the April elections. In the meantime, the carnage in that country continues unabated and most people think we are crazy. "Aren't you afraid?" or "Will you be safe?" are frequently asked questions.

I think of Miriam's ramrod-straight back, the way she held her head high as she said to me once, "I am a *sangoma*, nothing can hurt me." I may not have her faith, but it is true, as Ron reminds people, that in all the time we have spent there we have never been in a threatening situation, we have never even seen a threatening situation. In South Africa, however, many whites are preparing for the elections by making plans to be away.

But as the time of our departure approaches, I am filled with a dread that even the thought of the elections cannot still.

32

A Country Reborn

❧

We leave America early in April. The plane from New York is filled with reporters and UN observers as exuberant as New Year's Eve revelers. As soon as the plane is in the air they are up off their seats, crowding the aisles, drinks in hand, caroling to one another, "Hello, there, didn't I see you last at Tiananmen Square?" As though that, too, had been a party.

Some ask if we, too, are with the press. When we answer no, but that we have been returning regularly to South Africa for several years and begin to talk a little of the country and its issues, their eyes quickly flick away. "Hey, man, look who's here . . ." and away they squeeze.

Joyce has a new student now, Emily. She is short and plump, and when she dances begins to wheeze almost immediately with the effort even though her feet hardly leave the floor. Joyce clucks that she isn't dancing properly. "Maybe it's because she's a little bit fat," I say.

Joyce laughs. "And you, you're looking much better now, not thin like when you started."

I have indeed put on some weight and in my face it does look a little better. But, oh, those other places it settles!

I often think of Greta Fritz, a friend of my mother's, saying, "There comes a time when a woman has to make a decision: whether to look like a cow going or a goat coming."

"Ego," I say to myself, "that is all, just ego."

July and Alvis are still living in the little shed in the garden. Alvis has gone from having a fat tummy to being decidedly plump, and July is worried about her emotional well-being. "She's just lying around doing nothing," he says, and she is. She has been unable to find work and still barely speaks English, which makes finding work even harder.

I can hardly point a finger at Alvis for her lack of English. While most Africans are able to speak three or four languages, my Zulu remains stalled.

"Can you still 'see'?" asks Joyce one night, and to make sure, I begin to dance and divine again. My spirit growl is quick to rise and transport me to some halfway place where I seem to be neither here nor anywhere else, and I am quick to see what it is Joyce has hidden.

Now that I am spending evenings with Joyce again, dancing and divining, the fact that I have to kill a cow becomes reality, and the event looms as dark as doomsday.

"Will you be able to do it?" asks Joyce one night. I'm not at all sure.

"Couldn't we hire a veterinarian who would come and give the cow a shot so that it will just go to sleep and die?" I ask. Joyce rolls her head and laughs. She thinks I'm joking. I'm not.

♪

Joyce," I ask one morning, remembering the work we did, "what happened with the woman who took us over to her house, the one where we felt those bad things?"

"I don't know."

"She never came back to you?"

"No."

She is buttering slices of bread for herself for breakfast. "And your friend, the one where we went and made the house safe?"

"I just spoke to her, and everything is fine. I think she just feels better, safer, since we did it."

"That's good."

"And our cars that you made safe, nothing has happened to them, but I think Ron still wants to get insurance."

"If he wants to get it, that's fine, but it will be O.K. because nobody will touch those cars." Indeed, I have frequently seen Africans eye the circle of beads that hangs from my rearview mirror.

We must go and buy the material for the skirts for when you kill your cow," says Joyce, "and we must buy the blankets."

My stomach knots tight. "Oh, Joyce, I really don't know if I can kill something."

She laughs. "No, it will be all right."

"I'm serious." But she slaps my hand. Does she still think I am joking? Why is she now so calm when before I found my goats she was so nervous?

We have the day arranged when suddenly there is an horrific bomb blast in downtown Johannesburg. Many are killed, some horribly injured by flying glass and the debris of destroyed buildings. The police mount a massive search, and blame falls on the lunatic right.

Our trip downtown is postponed, and I become terribly skittish, staying more and more in the flat, and when I go out, avoiding high-density places. But then, inevitably, all that is mundane slowly slides back and fills the hole that the fear created, and life goes on; so Joyce, Alvis, and I drive back down to Diagonal Street.

The first stop is at the fabric store where Joyce shows me the material she has selected for the skirts. We descend dimly lit narrow stairs to the cavernous, densely packed fabric section. It smells overwhelmingly of lint. When Joyce points to a very untraditional black-and-white tartan I am so surprised that I am speechless.

"Don't you like it?" asks Joyce eventually. And I stammer, "No, it's lovely," unintentionally using the very South African negative affirmative that probably captures what I feel.

Then the beads, small white ones for around the hem, and finally the blankets. Now it is my turn to buy the blankets, with one for me—my first. These we buy at yet another store filled with racks and tall stacks of blankets of every texture and hue, some leaning so perilously outward that it seems as though a butterfly fluttering its wings somewhere in the world could at any moment create a blanket avalanche.

Joyce marches purposefully over to a soft, fuzzy, pastel column shaded in pinks, peaches, and baby blues.

"What do you think?" she asks.

"Mmm, mmm, pretty," says Alvis, burying her fingers in the fuzz.

Joyce pulls out five of the pastel-shaded ones for herself and the other *sangomas*, but there are some with deep tones of royal blue and emerald green, colors of the earth in its time of mystery, its passage from day to night, and one of these I choose for myself.

We must think about where you are going to kill your cow," says Joyce one evening while we bead. "Kill your cow." I let the terrible words slough off me.

Traditionally this event is held in the home of the new *sangoma's* parents. "What about Ronny's sister?" This is Joyce's next thought. They have a house in the suburbs with a back garden.

I remember Madota's event, the procession down the street with the drums, the fire in her parents' driveway and the chickens that were beheaded there. Even if it were legal to have livestock in the suburbs, which it isn't, I somehow could not picture myself running through the streets of Sandringham, a quiet, predominately Jewish suburb, in my skirt and bra, with the rattles around my ankles, looking for the cow and the goat. I also had some concerns about it becoming a freak show. "I don't know, Joyce. I'm not sure I want to do it in a place where white people live; it has no meaning for them. I think I must do it with the people who know what it means."

So Joyce made the decision that we would do it again in Madadeni in her mother's house. Sylvia was alarmed. "You mustn't do this in the home of your teacher, your spirit will leave you." This leaves me unsure of what to do, and I waver back and forth, then finally consult a *sangoma* who is not a part of this group. After we weigh the options, the pros and cons, he says, "Go and do it in Madadeni, the spirits will understand. Just make sure that you take everything that is yours back with you; you must leave nothing in your teacher's home."

This final celebration is expensive. Not only is there the cow and the goat to purchase, which will come to about two thousand rand, there will also be food for around two hundred people and the minibus taxi that will take all the *sangomas* from Johannesburg down to KwaZulu. Joyce has offered to pay for a portable toilet and the tent in which we will dance through the night after I have killed the cow.

Dear Ron, who has unquestioningly paid for everything thus far, keeps paying. It is for him both a mission of love and gratitude, gratitude because this journey has brought me back to South Africa, a country that he loves on a continent that lures him always back.

And while we prepare for a thanksgiving, campaigning is at high pitch throughout South Africa, with each party promising the same as the other. It is almost impossible to find an ideological separation. Posters garland telephone posts, trees, lampposts—all in English. Why aren't there any in Zulu or Xhosa I ask, but no one knows. There is, however, a massive drive, via television, radio, and newspaper, to educate Africans on the voting process.

One evening as Joyce and I sit sewing beads, she suddenly says, "I don't know who to vote for."

I glance at her, her eyes down on her sewing, her mouth pursed. "I thought you weren't going to vote."

"No, I must vote, I just don't know who I must vote for."

I think about the profusion of posters, all alike with their promises of jobs, education, housing; and the campaign rhetoric, all parties singing the same resurrection song. "It's difficult," I say.

"Yes, it's very difficult. Mercia says I must vote for the Democratic Party, and I told her that it was my business who I vote for. But now I don't know." I wonder if it's hard for her to tell me this. "How do you think it would be if I vote for the National Party?"

I am surprised, this is the party of apartheid. "Well, they are promising all kinds of changes, but you know what they are and what they have been." She sighs and I feel her heaviness, her difficulty, but I don't want to interfere, to impose what might be my biases. "What if we talk about what we know about each of the parties?" And so we talk, our heads bent over the beads, about this new beginning, about this New South Africa and who it might be that would navigate its passage even while our fingers create the trappings of an other, far older tradition.

One morning we wake to a dull boom and for a moment the windows rattle. We know instantly—another bomb. As though it has opened a sluice gate, I am suddenly consumed with fear.

"Oh God," I moan, "I can't do it."

"What?" asks Ron. "What can't you do?"

"I can't do it." I begin to feel hysterical. "I can't kill a cow, I can't do it."

"Slow down, slow down," he soothes. "You know, you never thought you'd be able to drink the goat's blood, but you did it."

"But that wasn't killing something." I shake my head, it is filled again with those awful images of Madota's killing, the cow bellowing, snorting, drool and blood running from its mouth and nose; although I keep shaking my head, the images don't clear. "Oh, God, Ron, what am I going to do?"

"You'll deal with it when the time comes."

"But how will I live with myself after?" I am crying now.

"Sshh, sshh—it will be all right." He tries to rock me in his arms, but I am tight with fear.

This time the bomb was detonated at the airport. We talk about postponing the killing of the cow if the craziness continues. I don't know whether I want it to be postponed or not; the less time to think, the better. We decide to go ahead.

33

Elections

❦

And so it is now, just as I am contemplating my final ceremony in this reunion with my homeland, that my homeland is finally to be made whole. The land and I have arrived together at a place of conciliation. It is as though the one who weaves has spun the web with the most delicious symmetry. How could anyone have known, have planned in the beginning, the elegance and timing of this unfolding pattern?

Ron and I walk down the lines, those multicolored, multiethnic lines of people waiting to vote. Waiting patiently in the hot sun, young and old, for their first taste of participation in a process waited for, longed for, fought for, for so very long.

Police in pairs stroll the block in front of the school hall. No cars are permitted into the area for fear of bombings. Two enterprising young men push a shopping cart down the line, laden with a large block of ice and cans of soda. The old and the infirm are moved to the front and led into the school hall. There is a mood of such easy joy, such lightness, as though the atoms themselves have become gossamer shimmerings, engulfing this moment in time with a luminosity such as the country has never seen.

We walk around to the side of the hall, where those who have already voted emerge. Ah, the radiance on the faces! And not only those who have never voted before, but everyone seems to share in this delight; it is a first, after all, for everybody.

Later in the day we listen to the talk radio station. "This is the happiest day of my life." The caller is white. "This is the first time that I've ever voted." Over and over the calls come in, from those white, first-time voters. The airways are filled with them and their elation.

Perhaps it really wasn't so surprising. It is just that the world had forgotten them—those who were that other minority in the quilting of whites. There were those who opposed and fought; there were those who opposed and left; there were those who supported the Nationalist regime. But there were also those who, like me, did not have the courage to fight for their belief—and courage is what it took in those days of torment and unlimited detention—but for whom, unlike me, Africa nevertheless remained home; who covered eyes, ears, and mouth in order to stay in a place they loved. This day was for them, too, a reckoning.

And what love and acceptance poured from those black Africans who called in to the radio station; what forgiveness shone from their words. Would that country have ever reached this conciliation had they not carried in their hearts such true generosity of spirit? Not a word, not a sound, not a sigh of anger, of retribution, only delight and merciful inclusion. What gift allows them such graciousness?

For two days, then for three, the election continues while radiance shines on the land; then the waiting for the results. And it seems to matter not that those results take far longer than anticipated, still the joyous mood is pervasive. And then the results; no planning could have ordered a more equitable spread. We all, as a nation, heave a sigh of relief and gratitude.

And now, as we still breathe the heady air of the New South Africa, once again our things for the trip to Madadeni begin to be laid out. Again Joyce, Alvis, and I, with three shopping carts, buy groceries for the feasting. So that as little baking as possible will need to be done in Madadeni, I order two sponge cakes, each three feet square. Next door is a butcher shop.

"I have to kill a cow, and I'm supposed to do it with a spear, but if that doesn't work I will need a good knife." They look at me as though I am mad. Eventually a row of long, thin knives lies on the counter while the butchers debate the merits of each. I buy an expensive, lethal-looking thing with a black handle.

The money for the cow and the goat is sent to Joyce's daughter in Madadeni; the taxi is arranged. The young taxi driver comes to the flat to make sure he knows where it is and to meet me. He takes my hand shyly. "Are you really *sangoma*?"

"Yes."

"*Hau!*" After that he is pretty speechless.

"Are you excited?" asks Ron. I shake my head. I have been walking around feeling sick with fear. Murderer, I will be a murderer. I cannot purge the thought from my head.

But inexorably, time has brought us almost to the moment. All the pieces are in place. Joyce and the *sangomas* and I will leave on Friday night with the food and the blankets. Ron and Dennis, his brother and again the photographer, will drive down Saturday morning.

The taxi driver arrives early, but our belongings already make mountains on the sidewalk.

"This will never work," Ron says over and over as he watches the driver arrange and rearrange the women, the food, the blankets, the overnight bags, the heater, and all the things Joyce is taking home in the minibus. Finally there is only one plump *sangoma* with a large derriere to get into the taxi.

She takes one step up, stops halfway through the side sliding door, and gets no farther. The taxi driver leans his shoulder up against her derriere and heaves. She moves maybe a few inches into the vehicle. Again he leans into her and heaves while she begins to wail and the other woman cackle like geese.

One more time the driver shoves and then quickly, while most of her disappears, he begins sliding the door behind her. For a while her rear end bulges out of the bus like a colorful balloon, then, with a last heave, she is in and the door slides closed.

Because of all the terrible accidents involving these taxis, I'd told Joyce that I would be sitting in the middle somewhere, but she shook her head. "You and me, we must sit in front with the driver."

"Joyce, if we have an accident, we'll be dead."

"No, we're not going to have an accident."

But now my anxiety clamps onto the fact that we will be killed on the way down. "Do you know how many people have died in the last few weeks in these taxis?"

"No, it doesn't matter," says Joyce.

"It doesn't matter!" I sputter. "I'm too young to die."

Joyce laughs. "You're just a baby," she says. It doesn't sound like a comment on my age.

Joyce nudges me in first, next to the driver, and with great relief I notice seat belts, but when I pull the center one across my shoulder and search for the latch into which it locks there isn't one.

"No, it doesn't work," says the driver.

Oh, why do I feel such a sense of doom about this whole thing? I pile my lap high with blankets and practice, in my mind, how I will take cover under them.

For the first hour I sit as stiff as a ramrod, my eyes glued wide to the road while the *sangomas* sing. But the driver is careful and somewhere in the second hour I relax.

We arrive in Madadeni at one in the morning. Again, before anything else, before relatives are greeted, before any hellos are said, the reed mats are laid out on the floor, the drums are pulled between legs, and the spirits are greeted in dance. Only then do we say hello to Dorkus, Joyce's daughter, and the family and friends who are here to help. Then we make tidy hillocks around the perimeter of the room with our things and settle down to dinner.

What a strange reversal this visit is. The last time we were here it was Joyce who was so nervous that she was solemn and withdrawn, while I flowed with ease. Now I am held tight within myself with fear, while Joyce is gregarious and unconcerned.

It is not till five in the morning that the blankets are pulled out of the cupboard and we roll up in them. Next to me Miriam begins to snore almost immediately. Joyce is in the kitchen with Dorkus; their voices chatter on and on, the light casts large square shadows of the dining-room chairs against the far wall, the slatted backs making lines like prison bars. Somewhere close by a rooster crows.

My eyes are clamped open, my feet are freezing. Eventually I get up and sit with Joyce and Dorkus in the kitchen. A huge kettle splutters on the coal-fed range. We cradle tin mugs and drink tea. It is getting light.

34

Giving Thanks

The winter sun is thin and silver. We lean outside against the east wall of the house, allowing the warmth to soak into our closed eyes. "Are you all right, Melisande?" they ask. I nod. I feel alien, unreal. Later, someone comes with a truck to take Joyce and Miriam to fetch the cow and the goat. Dorkus makes a list of things we still need from the market: bags of potatoes, tomatoes, onions, pumpkins, cabbages, and beets.

A small group of us leaves the house, five or six in red skirts with our *ibayi* wrapped around our shoulders. As we make our way down the dirt road, the wind begins gusting, whipping our skirts tight against our legs. At the corner we head diagonally across the field. There is a slim path worn through the meager clumps of dry grass, lined with broken glass, bits of plastic, paper; goats, some black, some dirty white, nibble at the yellowing clumps, at the plastic.

The wind grows, sweeping up the red earth-sand, and we turn our backs and shield our eyes and tie tight the *ibayi*. Our skirts hug our thighs. Furiously now the wind blows, swirling sand like swarms of locusts, bits of paper and white plastic flying high in the sky like inland seagulls.

"*Hau*, I haven't seen anything like this," grumble some of the *sangomas*. But I know, knew almost immediately, that it was for me. *Ngicabange ukuthi akusiwo umoya.*

"This is not just a wind." I know this is not just a wind. My breath lifts; for a moment, the chilling grip of fear lifts as my cells become aerated, filled with energy.

I turn to face it, to greet it—the Great Spirit, *Umoya*. Strange, the Zulu word has both meanings, both wind and spirit. The wind barrels into me, rocks me, whips the red skirt and the *ibayi* around me, and like an enchanted eye, I am enveloped within.

We cross the field, now leaning into the wind, now pushed along, shading eyes, nose, mouth, holding tight wraps and skirts.

It blew as we bought the pumpkins and potatoes and cabbages, going from one small stall to another. It blew as we made our way back down the dirt roads, across the field to the house. It blew when Ron and Dennis arrived, so that we did not dance to greet them and they came quickly into the house. It blew even at four o'clock when the *sangomas* led me away, away down the road to await the drumming that would signal the start of the event.

It has an icy edge to it now as we wait on the corner farthest from the house. Desolate is this corner, with no one out other than this huddled knot of *sangomas*, whipped by the wind.

The drums begin their call. The wind tears the sound from our ears and sends it hurtling across the empty field. The *sangomas* drape the *ibayi* over my head so I cannot see, and lead me back to the house, slowly dance-stepping and singing. In the driveway where I know the small fire has been lit to welcome in the spirits, we stop. This is where the chickens will be sacrificed.

I am shaking as I kneel in the driveway in front of the fire, the shawl still over my head. Joyce's and Miriam's voices lift, chanting.

I hear the chickens begin to squawk and suddenly a spray of wind-carried blood splatters my leg from foot to knee. They have been beheaded. The drums lift as the *ibayi* comes off and we dance.

The wind still blows when the dancing is done and we run through the house to chase away any lingering bad spirits, and it blows as I come to a stop before Joyce and Miriam.

On my knees now, I rub my palms together, click my trembling fingers. "Yeh, yeh," the long-drawn-out sound arises from my diaphragm.

"*Yezwake,*" the *sangomas* chorus, "*yezwake.*"

"*Shaya ngikutshele, shaya ngikutshele,*" I begin the chant.

I no longer know if the wind blows or not.

"What is it?" It is Joyce's voice.

"The cow."

"*Yezwake!*"

How do I know that it is in front of me somewhere, not far from where I kneel? How do I know that it stands around the side in a small enclosed space? I have heard it, seen it somewhere in my mind.

"*Yezwake, yezwake!*" they shout, and "Fetch it," says Joyce.

When I reach the cow Margaret, who is close behind me, says, "You must touch her with your whisk and run back," but as I round the corner Joyce waves me back. "No, you must bring her back."

But she had come away from her rope and loped off across the field. With much whooping and cheering, the young men and children gave chase. Since I was barefoot, and the field hard with winter stubble and bits of broken glass, I waited and watched as she trotted first this way around a tin shed at the far end of the field, and then that way, until finally the youngsters circled the shed and she was recaptured. I went to meet her then and took hold of the rope that was tied around her neck.

I talked to her as we began walking back, back across the field. I told her she was beautiful; I thanked her for walking softly with me, for being my cow. I told her how sad I was that she had to die, again and again I asked her forgiveness for the act I would have to perform. The words came out gently, soothing, and she came quite docilely. All the way back to the house I talked and all the way she walked, like a child, beside me. Only at the entrance to the drive-way did she stop, but then, after a few more soft words, she moved up the driveway and allowed the men to tie her to the tree. And it was then, in the gathering dusk, the ground already cold underfoot, that I realized that the great wind had stopped.

We waited inside while the men did what was needed to ready the cow. When Miriam said, "It's time," I wished more profoundly for divine intervention that I had ever remembered doing before. Like a child who believes that if she closes her eyes and wishes hard enough, something will change, I wished and waited for some miraculous intercession, my bare feet glued to the kitchen floor. So profoundly did I wish, that I did not see Joyce standing before me with the spear until she held it out to me.

My body drained then, drained, it seemed, of blood, of life. A great sense of abandonment filled me; all connections, all connect-edness dropped away. In a cold enclosure of aloneness, I took the spear, and because my eyes had teared when I took it, I held onto Joyce as we walked out.

A lone bulb strung on a slim line of wire stripped the scene of color, framing it in bleak outline like a stage set lit with only one working light: the cow, her head close to the tree; the men, ten, maybe twenty of them, their dark faces disappearing into the night. Along the back wall of the house, sitting on the reed mats, were the drummers. I saw only their rough, earth-scuffed feet and knew by the sound that they were there. And around the perimeter, made ghostly in the eerie light, the children and the women of the township.

For what seemed a long while Joyce stood between the cow and the group of men while the drums sounded their beat, I stood icily rooted behind her. Then the rope holding the cow was loosened, the position of her head changed, and Joyce beckoned to me.

I walked across the earth feeling an ashen cold in my brain, in my marrow, never before so afraid, never before so alone. Some of the men came in close and one put his fingers high in the spine, between her shoulders and her head, pushing into the softness between her vertebra. My white fingers joined his as I felt for the same spot, all the while my bones chilled, my mind frigid. Then I wrapped my fingers high around the haft of the spear and lined the spear point up with the soft place in her spine.

"Now," Joyce shouted and the drum sound intensified. I shut tight my eyes and pushed the spear hard downward, and at the same time let out a roar from deep inside me, a roar to release energy and drown out any bellowing the cow might make. But she had remained silent and I felt the spear roll away as she moved her head to the side. "No, you must not make a noise," admonished Joyce.

Again the drum sound rose, and I lined up the spear and pushed; but again she moved her head away. Three times with icy fingers I felt for that soft spot between her vertebra, three times I pushed with the spear tip, but each time she noiselessly moved her head to the side and the only sound was the hard pounding of the drums.

Then one of the men came forward, and after a quick exchange with Joyce, took the spear and handed me the slim-bladed knife. Again he felt for the spot just behind her lowered head and my fingers joined his, again Joyce said, "Now," and I closed my eyes and pushed.

Suddenly my body was following my hands down, down almost to the ground. The cow had dropped without a sound. In surprise I pulled back, but Joyce shouted, "Push, push," and I ground the knife between her vertebra to make sure. But she was already dead.

Much later, when Ron and I talked about the killing of the cow, his eyes grew misty, not at her death, but at her quiet willingness.

"It was so strange," he said, "it was as though she was offering herself to you."

And indeed it had seemed so. Not for a moment had she struggled or bellowed. There was none of the horrifying trumpeting and blood drooling of Madota's cow. She had lowered her head to me and had gone, in the blink of an eye, from something living to a thing dead. There was nothing haunting about it, nothing ugly in the experience for me to carry away. Perhaps I shouldn't have been surprised, given the embrace of the great spirit-bearing wind, and yet I was, filled with wonder at the strange grace of the event, at something that came mysteriously close to beauty in this death.

Back there, in the dark yard with the drums beating, my eyes flicked just for a quick moment at her lying on her side, then I turned away and walked back into the house. I did not see as the men pulled her away and began to remove her pelt; I did not want to see.

The next time I saw her was when she was brought into the house, into the bedroom where we sat. She was already carved into large sections as Madota's cow had been, and eventually candles in blue saucers were lit around her.

A short while later Joyce called me out to kill the goat, but it was only a symbolic thrust I made with the spear, then the men took her and quickly slit her throat.

In the early hours of the morning, Sunday morning, when most of the night's dancing is done, the sections of the cow that will be eaten are cut away and carried off into the large black cauldrons, set up over fires in the backyard. Nothing of her will be wasted—every part of her, except her hide and her tail, will be eaten. Her hide will be made into drums, wraps, a rug; the tail, black on top with a long white mane, will be wrapped around a rod and given to me.

It is at noon that the great feasting begins. There is a constant procession of plates from the kitchen out into the tent. We, the *sangomas*, eat in the room in which the cow had lain during the night, the room in which parts of her still lie. But these are the parts that will be shared among the visiting *sangomas*, to take home to their families.

When we were done eating, and had raised our plates high and given thanks, Ron called me outside. "I want you to see something." I follow him out, past the tent, out onto the dirt road. "Turn around and look up."

In a cornflower-blue, otherwise cloudless sky, is a semicircle of radiating lines of only slightly puffed whiteness, clouds like the spokes in a great half wheel that come together directly over Joyce's house. It is an uncanny sight and we stand quietly, Ron and I, gazing up at that half halo until we are slowly joined by others. Together in silent wonder we stand, our faces raised to a sight that seems so purposeful in its design.

Coincidence? Or did we in our ritual, as American Indians and Africans believe, create it?

For me it appeared as acknowledgment, acknowledgment of a sacrifice given and received, and as a benediction, a blessing that had come at the end of a service. Certainly not a service in a traditional western sense, but a service nonetheless, steeped just as deeply in ancient tradition and that had evoked this answer, this magical white-puffed sky wheel of acceptance.

And that was not the end of it, for later, as we were driving back to Johannesburg, there lingered in the cloudless sky a sunset—no, much more than a sunset—a dance of color and light that for more than an hour hung in our path. Golden chalices, blue and green spears, fannings of deep orange, violet orbs. A ballet of sky color—on and on those shapes glowed in a country where day turns to night with certain swiftness, while we drove toward them in hushed reverence.

I felt honored and humbled, doubly blessed and yet so small. I felt as though not only had the Great Spirit been there with me through these two days, but that now the Great Mother was comforting me, too, letting me know that this killing had been conceived and received as a sacrament. And I, so earthbound and mundane, felt caught up in something so mystical, so magical.

And my reflections turned again and again to my recent past, to this strange journey of signs and portents, this journey of synchronicity tinged with magic and with the sacred. Where did it begin?

Was it the time of depression, when, as Anne the Elder said, it was as though I had separated myself from the world, as though I had gone deep inside to prepare for something to come? Did it begin in the desert, with the meditations, listening to the winds, turning to the four directions, calling up the spirits, the wisdom of the ancients?

As the mountain I'd climbed had no top, so perhaps there was no beginning. For is it not all a circle? Singing alive the stars so that they should return again and again to dust the night sky with their magic. Treading barefoot on the earth; feeling deep in our skin her stones and her spines. Listening to the words in the wind and chanting with her song. Seeing the spring of a grasshopper and delighting in the life of it, and saying so; inhaling deep the sap smell of a tree trunk, hearing it run. And lifting our arms to the universe, allowing our joy, our wonder, our thanksgiving to flow back to that with which creation has surrounded us.

It is here that the dance begins. Not in the wind sound alone, or the running of the sap or the spring of the grasshopper, but in our union with the acts. It is in the exchange that sacred passages are born.

For an eternity we rode into that enchanted sunset. I was tired; the soles of my feet hummed with pain from running on the dirt roads, across fields, dancing, dancing, dancing on the winter dry grass, so when the colors finally faded, I put my feet up on the seat, wrapped my first *sangoma* blanket around me, and slept.